The Perils and Promise
of
Global Transparency

D1738784

SUNY series in Global Politics
James N. Rosenau, editor

*A complete listing of books in this series can be found
at the end of this volume.*

The Perils and Promise of Global Transparency

Why the Information Revolution May Not Lead to Security, Democracy, or Peace

Kristin M. Lord

State University of New York Press

Published by
State University of New York Press, Albany

© 2006 State University of New York

All rights reserved

Printed in the United States of America

No part of this book may be used or reproduced in any manner whatsoever
without written permission. No part of this book may be stored in a retrieval
system or transmitted in any form or by any means including electronic,
electrostatic, magnetic tape, mechanical, photocopying, recording, or otherwise
without the prior permission in writing of the publisher.

For information, address State University of New York Press,
194 Washington Avenue, Suite 305, Albany, NY 12210-2384

Cover photo © iStockphoto.com/Vladimir Pomortsev

Production by Diane Ganeles
Marketing by Anne M. Valentine

Library of Congress Cataloging-in-Publication Data

Lord, Kristin M.
    The perils and promise of global transparency : why the information
revolution may not lead to security, democracy, or peace / Kristin M. Lord.
        p. cm. — (SUNY series in global politics)
    Includes bibliographical references and index.
    ISBN-13: 978-0-7914-6885-2 (hardcover : alk. paper)
    ISBN-10: 0-7914-6885-2 (hardcover : alk. paper)
    ISBN-13: 978-0-7914-6886-9 (pbk. : alk. paper)
    ISBN-10: 0-7914-6886-0 (pbk. : alk. paper)
    1. Transparency in government. 2. Freedom of information. 3. Information
society. 4. World politics—21st century. I. Title. II. Series.

JC598.L67 2006
303.48′33—dc22

                                                                        2005033342

10 9 8 7 6 5 4 3 2 1

To Jeff and Max

Contents

Preface

I owe a great deal of thanks to many people. For commenting on early drafts of the manuscript—the most painful to read—I thank Robin Brown of the University of Leeds, who also was kind enough to host a helpful seminar with his students. I would also like to thank George Washington University student Lee Ann Fujii for her help on the Rwanda case study (and for taking the time to read the chapter while actually *in* Rwanda doing fieldwork); an anonymous journalist from Singapore for help on the Singapore case; Jonathan Frankel for helping me to understand American and foreign free speech laws; Christopher Langton for background information on the Institute for International Studies' excellent publication, *The Military Balance;* Loch Johnson, who provided encouragement at a difficult time; former congressperson Steve Solarz, who has devoted much of his career to understanding and resolving conflicts; and Serif Turgut, who herself has reported on some of the world's most dangerous conflicts and understands all too well the forces that limit media coverage. I owe a special thanks to my mother, Jean DeBarbieri, a professional indexer whose careful handiwork can be seen at the end of this book.

I am also indebted to my wonderful colleagues at The George Washington University's Elliott School of International Affairs. Martha Finnemore, James Lebovic, Henry Farrell, Leon Fuerth, and Joanna Spear all read and commented on various chapters. Their input was invaluable. Thanks also to Jim Goldgeier who generously spent significant time one afternoon to help me rethink the book's conclusion. Students in the mid-career Master of International Policy and Practice program provided excellent feedback and questions that made me rethink my manuscript at various times. Thanks also to undergraduates in my causes of war course who discussed the manuscript in class. I am also indebted to my colleagues in the Elliott School dean's office, especially Ed McCord, for their support. I am deeply thankful to my former boss, Harry Harding, from whom I have learned and continue to learn, a tremendous amount.

I must offer a special thanks to Bernard Finel, who not only read and commented on parts of this book, but helped spark my interest in transparency to start with, and served as my coauthor on several papers and on an article in *International Studies Quarterly*; he was also my coeditor of an earlier book *Power and Conflict in the Age of Transparency* (New York: Palgrave Macmillan 2000).

I owe thanks to several institutions. The International Studies Association and the American Political Science Association both sponsored conferences at which I presented papers related to this book. I took advantage of the excellent library at the Institute for International and Strategic Studies, of which I'm a member, while I was residing in London. My thanks to the staff for their assistance. I also would like to recognize The Elliott School of International Affairs for summer research assistance, which provided funds for a research assistant. These funds enabled support from Debbie Toy, who helped with both research and manuscript preparation. I appreciate all her hard work.

Most importantly, I would like to thank my husband, Jeff Lord, my toughest editor and the love of my life.

Chapter 1

The Complexity of Transparency

"No government can control the global information environment."
—Former U.S. State Department official, Jamie Metzl [1]

"Information, whatever the quantity, is not the same as understanding."
—*Financial Times* writer Christopher Dunkley [2]

In November 2002, Severe Acute Respiratory Syndrome (SARS) broke out in the Guangdong Province of China. The virus ultimately killed nearly 800 people, and infected approximately ten times that number around the world. [3] The Chinese government initially ignored the disease. However, though the government issued no official reports during the first months of the epidemic, news spread quickly via mobile phone text messages, E-mail, and Internet chat rooms. [4] A regional Chinese newspaper broke the story, reporting that word of a "fatal flu in Guangdong" had reached 120 million people through mobile phone text messages. With the news so widely known, Chinese authorities were forced to acknowledge and respond to the outbreak. [5] Officials were reluctant to report the full number of SARS cases at first, but the World Health Organization (WHO) began reporting its own data, which pressured Beijing to bring its figures in-line. [6] When the government announced that the number of SARS cases was ten times higher than reported earlier, one Chinese student expressed no surprise. "We already knew it was much worse from reading about it on the Internet," she said. "I don't think they can continue to cover up the truth." [7]

More than two years later, on May 9, 2005, *Newsweek* magazine published a two-sentence article reporting that an American interrogator at the U.S. Guantanamo Bay prison in Cuba had flushed the Koran of a Muslim detainee down a toilet.[8] The story, which *Newsweek* later retracted after an anonymous Pentagon source said he could no longer stand by it, prompted a press conference by a Pakistani opposition party member named Imran Khan. Khan called on his government to request an apology from the United States and announced that "Islam is under attack in the name of the war on terror."[9] Urdu- and English-language newspapers in Pakistan gave the story front-page coverage and the Pakistani parliament debated the matter. The governments of Egypt, Saudi Arabia, Bangladesh, and Malaysia issued critical public statements and mass protests followed in Pakistan, Gaza, and Indonesia. Protests in Afghanistan spread to several towns and turned violent, leading to the deaths of seventeen people and injuries of over one hundred more. Though there are numerous credible reports of other cases of Koran desecration, the *Newsweek* story appears to be false.[10]

These events show two faces of rising global transparency, the increasing availability of information around the world. The first depicts the conventional view: authoritarian governments losing control over information thanks to technology, the media, and international organizations. The second shows the darker side of global transparency, in which some of the same forces spread hatred, conflict, and lies. This darker side of transparency is less noted but, unfortunately, it will be at least as influential in the coming decades. Global transparency will indeed bring many benefits, but predictions that it will lead inevitably to peace, understanding, and democracy, are wrong.

The trend toward greater transparency *is* transforming international politics. Greater transparency reduces uncertainty, which can decrease the likelihood of war and increase international security if it shows that nations have neither the intent nor the capability to harm each other. Greater transparency also increases knowledge of other peoples, which can increase tolerance toward others and decrease the likelihood of conflict. When armed conflicts do break out, greater transparency may facilitate grassroots support for intervention. Finally, greater transparency decentralizes global power by breaking governments' monopoly over information and by empowering Nongovernmental Organizations (NGOs) and citizens. Armed with information, NGOs build coalitions in order to encourage political change, spark public protests when they publicize transgressions, or merely threaten publicity—a phenomenon known as "regulation by shaming."[11] Citizens, for their part, can use information to mobilize support for change and even overthrow authoritarian governments. Greater transparency gives citizens and NGOs new tools of influence and, when wielded appropriately, can be a force for good governance, freedom, and democracy.

These possibilities have raised hopes that transparency will usher in an era of unprecedented justice and peace.[12] Optimists predict that greater transparency will reduce the incidence of conflicts caused by misunderstandings. It can facilitate international agreements and deter cheating. It alerts the world to disturbing events and gives governments, NGOs, and international organizations the opportunity to respond. Transparency also promises to improve governance and to make powerful organizations of all stripes more accountable. As a result, groups across the political spectrum advocate greater transparency of corporations, universities, police departments, local governments, national governments, and international organizations like the European Union, the World Trade Organization, and the World Bank.

Yet greater transparency is not an unmitigated good. In all likelihood, the trend toward greater transparency will be at once positive and pernicious. More information about other societies may reveal conflicting values and interests as well as shared ones. More information about the military capabilities of other states may show vulnerability and encourage aggression by the strong against the weak. Greater transparency can highlight hostility and fuel vicious cycles of belligerent words and deeds. It can highlight widespread prejudice and hatred, encourage the victimization of out-groups and by showing broad acceptance of such behavior without repercussions, legitimize it. Greater transparency can undermine efforts at conflict resolution and, when conflicts do break out, it can discourage intervention by third parties. Transparency sometimes can make conflicts worse.

Greater transparency will not necessarily promote democracy and good governance. Though transparency is partially credited with encouraging the democratic revolutions in Eastern Europe at the end of the Cold War, in some cases, more transparency may actually strengthen illiberal regimes and increase their legitimacy. To the extent that transparency empowers transnational NGOs, it does so indiscriminately, aiding terrorist networks as well as human rights advocates. Moreover, the power of NGOs is likely to remain limited relative to sovereign states, regardless of the merit of particular NGOs' goals. Within states, greater transparency will not necessarily lead to democracy or undermine authoritarian regimes.

In short, the trend toward greater transparency is a complex phenomenon with complex implications. It will benefit the world in many ways, but sometimes at a price. To a large extent, the effects of transparency depend on what transparency reveals, who benefits, and how people interpret the information they receive in a more transparent global society. Transparency may reveal positive trends and an environment conducive to peace; but it may also reveal negative trends and an environment of suspicion and hate.

By highlighting the double-edged nature of transparency, this book strips predictions about the effects of greater transparency from value-laden assumptions about what transparency will reveal. Especially in the realm of international security and conflict, many discussions of transparency assume that when the fog of ignorance lifts, we will see harmony rather than conflict, and tolerance rather than hate. They assume that people will interpret new information in a particular way and hold a particular set of values. Their predictions are not false, but incomplete. When their assumptions hold, transparency is likely to have exactly the effects that optimists predict. However, when (equally plausible) assumptions are less rosy, greater transparency can produce more destructive results.

Optimists focus on how the availability of information will transform world events, but where people seek information, what information they trust, and what meaning they draw from that information will be more powerful. Regardless of whether the *Newsweek* article at the beginning of this chapter is true, it was quickly believed and treated as further evidence of an American war on Islam. Arguments that the United States has gone out of its way to respect the religious rights of Muslim prisoners, or that any violations are aberrations, have been quickly disregarded.[13] Such views have damaging implications for American interests. Wars, ever more, are wars of ideas and credibility as well as wars of might.

Though this book is about information, it is also about power. If knowledge is power, then transparency, by diffusing knowledge, empowers some groups and not others. This diffusion of information is not politically neutral, since when information changes hands, so too does influence. Moreover, the diffusion of power is not a one-way street. Transparency can make the strong stronger as well as empowering the weak.

Inevitably, this book is also about human nature. Because the trend toward greater transparency is about the relationship between people and information, the values and ideas that people use to evaluate information are crucial in analyzing the effects of greater transparency. Information is disseminated and interpreted by people, so human instincts and biases are always evident. People *choose* how to respond to new information and, indeed, whether to respond at all.

The Nature of Global Transparency

We live in an age of transparency. Nearly two-thirds of the world's countries are now democracies, which release vast amounts of information about their policy making.[14] Technological innovations, ranging from commercially available high-quality satellite imagery to the Internet, radically reduce the cost of obtaining information and transmitting it across borders. The twenty-four-hour news media ferrets out news and broadcasts it globally. Nongovernmental organizations document and publicize abuses of state power around the world. International organizations monitor the behavior of governments and determine whether they are adhering to international agreements. Together, these forces are making governments more transparent to outside observers than at any other time in human history.

Transparency is a condition in which information about the priorities, intentions, capabilities, and behavior of powerful organizations is widely available to the global public.[15] It is a condition of openness enhanced by any mechanism that discloses and disseminates information such as a free press, open government hearings, mobile phones, commercial satellite imagery, or reporting requirements in international regimes. Transparency is not synonymous with truth. It may reveal actual or perceived facts, actual or perceived falsehoods, behavior, intentions, ideas, values, and opinions. It may reveal neutral, empirically verifiable information or propaganda specifically designed to advance a particular cause or view. The term *transparency* does not necessarily require premeditated acts of disclosure by organizations, nor does it imply anything about the nature of the information revealed or what types of actors will gain from that information. Transparency increases due to major initiatives by governments to open up but it also increases through the cumulative effects of small acts. Much transparency occurs due to the aggregate, often unintended, acts of individuals or small organizations that spread information. In an age of transparency that dissemination of information is magnified and multiplied by information technologies, the media, and human networks. Transparency, in sum, describes the relative availability of information, without respect to content.[16]

Five factors in particular have led to the rise of global transparency: the spread of democratic governments, the rise of the global media, the spread of nongovernmental organizations, the proliferation of international regimes requiring governments to disclose information, and the widespread availability of information technologies. Of these five factors, the first four involve governments or organizations whose actions lead to the dissemination of information across borders. The latter is not an organization but a tool used by individuals or groups of individuals to disseminate information. Information and communication technologies have no agenda; they are neutral transmitters of content. Just as paper may be blank or printed and may be used to transmit all sorts of messages, information technologies are not themselves information providers.

These five factors can be mutually reinforcing, with each factor enhancing the power of the others to further increase transparency. To give some examples, information and communication technologies make it possible for nongovernmental organizations to disseminate information. International organizations publicize information that is reported by the media, which in turn is used by domestic opposition groups to pressure governments to release more information or to explain differences between official policy and information made available by nongovernmental sources.[17] The plurality of sources also matters. When there are discrepancies between information provided by one source and information provided by another source, that discrepancy can lead to questions that in turn clarify and improve the quality and credibility of that information, and sometimes produce more information.

The Spread of Democracy

Between 1950 and 2000, the number of democracies in the world rose from 22 to 120.[18] Democracies generally are characterized by a free press, public hearings, freedom of assembly, competing political parties, and contested elections—all of which facilitate the release of information to both the domestic population and observers worldwide. As a result, "[T]here is no way you can talk only to [your own population]. Other people listen in."[19]

Though there are variations in openness, democracies generally release more information than their nondemocratic counterparts. They have so-called sunshine laws requiring public disclosure of sensitive information.[20] They have free presses that report on issues that are sensitive or embarrassing to the government. And, democratic elections create pressure for otherwise tight-lipped officials to share information with the media, interest groups, opposition parties, and the general public.[21] Observers both inside and outside democratic societies process this information and draw conclusions about leaders' opinions, preferences, and intentions. They can attend public hearings and access government documents; evaluate public opinion by reading poll data and reading the public materials of thousands of interest groups that influence decision making; and read newspapers, magazines, and websites produced by independent media or groups promoting a particular view. The information released by democratic governments is incredibly helpful to interested analysts, especially for those who are knowledgeable about government structures and processes and about the history and culture of the democratic society in question.

Global Media

CNN, the BBC, Al-Jazeera, and other 24-hour news services provide nearly instant, real-time coverage of breaking news around the world. The scope of this coverage has expanded remarkably in the past twenty years. In 1980, CNN had 8 U.S. bureaus, 2 international bureaus, and an audience of 1.7 million. By 2000, it had 10 U.S. bureaus and 27 international bureaus, which delivered news to 78 million U.S. homes and an additional 212 countries and territories.[22] Al-Jazeera, which launched in 1996, has more than 30 bureaus and its website is among the 50 most visited sites in the world.

As live coverage is broadcast into homes worldwide, public officials are pressured to respond quickly to breaking crises and to avert the suffering that citizens see on television.[23] In the words of former CNN anchor Bernard Shaw, they have much less time to "perceive, react, and respond" to world events.[24] Though there are reasons to be skeptical of the most ambitious claims regarding the so-called CNN Effect, governmental officials agree that it has radically changed the way in which foreign policy is conducted and it has increased exponentially the amount of information in the public domain.[25]

Spread of Nongovernmental Organizations

When it comes to publicizing information that governments would prefer to keep secret, NGOs like Amnesty International, Greenpeace, and Transparency International are thorns in official sides worldwide. Despite their diverse missions and philosophies, NGOs call attention to embarrassing problems such as human rights abuses, toxic waste dumps, and corruption in order to promote particular causes. In the past few decades, NGOs have grown in both number and power. The Union of International Associations now lists over 15,000 transnationally oriented NGOs and the growth of informal coalitions is outpacing the increase in formal organizations.[26] Many of these organizations are small and poorly funded, but some are extremely influential and sophisticated, with global networks of researchers who scrupulously document abuses by even the world's most secretive regimes.[27] These NGOs have become influential players in world affairs. To give an example, NGOs mobilized the political support that was necessary for the implementation of the international treaty to ban land mines, despite American resistance. Though the treaty is not yet legally enforceable, the initiative is helping to change views about the acceptability and practice of using land mines. NGOs also had a significant impact on the agreement behind Africa's largest oil pipeline and successfully pressured the signatories to take the pipeline's environmental and social effects into account.[28]

International Organizations

International regimes and organizations such as the Organization for Economic Cooperation and Development, the International Convention for the Protection of the Sea from Ships (MARPOL), and the United Nations Register on Conventional Arms, often require their members to disclose a wealth of information to each other and to the global public.[29] Though they are more likely to require participants to disclose information on issues for which there are fewer benefits to asymmetrical information, some disclosure regimes touch on the most sensitive data of all: information related to national security and defense. These agreements force their members to disclose information that they would rather keep secret in order to achieve some outcome that is desired even more than the benefits of asymmetrical information.[30] This information may include data that governments are loath to disclose domestically. However, in an age of transparency that information often finds its way back home and enables citizens successfully to pressure governments to be more open domestically as well.[31]

Notably, international organizations are themselves becoming more transparent, which releases even more information to the international community and can help citizens and member governments hold these organizations more accountable. To give just a few examples, the World Bank, the International Monetary Fund, and the European Union have all launched initiatives to make themselves more transparent.

Information Technology

Information technology is revolutionizing global communications, making it easier and cheaper to share information than ever before. Though this revolution still bypasses much of the world's population, the trends are staggering. To give just a few examples:

- There were 940 million Internet users worldwide by 2004,[32] and the Computer Industry Almanac estimates that this number will jump to more than 1 billion users by the end of 2005.[33] Internet users in Russia alone, jumped from 1.4 million in 1998, to 7.5 million in 2000—a fivefold increase in just two years.[34]

- Every country in the world now has some sort of Internet connection.[35] With the development of wireless applications, Internet access is available without a personal computer, which will make communication even cheaper and more widely accessible.
- There are 418 radios and 247 televisions for every 1,000 people worldwide. In the United States, the country with the highest radio and television penetration, there are 2,146 radios and 847 televisions for every 1,000 people.[36]
- The number of cellular connections worldwide is projected to grow from almost 727 million at the beginning of 2001, to 1.26 billion in 2003, and to more than 1.76 billion in 2005.[37]

In addition, anyone with a credit card can now purchase sophisticated satellite imagery of almost any site on earth. These photos are available at one-meter resolution—a quality previously reserved only for superpowers. In 2004, the industry leader in commercial satellite imagery began selling photographs at one-half meter resolution, which allows photographs to distinguish anything larger than nineteen inches. An analyst would be able to identify something smaller than a picnic table and distinguish a cow from a horse.[38]

Economic pressures encourage the trend toward greater transparency. Investors want to invest their scarce resources in countries where they have credible information about risks and rewards. They want to be able to predict what the investment climate will look like in the future and ascertain that the government upholds its commitments. Consequently, investors—particularly direct investors who wish to build factories or offices, but also portfolio investors—tend to put their money into more transparent countries and shun less transparent countries. To attract investment, countries must don what Thomas Friedman calls "the golden straitjacket," a set of policies that may constrain governments' behavior but allows them to attract needed resources.[39] Greater transparency is a key requirement for those who don the golden straitjacket.

Values reinforce the trend. As transparency increases, more and more governments and international organizations conclude that transparency is not only inevitable, but also morally right. As Ann Florini writes, "The world is embracing new standards of conduct, enforced not by surveillance and coercion but by willful disclosure: regulation by revelation."[40] The expectation that powerful organizations will be transparent creates additional pressure for secretive organizations to open up because secretive organizations look like they have something to hide. When transparency is prevalent, acts of secrecy are themselves suspicious. President George W. Bush justified the 2003 invasion of Iraq at least partly because of the regime's lack of transparency and because of the consequent suspicion that it was building weapons of mass destruction. To quote President Bush, "A country that hides something is a country that is afraid of getting caught, and that was part of our calculation."[41]

Predicting the effects of greater transparency requires delving through many layers of complexity and understanding what information is available, who gets what information, and how they interpret and act on that information. The sources of transparency in international politics—democratic governments, the global media, nongovernmental organizations, and international organizations—all report information selectively, which is reasonable for some organizations and a fundamental responsibility of others. Citizens of democracies do not want to become informed about every issue in detail, which is why we elect representatives and maintain permanent government bureaucracies. Similarly, we would not want to read newspapers that reported every significant event or all stories in equal depth; we buy newspapers precisely because they filter information for us. Nonetheless, consumers of information rely on organizations with goals such as profit, entertainment, or the promotion of a particular political agenda that takes precedence over their role as public educators. Consider just a few examples of how the very factors that create and disseminate information also affect our understanding of the world both by what information they spread and—more importantly—what information they do not:

- Democracies still keep millions of secrets despite their openness. The United States, one of the world's most transparent countries, creates more than 3.5 million secrets each year, almost 10,000 secrets per day.[42] More than 32,000 full-time employees at 20 departments and agencies are involved in classification activities and approximately 1.5 billion pages of records at least 25 years old remain classified.[43]
- An extensive literature documents the forces that distort media coverage of international events due to the fact that (1) many media organizations are businesses with a profit motive; (2) the media must report on the government's activities while simultaneously relying on the government as a source of that information; and (3) the media has significant influence over which stories get coverage, which do not, and how those stories are

presented. Those decisions are in turn affected by costs, geography, what else is happening in the world at the same time, and the interests of viewers and readers.[44]

- NGOs focus on some issues and not on others. What issues they do cover, depends on a confluence of circumstances including leadership, timing, funding, and technology. Notably, attention and money do not always go to the most deserving causes, and groups that are supported by larger international organizations, often drown out small, indigenous groups. As Clifford Bob writes, "In a context where marketing trumps justice, local challengers—whether environmental groups, labor rights activists, or independence-minded separatists—face long odds. Not only do they jostle for attention among dozens of equally worthy competitors, but they also confront the pervasive indifference of international audiences."[45]

- Information released by international organizations and regimes is limited by selective participation, including nonparticipation by some of the worst offenders. Moreover, disclosure regimes exist in only a small number of issue areas and, even in those areas the high costs of collecting and reporting information limit their scope.

- The reach of information and communication technologies is still extremely limited. Two out of every three human beings have never made a telephone call. Nineteen out of twenty people in the world lack Internet access. For every two telephone lines in all of sub-Saharan Africa, there are three in Manhattan alone.[46]

Complicating matters further, information is collected, analyzed, and disseminated by human beings (or at least by computers programmed by human beings). Humans often have trouble processing information and even more trouble processing large amounts of information—something that transparent organizations provide in abundance. Decades of scholarship indicate that human beings rely on cognitive shortcuts to help them cope with large volumes of information. We form theories about the way things work and we may resist new information that does not fit our preexisting views. Though these cognitive processes help us to cope with information and form opinions, they can also lead us astray. Thus, even when the information we receive because of greater transparency is excellent and unbiased, we may not interpret it accurately. We may fail to recognize important information amid the "noise" of constant information streams or we may fail to recognize its implications.[47]

Three key factors affect the ability of people to recognize important information when they see it. First, correct interpretation is more likely when the "signal-to-noise" ratio—that is, the strength of the signal relative to the strength of the confusing or distracting background stimuli—is low. When there is simply too much information, people may disregard important data.[48] Second, people are more likely to recognize important information if they expect to find it, and if it does not contradict their existing beliefs. Third, people are more likely to recognize important signals if they work in an environment that rewards correct appraisal and that does not punish people for coming up with the "wrong" answer.[49] Though the first factor may seem to be the most important, controlled laboratory tests show that information overload is less important than the second and third factors.[50]

Humans filter information through their own cognitive processes, but also interpret information in the context of broader social relationships. As part of this process, humans tend to sort others into categories such as friend or foe. Assigning this identity makes the world easier to understand and helps us to predict how others will behave.[51] Governments, too, predict each other's actions not in isolation. but as part of a history of social practices, a fact that affects whether certain actions by governments are considered threats or not.[52] For example, we normally consider the possession of nuclear weapons as a threat. But, as Benjamin Frankel indicates, "If we base our judgment of a country's intentions concerning nuclear weapon development on capabilities alone, then we would have to regard some thirty countries as proliferation suspects."[53] That is obviously not the case and governments worry about some countries' nuclear capability far more than others. The United States, for instance, would be far more concerned if Iran developed theater nuclear weapons than if Canada did likewise.

People must also draw meaning from information, which can be complicated, even when that information consists of tangible, measurable facts. Consider two examples: the level of pollutants in a river or the number of missiles near a border. Both pollutants and missiles are observable, physical entities that can be counted using established scientific methods. However, interpreting the data is still problematic. What exactly should be counted? What exactly qualifies as a "pollutant"? Do a pile of unassembled parts count as a missile? What level of chemicals or missiles is acceptable? At what level do we treat the chemicals or missiles as dangerous? Should people bother to change their behavior based on the new information? Complicating matters further, the intellectual and normative frameworks we use to interpret information constantly evolve. Standards of behavior change. As a result, levels of pollution that were once acceptable, may no longer be tolerated. People may no longer feel safe with a certain level of defense, even though that same level made them feel safe in the past.

The fact that intellectual and normative standards change, shows that people's views are malleable and can be influenced by information. People can persuade others to change their minds, a fact that makes transparency more complex than simply removing obstacles to understanding or giving more people access to information. By disseminating information and giving people different types of information from different sources, the trend toward greater transparency can change how people interpret information. Merely by packaging information in a certain way, people may in a sense create new knowledge.[54] When organizations aggregate existing information or present information in ways relevant to political debates, they have the potential to change the way in which people think and behave and what issues they feel are important. Transparency International did not discover corruption and reveal it to the world's surprise. Rather, it measured, analyzed, and publicized corruption in order to persuade governments and international organizations that they must confront the problem and change their own behavior.

Why Transparency Matters

The trend toward greater transparency deserves attention because it affects international relations, because influential leaders advocate greater transparency as a solution to many problems, and because it bears on many important debates about international politics and security. Indeed, growing transparency affects the lives of citizens around the globe. It affects the fundamental security of societies by influencing the likelihood of war and peace and influences the success of cooperative efforts to reduce violent conflict. The trend toward greater transparency affects the quality and efficiency of governance, at all levels of government within states, and internationally. Greater transparency also empowers citizens directly and allows them to monitor world affairs themselves instead of relying on a single official source of information. For these reasons alone, transparency merits greater scholarly attention.

Technology experts, peace advocates, political scientists, politicians, business leaders, arms control experts, and international lawyers all cite growing transparency as a trend that may solve a host of global problems. Their faith in transparency leads them to advocate transparency as a matter of policy and to make predictions about what greater transparency means. However, many "transparency optimists" have not examined carefully their assumptions about transparency, which is dangerous since greater transparency may not always have the effects optimists expect. That transparency sometimes has negative consequences is no reason to restrict it, but leaders should anticipate and prepare for transparency's complex effects.

Transparency also merits further study because the effects of greater transparency bear on important debates about international politics. This book sheds light on these debates and on whether transparency will have the effects that scholars and policy makers expect.[55] For instance, the trend toward greater transparency should bear on several theories regarding war and peace. Some analysts believe that transparency will make the world more peaceful by clearing up misunderstandings that can lead to war.[56] Governments will have better information about opponents' intentions and capabilities. Consequently, they will not start wars because they overestimate an opponent's aggressive intentions and enter a conflict neither side wants, or because they underestimate the other side's strength and start a war they wrongly think they can win.[57] Greater transparency may also reduce conflicts by easing what political scientists call the security dilemma. According to this concept, wars and arms races occur in international politics because states cannot be sure of each other's intentions. As a result, when states arm themselves, expand, or form alliances to increase their own security, other states view those actions as threatening, even when such measures are purely defensive and not motivated by any aggressive intent.[58] Political scientists view this scenario as tragic because states, interested only in increasing their security, end up being even less secure.[59] Some scholars argue that transparency can end the tragedy of the security dilemma. If states can readily discern that others are not aggressive, have limited objectives, and genuinely want peace, then international conflict can be reduced significantly.[60]

Some observers believe that greater transparency will allow us to know one another better, which will help to prevent conflicts. We can see this sentiment in the statements of technology enthusiasts like Michael Dertouzos, who argue that "Any new channel of communication among the people and organizations of this world is likely to contribute to increased understanding and hence greater peace."[61] Advocates of international exchange and youth programs echo this sentiment, though they favor face-to-face contact versus contact via technology. Whatever this means, advocates of this idea agree that increased contact improves relations between groups, which inevitably decreases the chance that conflicts will escalate to violence. Some analysts expect transparency to reduce the incidence of intergroup conflict by preventing political leaders from demonizing other groups.[62] The ability to dehumanize enemies through propaganda, they argue, is a necessary condition for waging war.[63] Dehumanizing enemies, in turn, requires the government to control information—something that is increasingly difficult in the age of transparency—to avoid contradiction or the spread of information that humanizes other groups. Common examples of this phenomenon are ethnic conflicts in Bosnia and Rwanda, where controlling the media was critical to mobilizing the political support that was necessary in order to wage campaigns of ethnic cleansing and genocide.[64]

When conflicts do break out, greater transparency will lead to more frequent acts of intervention by third parties, according to some analysts. Theoretically, by providing early warning of impending conflicts, transparency should allow outsiders (often NGOs) to identify trouble spots and to encourage governments or international organizations to intervene before conflicts get out of hand. Greater transparency also makes foreign conflicts more visible to the world and therefore harder to ignore. In an example of the so-called CNN effect, people who watch scenes of horrible violence on their televisions may pressure their politicians to intervene in the conflict, in order to end the violence.

Other analysts hope that greater transparency will empower NGOs at the expense of sovereign governments, and topple authoritarian regimes, trends they present as unambiguously positive. With respect to authoritarian governments, observers argue that the free flow of information will erode the power of authoritarian regimes and allow citizens to challenge their governments' authority.[65] Former Citibank CEO Walter Wriston predicts that the spread of information technology will eradicate authoritarianism around the globe by opening people's eyes to the democratic freedoms they are denied. Aware of what they are missing, citizens will demand more say over their destiny and topple governments that do not comply.[66] According to Wriston, transparency empowers citizens "to watch Big Brother" instead of the other way around, unleashing "a virus of freedom for which there is no antidote" that will be "spread by electronic networks to the four corners of the earth."[67] The most commonly cited prediction concerns the People's Republic of China, where approximately one hundred million Internet users are viewed as increasingly slipping beyond the government's control.[68] Indeed, President Bill Clinton boldly announced that the Internet will make a closed political and economic society "impossible" and ultimately bring down the Communist regime.[69]

About this Book

This book presents a view of transparency that is more complex than the conventional wisdom. Though the trend toward greater transparency will have major effects on international politics—by reducing uncertainty, helping people to know each other better, and decentralizing power—greater transparency will not always reduce international conflicts; it will sometimes make them worse. Transparency, furthermore, will not always promote cooperation and good governance; it may sometimes strengthen illiberal regimes rather than weaken them. Transparency does empower transnational NGOs, but it does not always empower them as much or in the ways we might like.

Why is this prognosis gloomier than most of the discussions of transparency to date? First, comprehensive analyses about the impact of greater transparency are relatively rare. Analysts mention transparency as part of a solution to particular problems in international affairs, but do not take a broader perspective. The result is that discussions of transparency are often one-sided and are focused on its positive effects with little, if any, discussion of costs. Such analyses are not necessarily wrong, but they are incomplete. The cumulative effect is an overwhelming focus on the positive aspects of transparency. To address this imbalance, the major purpose of this book is to discuss the complex implications of growing transparency, with particular attention to the circumstances under which transparency's effects are negative.

Second, many discussions of transparency contain unanalyzed assumptions based on a particular set of values. Analysts often assume an underlying harmony of interests in discussions of international affairs.[70] When that assumption is accurate, clearing up misperceptions and uncertainty should allow governments to see their common interests and encourage cooperation, mutual understanding, and peace. However, harmony is not always the underlying condition of international affairs, an unfortunate reality that greater transparency may only expose. Nations sometimes have real conflicts of interests and values and will want to protect them, often resorting to violence.[71]

Third, some discussions of transparency focus exclusively on deliberate acts of openness, which inevitably lead to more optimistic predictions.[72] Deliberate acts of transparency by governments signal that those governments are trustworthy and adhering to certain standards of behavior. If governments desire friendly political relations and have cooperative intentions, transparency highlights this inclination and may encourage like responses by other states. In this way, transparency fuels virtuous cycles in which clearly visible cooperative gestures are reciprocated, and further reinforces the friendly relationship. Because of this dynamic, sometimes transparency may be more meaningful as a political signal about identity and intent than for the specific information it reveals.

Whereas deliberate acts of openness can lead to better relations among governments, we should not expect involuntary transparency due to technological breakthroughs, investigative reporting by the global media, or reports by NGOs to have the same effect. Instead, involuntary transparency may lead to many of the more pernicious outcomes elaborated earlier in this book. Involuntary transparency is not a signal, nor is it as likely to spread information that indicates cooperative or at least benign intent on the part of governments. It may show arms buildups and hostile intentions, which may make political relations worse. In this context, transparency may fuel vicious cycles by demonstrating a high level of threat, which leads to hostile rhetoric and military preparations, which leads to even worse relations. Involuntary transparency is also likely to spread information that governments would prefer to keep secret such as corruption, human rights abuses, environmental degradation, oppression, the desire to overrun or otherwise abuse their neighbors, or plans to kill members of their population.

Importantly, a lack of transparency itself sends a signal that more transparent governments may perceive as threatening. The trend toward greater transparency is a condition, but a commitment to transparency is a value, motivated by a particular view of morality or justice. Like transparency, its absence sends a political signal about identity and values, whether governments wish to send that signal or not. Secrecy implies that states have something to hide. It also suggests that a regime does not fully embrace the prevailing norms of the international community.

Finally, greater transparency can mislead us. Transparency does make more information about the intentions and capabilities of governments and powerful organizations widely available to the global public. It does not mean that information is correct, unbiased, or complete or that we will interpret that information correctly. As a result, greater transparency is no guarantee of fewer misunderstandings.

Outline of the Book

This is a conceptual book. Its goal is to examine what transparency is, and how it will affect international politics and security. Its purpose is not to test specific hypotheses—a goal that the author and others have pursued in other publications—but to integrate existing knowledge and to determine what it tells us about the trend toward greater transparency and its implications. The book includes several case studies: one on the 1994 genocide in Rwanda, one on the international response to that genocide, and one on transparency in Singapore. The purpose of these

Figure 1.

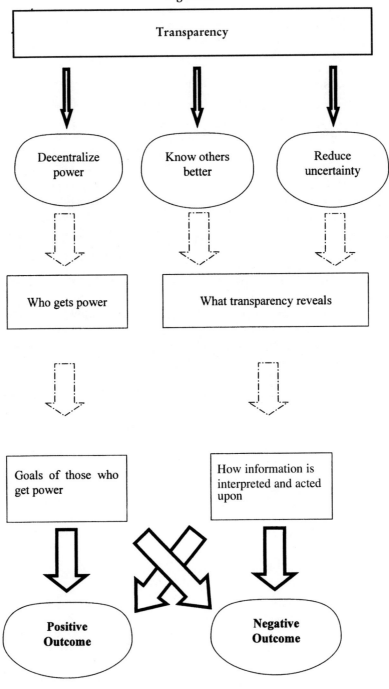

case studies is to illustrate the complex dynamics of information flows and the implications of greater transparency.

The book draws extensively on scholarly research, but always with an eye to its practical application. It intends to bridge the worlds of theory and practice. Making this goal explicit is important because it has costs and benefits. The cost is that this book cannot possibly engage every scholarly debate in adequate depth or resolve those debates. It also cannot give policy makers extensive details about how to implement the book's conclusions. The benefit is that it can ask both scholars and policy makers to consider the broader context of their work and to recognize how flawed or incomplete assumptions can lead to flawed understanding and action.

Chapter 2 analyzes how transparency reduces uncertainty in international politics and argues that less uncertainty will not always lead to more cooperation and less conflict. Greater transparency can illuminate hostility, invite aggression, and exacerbate conflicts. It can undermine efforts at international cooperation and conflict resolution.

Chapter 3 examines how transparency increases knowledge of other peoples and argues that more contact with, and information about, other groups will not always lead to peace. Although greater transparency can familiarize "the other" and in so doing, reduce intergroup animosities and prejudice, it can also show conflicting values and interests. Under some conditions, greater transparency can exacerbate hostilities and spread prejudices about out-groups.

Chapter 4 analyzes how transparency disseminates information about foreign peoples and disputes and argues that information will not always result in earlier and more frequent conflict intervention. Although greater transparency can help the international community to overcome informational obstacles to early intervention and even help to create the political will to intervene, sometimes greater transparency will make conflict intervention less likely.

Chapter 5 discusses the tendency of transparency to decentralize power and argues that greater transparency will not necessarily empower democrats and peace-loving NGOs. Sovereign states, including those run by authoritarian governments, retain significant control over information and, when they do not, the results may not always be positive. Greater transparency empowers terrorists and activists alike.

Chapter 6 summarizes the book's arguments and emphasizes the importance of stripping predictions about transparency's effects from value-laden assumptions about what transparency shows. That approach reveals transparency as a complex phenomenon, the effects of which can be either positive or negative depending on what transparency reveals, how people interpret the information they receive, and how people respond to that information.

Though the purpose of this book is to separate the effects of transparency from false assumptions about what transparency will reveal, ideas and values are critical to understanding the effects of greater transparency. They influence what information people seek and how people interpret and act on that information. They affect the behavior of governments. Because ideas and values evolve, transparency will have different effects at different times. Moreover, these ideas and values can be actively influenced. That possibility gives governments and other powerful organizations a potent source of power in the age of transparency because they can reach foreign audiences quickly, cheaply, broadly, and directly. They can persuade people to change their minds and look at information in new ways. The ability to convince others to share one's ideas and values conveys extraordinary power. When others "want what you want," accomplishing goals is easier and success is more likely.[73] Those who can persuade others to share their values and interests through a compelling message, will be the true winners in the age of transparency.

The scope of this book is ambitious. By definition that means that many issues are not covered in depth and many more are not covered at all. The book does not discuss at all, for instance, transparency of financial institutions, central banks, or fiscal and monetary policy making. It does not discuss at all the effects of transparency on currency markets. The book also does not discuss the relative transparency of international institutions, ranging from the European Commission to the World Trade Organization, or the effects of transparency on negotiations. Instead, this book focuses on broad issues of security and governance and on the transparency of national governments to their citizens, to transnational organizations, and to one another. The reason for this choice is that sovereign states and their governments remain the single most powerful actors in international politics, and by focusing on them, we can analyze global transparency and explain its most important effects. Though the broader phenomenon of transparency is an interesting one that deserves further attention, especially analyses that examine both the pros and cons of greater transparency, it is beyond the scope of this book. This book also does not concern operational issues related to transparency. Though it discusses, for example, the relationship between transparency and accountability and transparency and conflict resolution, it does not discuss how to increase the accountability or how to resolve conflicts. A "how-to" guide to these and other objectives would undoubtedly be valuable, but those are separate endeavors.

Most importantly, this book is not a defense of secrecy. More often than not, secrecy is a bad policy for governments, which all too often classify information for the wrong reasons. Secrecy covers up missteps and corruption. It prevents leaders, who sometimes become over-enchanted with their own ideas, from defending them to skeptics. Criticism is good for governance and transparency ensures that governments face criticism. Secrecy makes governments weak. Transparency is also morally right. Governments should be held accountable to the governed. Holding leaders to high standards, and punishing leaders who fail to meet them, mandates that citizens know what their leaders are up to. Citizens pay taxes and have a right to see how they are spent. They fight in wars and have a right to understand why they must sacrifice their lives. Citizens abide by laws and are punished if they do not. They have the right to expect that their leaders will uphold similar standards. Transparency does not ensure accountability, but accountability without transparency is nearly impossible.

Chapter 2

Transparency and Conflict

"If states knew with certainty that other states sought only to be secure, they could refrain from attacking each other and be perfectly secure.... Democracies are particularly good at dispelling uncertainty and... this fosters peace."

—Political scientist Andrew Kydd[1]

"Uncertainty... is threatening itself."

—Psychologist Reginald Adams[2]

Uncertainty is dangerous, according to the conventional wisdom regarding international politics. Uncertainty about how others could use their military power leads states to regard all power as a potential threat, regardless of who bears that power. This makes states perpetually insecure and leads them to spend money on guns rather than on butter, diverting scarce resources away from other needs.[3] Military spending, reciprocated by equally nervous societies, encourages arms races that make no one more secure and sometimes escalate to war. Uncertainty also leads states to make poor or counterproductive decisions. Inaccurate estimates of relative military strength lead states to initiate wars they will lose. Ill-informed states misperceive their neighbors' intentions and inadvertently provoke wars. Conflicts of interest escalate to violence when states fail to recognize mutually acceptable solutions short of war. Fear that others will cheat prevents states from forming agreements such as arms control treaties that could make them more secure. Though nations willingly enter conflicts when threats are real, they do so needlessly when conflicts result from misperception,

23

miscalculation, or uncertainty about the motivations of other states. Such unwanted conflicts should be the easiest to prevent. The hope for transparency is that increased knowledge and international understanding will help states to prevent unnecessary wars and to devote their resources to more productive causes.

Greater transparency should reduce—though not eliminate—international uncertainty by providing states with more and better information about the intentions, capabilities, and priorities of other states. This information, in turn, should reduce misperceptions (defined as false interpretations of information) and miscalculations (defined as plans based on misperceptions). A lack of information is certainly not the only reason for misperceptions and miscalculations, but misguided views are harder to maintain in the face of overwhelming evidence to the contrary.

Unfortunately, transparency is a double-edged sword. Though transparency does reduce uncertainty, less uncertainty will not always mean more security or peace. Rather, the effects of greater transparency depend on what it shows and how states react. We cannot assume that transparency will show behavior that supports peace and cooperation or that states will react to information in ways that will lead to a more just or peaceful world. Greater transparency can indeed enhance international peace and security if it shows that other states are genuinely peace-loving, but transparency can make conflicts worse if it illuminates hostility, aggression, or arms buildups. By illuminating weakness, transparency can undermine deterrence and encourage aggression. It can alert states to closing windows of opportunities and give them incentives to fight. By taking away strategic ambiguity, transparency can encourage states to find less visible, more pernicious means of defending their interests.

This chapter explores the role of uncertainty in international politics and the complex implications of greater transparency for international security, conflict resolution, and security cooperation. It argues that greater transparency can be a mixed blessing. This view contrasts with prevailing opinion, which assumes that decreasing uncertainty will reveal information that enhances international cooperation and security. That outcome is possible, but not assured.

Uncertainty, Security, and Conflict

The lack of a world government to protect states from acts of violence, and to enforce agreements between them, means that states must protect their own interests and citizens.[4] In this environment, states are perpetually insecure. Uncertainty about how other states will use their power in the future means that all power is a potential threat. States, therefore, build military strength and maintain standing armies even in the absence of direct threats to their security.

Paradoxically, building military strength may actually make states less secure. Even though a state may arm only to defend itself and its interests, other states cannot be certain of this motivation. To be on the safe side, those states arm in response, creating a spiral of suspicion and insecurity even when none of the parties has aggressive intentions.[5] This "security dilemma" is a rational, if unfortunate, side effect of an international system in which states must protect their own security and interests. States can try to avoid this dilemma by predicting which states have peaceful or aggressive intentions, but the costs of guessing wrong are high. Consequently, states tend to assume the worst unless they have substantial information to the contrary and a level of confidence that is difficult to come by. Unfortunately, such behavior is counterproductive since treating other states like enemies can sometimes become a self-fulfilling prophecy.[6] According to some theories of international relations, under conditions of uncertainty, even states that are not aggressive can get drawn into war.[7] Unsure of an adversary's motivations, a state may interpret that adversary's behavior in the worst possible light. The steps they take to defend themselves appear threatening to the adversary, which may attack in order to defend itself against the perceived threat.[8]

Uncertainty also affects wars involving states that want to fight. Arguments about the security dilemma typically assume that states wish to avoid violence and only wish to protect their own security. In the lingo of political science, most states are assumed to be "security seekers." States—sometimes rightly and sometimes wrongly—do choose to fight to protect or acquire something of value, be it territory, oil, or people. Whether or not these states use force to achieve specific objectives depends on the costs and benefits of war.

When states consider whether to fight, uncertainty about other states' military capabilities can lead them to fight wars they would otherwise avoid. Clarity about the distribution of state power should lead to peace, according to some scholars, because states typically fight wars only when they think they can win.[9] Leaders weigh the costs and benefits of using force and attack when the costs are low relative to the rewards.[10] When they have accurate information about the military capabilities of potential rivals, wars often will be unnecessary or unlikely. States normally avoid fighting stronger states since there is no point wasting lives and treasure if they know they are going to lose. Wars with weaker states may be unnecessary since less powerful countries often will comply with stronger states' demands rather than suffer the costs of war. Geoffrey Blainey summarizes this argument: "On the eve of each war at least one of the nations miscalculated its bargaining power.... And in that sense every war is an accident."[11]

Recent exponents of Blainey's theory assume that states would always prefer an alternative to war if only they could identify it.[12] However, uncertainty about adversaries' priorities sometimes prevents states from identifying an acceptable settlement. The parties then give up on negotiations and turn to violence. If states had perfect information about the preferences of other states, these scholars argue, we would see very few wars since states would simply negotiate their way to an acceptable settlement and avoid the costly outcome of war.[13] Empirical studies support this view, demonstrating that imperfect information makes conflict more likely.[14]

Uncertainty about priorities can lead to unintended war when states underestimate the importance of a given issue to another state. When states do not understand what policies constitute "red lines" that they should not cross, they can unintentionally start a war. As Kenneth Schultz writes, "A state may be unsure, for example, how its opponent would respond to a demand to change the status quo: will it acquiesce to such a demand or will it resist?"[15] Similarly, unintentionally provoking a war is possible if states underestimate another state's resolve or willingness to intervene in support of an ally. Numerous examples of these dynamics are evident in the relationship between the United States and China over the last few decades. Mao Zedong supported Kim Il-Sung's invasion of South Korea, never imagining that President Harry S. Truman would respond with massive force.[16] In 1958, the strength of President Dwight D. Eisenhower's response surprised Mao after a military crisis in the Taiwan Straits. In 1996, when China conducted missile exercises off the Taiwanese coast, Beijing did not expect the United States' rapid dispatch of warships to the Straits.

Uncertainty also leads states to forego cooperation even when they could increase their security. What explains this apparently irrational behavior? States fear a sucker's deal in which they change their behavior but others cheat and gain an unfair advantage.[17] In a world where states must protect their own security and interests, relative losses of power to other states can present serious security problems if the cheaters exploit their gains to the detriment of cooperating states. The barriers to cooperation are highest when members of an agreement benefit collectively if the agreement is upheld, but each member individually has incentives to cheat. Arms control agreements are a classic example of this dilemma. All parties would benefit if they collectively reduced arms buildups or stockpiles. However, if all parties but one comply, the "defector" gets the double benefit of increasing its own military strength while others reduce theirs.[18] Uncertainty about compliance, therefore, is a central obstacle to international cooperation.[19] This uncertainty makes verification a critical component of many security agreements, though of course, even intensive verification efforts may not be sufficient to allay distrust.[20] As indicated by both the North Korean and Libyan nuclear weapons programs—which were developed in spite of international agreements, verification protocols, and inspections—states do sometimes cheat.

In addition to reassuring states that others are also complying with agreements, transparency facilitates security agreements that aim to prevent surprise attacks. Because of the military advantages of attacking first and the incentives for attacked states to respond rapidly, the risk of surprise attacks is extremely destabilizing. Transparency measures reduce that risk by providing early warning of troop movements and military exercises and by helping states to "separate unambiguous signals of hostile intent from the random noise of continuous military activity."[21]

When states have credible information that others will not launch surprise attacks, they can maintain a lower level of military readiness and avoid miscalculations that can escalate to an accidental war. Avoiding such miscalculations through early warning was a major concern in the Cold War when the stability of nuclear deterrence depended on the ability of the two superpowers to respond in minutes to a surprise nuclear attack. That strategy also increased the risk of accidental war, however, because wrongly concluding that a surprise nuclear attack was underway could lead to a nuclear response and annihilation.

We now turn to ways in which transparency can increase security and decrease the likelihood of conflict by reducing uncertainty—and why transparency will not always have that effect.

Transparency and Conflict

Greater transparency reduces uncertainty, which leads many analysts to view greater transparency as a force for international peace and cooperation. If states knew with more confidence the intentions, capabilities, and priorities of other states, the argument goes, they could abandon worst-case assumptions and make more effective policies. Transparency should help states that do not want to fight avoid conflict in the first place. It can help states that are content with the status quo to recognize each other and to reinforce peace. It can illuminate military strength and deter states that do want to fight from initiating wars. Transparency of military capabilities can encourage restraint and provide a foundation for security cooperation. It can help states form agreements that enhance their security.

Greater transparency should reduce the likelihood of international conflict caused by uncertainty about other states' intentions since states would then have a clearer understanding of whether the military strength of other states constitutes a threat.[22] Better information about other states' intentions and preferences would allow decision makers to not always assume the worst and to pay the high price of that assumption.[23] It would allow states to coexist peacefully and to redirect resources from military spending to more productive purposes. Theoretically, states seeking security only for defensive purposes could enjoy that objective without reducing the security of other states, so that only some sort of misperception about motivations should lead "security seekers" into conflict with each other.[24] Without uncertainty, in other words, "the security dilemma is no dilemma and the search for security leads to peace, not war."[25]

Transparency helps states estimate threats more accurately. Better information can prevent states from initiating wars they will lose due to mistaken estimates of others' strength or resolve. Knowledge of others' priorities and interests helps states avoid provoking unwanted conflicts and identify solutions to conflicts. Transparency can reassure states and their citizens that others are complying with arms control agreements that make everyone more secure. It can contribute to greater confidence and trust.

By giving states a window into other societies, greater transparency allows leaders to see how their states' behavior is interpreted abroad. If others interpret a state's policies in undesirable or unexpected ways, leaders have the opportunity to adjust their behavior and rhetoric accordingly. In this way, greater transparency may help states to recognize when their actions are counterproductive and actually make them less secure.[26]

When states are not belligerent and seek only their own security, transparency can help them to signal their peaceful intentions credibly. The signals of transparent states are more credible because rival states can "see" that the signal is a public commitment for the regime, observe the domestic reaction, and generally get more clues about how committed the state is to the policy it signals.[27] Transparency also lets other states see that a state is abiding by established rules or norms.[28]

Since words alone are cheap in international politics, states also can signal defensive intentions through the configuration of their military forces. In this way states can signal that they will not threaten their neighbors and possibly escape from arms races or conflicts caused by misunderstandings.[29] When transparency demonstrates credibly that states possess weapons with only defensive applications and forces deployed only to defend rather than attack,[30] other states need not fear surprise attacks and feel that they must initiate an arms buildup in preparation for war.[31] States can signal defensive intent through any of the following measures: a navy able to defend territorial waters but unable to launch offensive maritime campaigns, forces deployed away from the edge of expected battle areas so that an opponent would be able to detect significant forward movement, or fortification that would hinder or prevent force movement in sensitive areas. In addition, states can forego systems that are useful to take and hold territory like long-range weaponry and fighter aircraft in favor of more defensively oriented systems like mines, anti-tank missiles, and support aircraft with short-range abilities and no refueling capability.[32]

To reinforce that states have only defensive intentions or avoid accidental war, states may commit themselves to a formal treaty or regime, the most ambitious of which are cooperative security regimes. The purpose of such regimes is to create a stable, secure environment in which states pledge that they will not attack each other and back up that pledge with arms reductions or militaries deployed only for defense. Transparency plays an important role by reassuring members of the regime that all parties are complying with agreements and actively participating in the regime.[33] Cooperative security regimes can effectively help states to break out of the security dilemma when all members have "fundamentally compatible security objectives" *and* agree on how to configure their militaries for defensive purposes.[34] Restricting destabilizing arms acquisitions may have tangible security benefits, but the more important outcome may be agreeing on what behaviors are destabilizing and then visibly avoiding such behavior. Evidence that states share norms of behavior can build trust more effectively than any direct military effects of agreements.

With or without formal security agreements, transparency can encourage restraint if states see that they will be repelled either directly by the state they attack or by third parties. By clarifying whether allies or international coalitions will come to the aid of an attacked country, transparency can discourage aggression even when the intended target is itself weak. Before acts of aggression occur, transparency can also encourage collective defense by helping groups of states to identify threats and to join forces against them. Such multilateral actions can occur as part of a formal security organization or regime, but they may also consist of "coalitions of the willing" formed on an ad hoc basis to confront particular threats.

The possibility that identifying destabilizing arms buildups deters aggression either directly or by encouraging coalitions to balance against threats is the basis of arms transparency regimes like the United Nations Register of Conventional Arms (UNROCA).[35] The hope for such regimes is that transparency will facilitate a sort of diffuse deterrence. States with an interest in peace and stability will be able to identify potential aggressors and deter them, even when they themselves are not the target of aggression and the actual target of that aggression is weak. As the General Assembly Resolution that created the Register observes, "an increased level of openness and transparency in the field of armaments would enhance confidence, promote stability, help states to exercise restraint, ease tensions and strengthen regional and international peace and security" without any formal rules or punishments for violating them.[36]

When states wish only to protect their own states' security and have no interest in threatening others, transparency can help start or maintain virtuous cycles. When states genuinely want peace, transparency makes that clear, which reassures others. Those states then take steps such as reducing military spending that make the first state more secure. That state may take similar steps and so on. Transparency encourages the cycle by indicating peaceful intentions and defensive force postures. It then perpetuates the cycle by credibly showing the responses and by reassuring states that conciliatory policies are being reciprocated.

Transparency's role in encouraging virtuous cycles of security and cooperation may help to explain why democracies rarely fight wars with each other. States that are more open and share more information about their decision making can signal their intentions more credibly. Charles Lipson writes,

> Their public debates, relatively open decision making, and free press allow partners to make more confident estimates about how faithfully democracies will execute their promises, now and in the future. (This same open discourse probably allows democracies to make systematically better estimates of others' intentions, as well.) These procedures make democracies more trustworthy and allow partners to gauge the depth of support for policies and promises on a continuous basis.[37]

Thus, even when there is an arms buildup in democracies, other democracies may not perceive those actions as threatening if they can observe the motivation for arms buildups and ascertain nonaggressive motives.[38] Greater transparency also may allow fellow democracies to recognize shared interests and values as well as nonviolent solutions to conflicts.[39]

When states *are* inclined to fight, transparency clarifies the high costs of war and enhances deterrence. Since states usually do not initiate wars they expect to lose, better information about the military capabilities of other states should prevent wars based on miscalculations of relative power. Transparency may also reduce the incidence of war by facilitating coercion. Since weaker states can clearly see what they are up against if they do not comply with a stronger state's demands, they can make reasoned decisions about whether fighting is worthwhile.

The Complexity of Transparency and Conflict

Greater transparency will not always encourage peace and cooperation since the effects of transparency depend on what transparency shows, how that information is interpreted, and how states respond. Greater transparency does discourage conflicts when states genuinely want peace and the costs of war are high. However, greater transparency can also be ineffectual, exacerbate conflicts, or encourage aggression. Transparency is a complex phenomenon and provides no easy solution to the problem of international conflict.

A key reason why transparency will not always encourage peace is that, despite the attention paid to unwanted wars, not all conflicts are caused by misunderstandings.[40] States sometimes have conflicting interests and violence is an effective way to protect or advance them.[41] When states hold truly incompatible objectives, conflict and tension are predictable side effects of world politics. Policy makers can influence whether those conflicts are resolved peacefully, but they are unlikely to avoid violence altogether. Presumably, we can expect real conflicts of interest as long as nations are not all converging toward an ideal model of politics or economics—if, as Martha Finnemore argues, Weberian rationality is not "marching relentlessly across the earth, leaving in its wake a marketized, bureaucratized world of increasingly similar forms."[42] If the interests and values of countries are not converging, transparency may only make conflicts more evident.[43]

Even when transparency helps governments to see that an opponent's intentions are peaceful, the risk that states' intentions can change, may undermine some of transparency's pacifying effects.[44] John Mearsheimer's assertion that "states have little choice but to fear each other," is overly stark but contains a grain of truth.[45] Superior power is often threatening regardless of intentions because latent power can always be mobilized. This fact is particularly important because defense procurement must often be years, if not decades, ahead of current needs, while governments and their intentions can change quickly. As discussed earlier, however, preparations for possible future wars can ultimately reduce security further since such preparations are usually observable and encourage like actions by other states.

Greater transparency also makes states less secure if it shows that states are aggressive, greedy, or seek to maximize their power.[46] Just as transparency can illuminate peaceful intentions, it can emphasize hostility and a willingness to fight. In such cases, transparency acts as a megaphone that amplifies belligerent rhetoric and exacerbates conflicts. When hostile rhetoric is widely heard, rhetoric can build on itself and reduce the number of politically acceptable options short of the use of force.[47] In contrast to many liberal arguments, such rhetoric comes not just from leaders who will benefit from war, but also from mass publics. War can be popular and several cases, such as the Spanish-American War, illustrate that the general public can desire war even more than leaders and can pressure reluctant governments to fight. When domestic politics makes it difficult for politicians to defuse a crisis, transparency may constrain the options of negotiators and limit the political space available for peaceful conflict resolution. Transparency exacerbates conflicts if it shows that there is public support for war and may be particularly dangerous when it shows that there is widespread animosity toward some other nation or "out-group," which can heighten perceived threats and exacerbate conflicts.[48]

Aggressive nationalism is not limited to authoritarian states. Indeed, because democracies tend to be the most transparent of states, they may also send the most belligerent signals when roused. Democracies do not usually fight each other, but strong evidence indicates that democracies fight wars at least as much as other types of states. Classical liberals like Immanual Kant, failed to predict this phenomenon, believing that states ruled by the people whose lives and treasure would be lost by war, would also be the most pacific.[49] But, historically, war is often popular in democracies. Publics may support war even more than their leaders, thus constraining efforts at peaceful resolution of a conflict.[50] Democratizing states may be the most dangerous of all. When publics are able to express nationalism that authoritarian regimes suppressed, the results may be a more aggressive foreign policy.[51]

The 1898 Fashoda Crisis, which began when French and British forces met in the Upper Nile Valley, provides an example of how transparency can amplify hostile intentions in conflicts between democracies. Though tensions were high throughout the crisis and war seemed possible, neither government wanted war. Diplomats worked behind-the-scenes to resolve the conflict but, in public, politics trumped moderation. French Foreign Minister Théophile Delcassé, for instance, was willing to cut a deal privately but spoke "brave words...for public consumption." These words were so convincing that the British ambassador to Paris argued that Delcassé believed his own rhetoric and was unwilling to negotiate. The press and parliaments on both sides echoed the belligerent tone. A headline in the French newspaper *Le Matin* read, "The only answer worthy of France is No!" Though the British press generally advocated restraint at the beginning of the standoff, it became increasingly hostile as weeks passed. In France, public opinion grew more pugnacious and the Parliament and press picked up this tone. The crisis finally ended when France, the far weaker state in the standoff, chose a humiliating withdrawal over war. Transparency created more room for misperceptions between policy makers in Britain and France because the press and parliaments on both sides exacerbated hostilities, creating a vicious cycle of action and reaction. Negotiators were able to avoid war only by insulating themselves from public opinion and by quietly reaching a decision based on their complex interests.[52]

Uncertainty and Deterrence

The relationship between transparency and deterrence can be summarized in one simple question, does uncertainty breed aggression or restraint? Many analysts assume the latter and consequently, believe that transparency will increase international security by reducing uncertainty. But, in fact, transparency either supports or undermines deterrence depending on the military capabilities and intentions that uncertainty conceals.[53] Uncertainty can undermine deterrence if states overestimate their power or lead strong states to abandon peaceful efforts at coercion in favor of war. As a result, arguments that transparency of military capabilities or states' intentions will promote stability and peace are not wrong, but incomplete. Transparency may very well have those effects if it reveals information that is stabilizing, but that is not the only possible result.

   Deterrence theory is based on the idea that states will be deterred from fighting wars if they see that the costs of war outweigh the benefits. When transparency shows that a state is militarily stronger than a potential foe and will impose high costs on the battlefield, states can recognize in advance that they will either lose a war or win only at an extremely high cost.[54] By giving states better information with which to assess the costs of conflict, transparency in this circumstance can help to deter war. However, just as transparency can expose costs that deter war, it can expose net benefits and encourage conflict. Just as transparency can highlight strength, it exposes vulnerability, which may invite aggression by stronger states.

Recognizing that transparency can both strengthen or undermine deterrence is an important first step toward understanding the implications of greater transparency for international security, but the effects of greater transparency are more complex still. As analysts, we must predict the effects of greater transparency based not only on a snapshot of military capabilities but also on trends.[55] After all, transparency of military capabilities reveals not just how powerful states are, but how powerful they are becoming relative to other states. When less uncertainty leads governments to conclude that power shifts are not in their favor and windows of opportunity are closing, less uncertainty does not encourage restraint. In such circumstances, states feel pressured to act before it is too late, especially if that action will augment their power. States also may strike first to capitalize on the element of surprise. As Bruce Bueno de Mesquita observes, in this scenario "war can begin, even with full information if it is motivated by a fear of ceding any advantage, however small, that is attached to the first use of force."[56] To give a concrete example, the urge to leap through closing windows of opportunity may have led Japan to attack Pearl Harbor in December 1941. Until a few months before Pearl Harbor, Japanese leaders believed that Japan could secure the economic resources it needed through political pressure and limited use of force in Southeast Asia. But as war with the United States looked more likely and the United States and its allies increasingly cut off Japan's access to raw materials and energy, the Japanese navy high command—which had urged negotiations with the United States—suggested that any war with the United States must be initiated soon, if at all, before Japan exhausted its oil reserves. If war was inevitable, as Japanese leaders came to believe, Japan should strike while surprise was still on its side and prepared its December 7 attack even as negotiations continued.[57] Transparency, if it makes closing windows of opportunity more evident, could make these scenarios that much more likely.[58]

Transparency of military capabilities may also fail to enhance deterrence when the source of uncertainty is not inadequate information but a roughly equal balance of power. If states only fight wars they think they can win, states are most likely to miscalculate their relative power when military capabilities are roughly equal and superiority is difficult to establish. Transparency may provide information about military capabilities but the meaning of that information, that is, whether it means that another state will be militarily superior in battle or not, must be interpreted. Because competitors are unlikely to have exactly comparable weapons, force structures, skill on the battlefield, and so on, assessing the likelihood of success in war is both complicated and debatable. Though political scientists disagree about whether a balance of power between potential enemies or a clear power preponderance of one state over another is more likely to lead to peace, most scholarship indicates that power parity is more closely correlated with war, especially when power capabilities are shifting.[59] If this view is accurate, greater transparency of military capabilities may not deter war at all.

Greater transparency also will not enhance deterrence if states do not rely on a rational cost-benefit analysis when determining whether to fight. Indeed if states are sufficiently hostile toward one another, deterrence can fail even if capabilities are completely transparent. To give a particularly striking example, during the 1947-1948 partition of India and Pakistan, the military assets of the two newly independent countries were almost completely transparent while the joint Indo-Pakistan Military Commission divided the military assets according to a 2:1 ratio. Personnel on both sides served in the British Indian military in World War II and continued to serve together until August 15, 1947. However, this deep knowledge of the enemy's capabilities did not prevent Pakistan from launching a war a few weeks later—even as the Commission continued its work.[60]

Irrespective of the relative balance of military capabilities, clarity about the high costs of war also may not deter war if the *political* costs of peace are higher than the political costs of war. Arguments based on cost-benefit analyses assume that war is the most costly and undesirable outcome of any conflict and that states will therefore prefer other outcomes. But, historically, that assumption has not always proved accurate. Sometimes weaker states prefer violent loss to surrender because of the political or psychological costs of peaceful surrender. The 1973 Arab-Israeli War is the classic example of this scenario. Egypt attacked though its leaders knew full well that Egypt would lose a war against Israel. However, the political victory of launching an attack on Israel appeared to have compensated for the military loss.

States benefit unequally from military transparency. How states react to less uncertainty in the world depends on how strong they are. In many ways, transparency benefits the strong because it broadcasts that strength and discourages others from attacking. For this reason, it is not surprising that strong states are more likely to participate in arms transparency regimes than weak states.[61] For weaker states, ambiguity provides a shield that transparency takes away.[62] If, as J. David Singer argues, "ambiguity and uncertainty is what inhibits escalatory behavior," ambiguity may provide a security advantage for weak states since aggressors may be unsure about the extent or quality of a weak state's military capabilities.[63] Moreover, if weak states can convince potential aggressors that they have a "secret weapon," such as nuclear, biological, or chemical weapons, that potential threat may deter stronger states, even if that threat is obscure. Bluffing in this way can be quite effective as long as the adversary believes that there is some probability that the state will carry out the threat.[64] Since most leaders are risk averse and value what they currently have over possible gains in the future, the threat of heavy loss can be effective even when power is asymmetrically divided.[65]

Strategic ambiguity can benefit strong states, too, if they can make an adversary believe that they will carry out a threat, even if the state has no real intention of doing so. Prior to the 1991 Persian Gulf War, the United States intentionally gave Iraq the impression that using chemical or biological weapons would lead to nuclear retaliation even though President George Bush, Secretary of State James Baker, and National Security Adviser Brent Scowcroft had already agreed that the United States would not use nuclear weapons. However, as Baker noted in his memoirs, "There was obviously no reason to inform the Iraqis of this."[66] To enhance the credibility of the threat, President Bush announced on CNN that he would "preserve all options" and never told the Pentagon that he would not use nuclear weapons in Iraq. Though it is impossible to conclude firmly what Saddam Hussein's motives were for not using chemical weapons, there is some evidence that the Iraqi regime believed Bush's threats.[67] Bluffing tactics are risky in a relatively transparent state, but they can help to deter aggression if used carefully.[68]

If transparency takes away weak states' leverage, the clear strategy for weak states is to eliminate the need to bluff. And, in today's climate, the way for a weak state to quickly and cheaply increase its bargaining power is to acquire weapons that are so destructive or disturbing that they deter even states with significantly greater military power. The most disturbing example of a state pursuing this strategy is North Korea, which first pursued nuclear weapons clandestinely, but increasingly seeks to demonstrate its purported capabilities. As one Bush administration official put it, "What worries us most is that there is a progression of openness among the North Koreans about their nuclear capabilities. They have unfolded new phases of specificity about what they can do and they seem to have been on a long-term path of ending the ambiguity about their capability."[69]

A second strategy is to engage in a "rush to the shadows." When conventional arms transfers are monitored closely, desperate states may seek out less monitored weapons such as biological or chemical arms or use tactics like terrorism that are more difficult to monitor. They may seek to acquire weapons on the black market, as Libya did when it acquired high-technology equipment needed to enrich uranium. Moreover, when state actions are scrutinized, states might consider letting non-state actors, whose activities are harder to track, fulfill their more nefarious objectives.

In the Eye of the Beholder

Despite an unprecedented level of information about states' intentions, priorities, and capabilities, greater transparency will not necessarily reduce uncertainty in international relations. States interpret information in the context of existing political and security relationships. Consequently, while they may have extensive information about military capabilities, they do not necessarily know whether those capabilities are a threat.[70] The United Nations Register of Conventional Arms is based on the idea that military capabilities indicate aggressive intent and that transparency of these capabilities will discourage aggression. However, because military capabilities must be interpreted, the relationship between weapons and aggressive intent is not as clear as it might seem at first glance. According to the UNROCA framework, governments should be concerned when arms acquisitions are "excessive and destabilizing." But what exactly does "excessive and destabilizing" mean? Threats are often in the eye of the beholder and definitions, no matter how complex, cannot fully respond to these perceptions. Governments continue to disagree about the number and kinds of weapons, doctrines, and strategies needed to deter an adversary.[71] With no generally accepted answer to the question of how much deterrence is enough, even military power designed to deter and not to conquer can be interpreted as evidence of aggressive intentions. The United Nations Conference on Disarmament, which developed the UNROCA after large flows of arms to Iraq were blamed for facilitating in the 1991 invasion of Kuwait, failed when it tried to develop a definition of excessive and destabilizing acquisitions.[72]

The link between arms transparency and peace is complicated further by the fact that many weapons are difficult to classify as unambiguously offensive or defensive and give no clear indication as to strategy.[73] Many weapons, such as small arms, can be used for either offensive or defensive purposes.[74] The best defense against offensive weapons like tanks are strike aircraft and more tanks, both of which are classic offensive weapons.[75] Meanwhile, so-called "defensive weapons"—like advanced sensors, which provide early warning of conflicts and reduce the chance of surprise attack—can be used in offensive attacks. As Jasjit Singh explains, Israel used airborne early warning systems, electronic intelligence systems, and precision-guided munitions in an integrated manner to defeat Syria in the Beqa'a Valley in June 1982. Open source information as well as intelligence made the international community well aware of the type and number of Israeli systems (such as the E-2C), but most observers did not predict the way they were used or the effects of their use."[76] In 1973, Egypt acquired "defensive" military goods including advanced anti-aircraft missiles to shield its forces from Israeli air power, but these "defensive" arms were also critical to the Egyptian offensive attack against Israel. The Israelis failed to recognize that Egypt was preparing for war since they did not imagine that Egypt planned to rely on Scud surface-to-surface missiles for deterrence and on surface-to-air missile shields for attacking aircraft.[77]

Transparency of military capabilities alone will not reassure states of another state's peaceful intentions. If political relations are good or improving, and if transparency exposes a force structure that coheres with a government's overall political message, transparency may indeed reassure states that others are not aggressive and may enhance international security. If, however, political relations are characterized by suspicion and mistrust, transparency of military capabilities may not necessarily improve international security even if militaries adopt "defensive" postures. To give a concrete example, measured by economic power, Japan is the strongest state in history with such a weak military and defensive military doctrine. As per Article 9 of the Japanese constitution, use of military force for anything except national defense, narrowly defined, is illegal. Japan's military posture is relatively transparent to the region and to the world. And yet, Japan still faces deep suspicion in the region and transparency may not always help. Some Chinese analysts fear how Japanese power will be used in the future, whether or not Japan currently lacks offensive capabilities.[78] Because the security dilemma is driven by mistrust as well as by uncertainty, it can take significant time for states to change their interpretation of an enemy's behavior even when there is substantial information that a state's intentions are conciliatory.[79] Even after the former Soviet Union signed the 1987 Intermediate Nuclear Forces (INF) treaty, withdrew forces from Afghanistan in 1988, announced conventional force reductions in Europe, and acquiesced to the 1989 revolutions in Eastern Europe, many American policy makers questioned Soviet motives.[80] Six months before the Berlin Wall fell, Secretary of State James Baker praised the Soviets for releasing political prisoners and reforming emigration policies but said, "We must all, I think, face the fact that the Soviets continue to pose a significant military threat.... For all the talk of 'defensive defense,' Soviet military exercises still continue to show a marked inclination for taking the offensive. For all the talk of openness, the Soviets have yet to publish a real defense budget."[81] It took the extremely costly signal of acquiescing to the 1989 revolutions in Eastern Europe to convince American leaders that the former Soviet Union had changed truly and irreversibly. Even seventeen years later, American nuclear forces remain largely directed against Russia.

The impact of transparency depends not just on the nature of the information, but on whom that information is about. Mistrust is tightly linked to identity, because identity provides important clues about how a state will behave in the future.[82] Identity, in this way, reduces international uncertainty. For instance, the United States is more worried about North Korea's nuclear capability than Great Britain's nuclear capability not only because it has less information about how North Korea will use its power, but also because the United States trusts Great Britain not to use its nuclear capability to threaten American interests. As one commentator put it, "The real issue all along is what is the North Korean motivation, why are they doing this [developing nuclear weapons] and what do they want [from the U.S.]."[83] The ambiguity of North Korean intentions strongly influences the perception of threat. To give another example, despite Indian defense spending increases of 7.8% in 2005-2006 and 22% the year before, American leaders do not portray India as a threat. In contrast, China's military buildup (reflected in an 11% increase in defense spending in 2004), led the commander of the United States Pacific Command to state, "It's disconcerting to see this buildup, it seems to be more than might be required for their defense...it's certainly a cause for concern."[84]

Transparency, Conflict Resolution, and Cooperation

The idea that transparency facilitates conflict resolution and cooperation is widespread. However, that idea is based on an unanalyzed assumption about what transparency shows. If transparency shows that parties to a security agreement genuinely want peace or eases fears that a security agreement, hindered only by concerns about compliance, transparency measures can contribute significantly to security and peace. That assumption is not always accurate. Sometimes parties to conflict resolution or security cooperation agreements remain hostile and do wish to deceive others in order to reap some reward. Moreover, transparency measures are sometimes an excuse for avoiding real conflict resolution, which can exacerbate suspicions between states, or actively undermine cooperation. In such circumstances the risk is that transparency becomes the end and not the means to an end. Without further steps toward dialogue and toward the resolution of underlying security issues, it is not at all clear that transparency will improve security relations. Changing state behavior requires political will and transparency alone is unlikely to provide that will.

Confidence and security building measures (CSBMs) are efforts to signal through action, that a government or group would like to improve relations with a former foe. CSBMs offer observable changes in behavior that reinforce and provide a foundation for further efforts at reconciliation. Acts of military transparency (specific examples of which are provided in table 2.1) are commonly advocated CSBMs. Because military capabilities are integral to waging war, making such capabilities transparent, provides a powerful signal of intent. The assumption is that transparency reduces "mutual misperceptions, suspicions and fears by making military *capabilities* explicit."[85]

Table 2.1. Examples of Transparency CSBMs
- advance notification of troop movements
- advance notification of military exercises
- advance notice of advanced weapons tests
- expansion of military-to-military contacts
- observers at military exercises
- exchange of information regarding military budgets, procurement, production, weapons, doctrines, etc.
- overflights

The assumption that transparency CSBMs are effective tools of conflict resolution is often accurate. Because information about military capabilities is sensitive, deliberately sharing that information can build confidence, and possibly trust, among states and create a political climate conducive to resolving differences.[86] They can signal effectively a desire for better political relations and provide a "psychological benefit of increasing confidence."[87] In other words, the act of foregoing the military advantages of secrecy is a gesture that can reduce "the causes of mistrust, fear, tension, and hostilities" and generally create a climate of trust.[88] Obviously, CSBMs are most likely to have the desired psychological effect if the parties want better relations, recognize the legitimacy and borders of the other parties, and share an interest in better relations. However, advocates believe that CSBMs can help to rebuild even the most troubled international relations.

The fact that transparency CSBMs are not the ideal solution to conflicts does not necessarily mean that they are not better than no step at all—but in some cases it does. When CSBMs are complied with selectively, they may actually increase distrust and hostility. As Marie-France Desjardins notes, "Half-truths about the real purposes of some weapons acquisition are likely to reinforce patterns of suspicions and mistrust, especially if such semi-transparency is under the cover of an agreement designed to reassure others of peaceful intent."[89] Transparency CSBMs will work only when "perceptions of belligerence are wrong" and can be counterproductive if the opposite is true. Transparency is downright dangerous when participants are still hostile since it may only further undermine trust and damage relations so badly that dialogue is no longer possible.[90] In such circumstances transparency can publicly punish leaders who advocate CSBMs and reward leaders who do not. CSBMs, therefore, should be reserved for situations in which there is genuine interest in negotiation and peace.[91]

History demonstrates that transparency CSBMs are often employed as an alternative to meaningful arms control measures rather than as a means to achieve them. They may be used precisely when real arms control negotiations fail. For instance, talks to restrain global arms transfers in 1991 stalled due to the continuing economic interests of member states in arms sales. Unable to develop a true cooperative security regime, negotiators were left with the UNROCA as a second-best alternative.[92]

Another hope for transparency is that it will facilitate international cooperation, which it does in three circumstances: when states want to cooperate but need reassurance that others are complying with international agreements, when states want to cooperate and violations of agreements are punished, and when states do not want to be identified as not upholding some widely held norm in the international community. If uncertainty discourages states from forming mutually beneficial agreements, greater transparency can encourage international cooperation. When states agree to change their behavior, transparency reassures them that others are also changing their behavior. If others renege, the complying states can stop cooperating before ceding too much advantage and perhaps punish the offending state.[93] By easing the fear of undetected cheating, transparency removes a major obstacle to international agreements and is therefore considered one of the most important functions that many international regimes perform.[94] Within international regimes and institutions, transparency can facilitate cooperation between friends and enemies alike. As Antonio Handler Chayes and Abram Chayes summarize,

> A party disposed to comply with the norm needs reassurance. A party contemplating violation needs to be deterred. Transparency supplies both. The probability that conduct departing from the norm will be discovered operates to reassure the first and to deter the second, and that probability increases with the transparency of the regime.[95]

Some analysts believe that transparency also can facilitate cooperation even in the absence of any formal regime or agreement. Their hope is that transparency will illuminate undesirable behavior and encourage states, international organizations, and nongovernmental organizations (NGOs) to condemn such behavior. The prospect that undesirable behavior will be publicized and condemned can deter many states and organizations from actions unacceptable to the international community. This strategy can be effective, especially among organizations that have an interest in not looking disreputable. For instance, by requiring companies to register the emission of toxic chemicals, the American Environmental Protection Agency cut the emission of certain chemicals by 44 percent between 1988 and 1994.[96] Companies do not want to be known as polluters; it's bad for business and bad for relations with their communities. Transparency alone can be enough to change behavior in such instances. The hope is that, in a highly integrated world, this analogy will extend to states and include even matters of national security. When states depend on each other for many different things, the power of disapproval cannot be completely dismissed since it may lead to less favorable treatment on other important issues. Reputation is important.[97]

Yet, transparency will not always lead to "regulation by revelation." States sometimes need the prospect of genuine punishment to deter them from breaking international rules. When this is true, transparency and verbal expressions of disapproval may not be enough to rein in scofflaws. Powerful states in particular may be able disproportionately to ignore international disapproval since others will have fewer ways to punish them and incur high costs if the powerful state retaliates.

Transparency also may be insufficient when states feel that their national security is at risk. Because governments view arms acquisitions as core security issues, the opinions of other governments or organizations are less likely to constrain state behavior in this area. The 1990s arms race between Greece and Turkey is an example. Although the activities of these governments are highly transparent and both are members of the UNROCA, arms transparency did not prevent the arms race. Interestingly, both countries did keep acquisitions below the threshold required by the 1990 Conventional Armed Forces in Europe (CFE) Treaty in order to avoid penalties—which underscores the idea that formal sanctions may be able to deter behavior when transparency alone cannot.[98]

However, transparency does not encourage cooperation equally in all instances and is effective only when states truly do want to cooperate. It can encourage cooperation when uncertainty alone prohibits cooperation or when states are part of a formal transparency regime capable of punishing violations. However, when states feel that national interest is at risk or when violating an international norm carries no direct penalty, transparency will be less effective in changing international behavior. In such instances, transparency not only fails to encourage cooperation, but it illuminates the failure to cooperate. Thus, it may encourage international cooperation but possibly in a narrower and less troublesome set of circumstances than many analysts would hope.

Conclusion

The notion that transparency unconditionally will reduce conflict is wrong. That argument relies on certain assumptions, namely, that greater transparency will reveal either peaceful intentions or strength sufficient to deter war. This chapter argues that transparency can indeed lead to peace, but that is not the only possible outcome. The effects of transparency depend on what it shows. Transparency may show hostility or aggression. It may undermine deterrence by showing weakness, encourage aggression by the strong, or take away uncertainty that inhibits aggression. In the realm of conflict resolution, transparency may reveal that participants are not adhering to agreements and undermine efforts at peace. It may reveal information that undermines trust and makes states eschew efforts to cooperate or resolve conflicts. Sometimes transparency makes conflicts worse.

Greater transparency can encourage *either* vicious or virtuous cycles. When governments see peaceful behavior, they tend to respond in-kind, which can start a spiral of cooperation as action generates reaction. Transparency in this situation promotes international security and peace; it reinforces existing cooperation and encourages more. When transparency reveals arms acquisitions or hostile rhetoric, however, states may begin a dangerous game of tit-for-tat, in which backing down is public and the political costs are high. In such cases, transparency can fuel spirals of conflict that ultimately lead to war.

The implication of this argument is that there are no magic bullets to make states more secure. International security cooperation requires hard, deliberate work and transparency is likely to be helpful when it is just one part of a broader initiative. Transparency can be a first step; can be a bold signal in the manner of Libya's startling revelation and then renunciation of its nuclear weapons program. It can be part of an arms control agreement, like the Treaty on Conventional Armed Forces in Europe between the twenty-two members of NATO and the former Warsaw Pact. It can be an informal set of circumstances that reinforce and illuminate states' commitment to peace, as in the early twenty-first century rapprochement between India and Pakistan. But, whatever its role, transparency alone cannot resolve difficult security problems and can even make them worse.

Chapter 3

Transparency and Intergroup Violence

"A free marketplace of ideas has a self-righting tendency to correct errors and biases."
—Political theorists David Kelley and Roger Donway[1]

"One of the most effective policy instruments in the hands of international actors today is to ensure that objective, unbiased, and balanced information is made widely available in states threatened with intense conflict."
—Political scientists David A. Lake and Donald Rothchild[2]

Knowledge of other peoples and cultures can promote cooperation and peace, according to widespread opinion. When people see that they share a common human experience, that information humanizes those who seem different and makes people less willing to use force to resolve conflicts. When people understand each other better, they may recognize shared interests and values, which provide a foundation for conflict resolution. Better-informed people may also develop the ability to see the world as others see it, which may make them more sensitive to others' views and willing to change their behavior toward other groups, even if that behavior previously seemed justified. They may develop tolerance, empathy, or even friendship.

The idea that increased exposure to other peoples promotes cooperation and peace is evident in popular media, practical efforts to improve relations between groups, and scholarship. It is the basis of people-to-people exchanges, citizen diplomacy, and study abroad programs, particularly when those activities involve groups with a history of conflict. It is also the basis of optimism regarding innovations in information and communication technologies.[3] Though most recent arguments of this sort concern the Internet, the idea is not new. A century ago, a British ambassador lauded the telegraph, proclaiming, "It is impossible that old prejudices and hostilities should longer exist" with the newly invented telegraph to help people exchange thoughts with others around the world.[4] Academics study a related concept called the contact hypothesis, which postulates that "more contact between individuals belonging to antagonistic social groups (defined by customs, language, beliefs, nationality, or identity) tends to undermine negative stereotypes and reduce prejudice, thus improving intergroup relations by making people more willing to deal with each other as equals."[5] The contact hypothesis can apply internationally—the argument being that more contact with foreigners reduces xenophobia—as well as domestically to relations among ethnic or racial groups.[6] In both contexts, deeper mutual understanding increases positive feelings but a lack of dialogue breeds hostility and sometimes conflict.

A corollary to this idea is that just as more knowledge increases positive feelings toward others, ignorance of others breeds animosity. In other words, we are more likely to dislike or distrust those we don't know. Americans invoke this idea as a partial explanation for the September 11, 2001 terrorist attacks on the United States by the radical Islamic group, Al-Qaeda. As one American put it, "Why do they hate us? Because they don't know us."[7]

Greater transparency provides both more information about other peoples and more varied, decentralized sources of that information. If more contact with other groups creates more positive feelings toward them, more and more objective knowledge could decrease intergroup hostility and encourage peace. Foreigners, according to this view, would seem less foreign. Differences between ethnic majorities and minorities seem less important. Insiders would find commonalities with outsiders. Greater transparency also expands access to different opinions from within and outside a society, which can lead people to reexamine their beliefs. When they find that prejudices and stereotypes about other groups are not substantiated by fact, they may reject them and become more tolerant.[8]

Greater transparency also reduces the ability of governments to monopolize channels of information and to use that monopoly to demonize other groups. On an individual basis, people can choose to ignore propaganda that fosters hostility toward other groups, but numerous historical cases—in Nazi Germany, in the United States during the Pacific War with Japan, and in Bosnia—indicate that citizens often

embrace the vilification of so-called out-groups. When minorities or foreigners are dehumanized or portrayed as enemies, people are more willing to violate societal mores and to accept the use of violence against
them. For this reason, some scholars argue, states in which information
flows freely seldom fight with each other.

Unfortunately, greater transparency will not always encourage
international understanding and sometimes makes conflicts worse.
Instead of refuting stereotypes, greater transparency may spread information that confirms them. Instead of humanizing others, it may spread
information that dehumanizes them and therefore facilitates the use of
violence. Instead of showing shared values, it may make people realize
that they abhor the values of others. In such circumstances, greater
transparency only reinforces tension between groups and increases the
possibility of violent conflict.

This chapter argues that the conventional wisdom regarding the
role of transparency in conflict resolution is both naive and dangerous.
More widely available information about other groups sometimes exacerbates conflicts rather than prevents them. Though greater transparency
may indeed increase positive feelings between ethnic, racial, or national
groups, it can also illuminate and encourage the spread of hostility
toward other groups.

Transparency and the Social Psychology of Conflict

Theoretically, greater transparency could help to ameliorate conflicts
between hostile groups in three key ways. First, greater transparency
gives citizens access to information that humanizes others and encourages positive feelings and empathy toward them. The nonprofit organization Seeds of Peace, which brings together Israeli and Palestinian
youths, operates on precisely this premise. One Seeds of Peace partici-
pant articulated the organization's vision. "Once you learn about other
people's cultures, their points of view, you really can reach a compromise."[9] When people have more information about each other, they may
also realize that they share interests and values. Shared goals can provide
the foundation for long-term cooperation. Shared efforts toward reaching those goals can improve how each group views the other and can
build mutual trust.

Second, because transparency decentralizes control over information and increases access to a wide range of views, transparency encourages a marketplace of ideas, which helps to refute false arguments about
out-groups such as foreigners or ethnic minorities.[10] An enduring tenet
of classical liberal thought, the underlying philosophy is that in a fair

fight, truth wins and prejudices will wither under public scrutiny.[11] As John Stuart Mill wrote, "Wrong opinions and practices gradually yield to fact and argument."[12] The key, then, is to ensure that fact and argument are aired.

Because greater transparency tends to give people access to many different opinions, greater transparency makes it harder for governments to justify the killing of innocents without debate.[13] All leaders must manage information in order to wage violent conflict successfully since violent conflicts require the participation or at least acquiescence of large numbers of people.[14] The need to persuade citizens is obvious in a democracy, but persuasion is necessary in authoritarian systems as well. Leaders of more oppressive regimes need to convince a certain segment of the population, for instance, the military leadership, or they may need to convince citizens that there is a threat to their own safety, perhaps from their own government, if they do not cooperate. In some senses, all conflict involves the intersection of information, group behavior, and violence.

Governments can manipulate the social dynamics of in-groups and out-groups, "us" and "them," more adeptly when they control the channels of information in a society but they lose that advantage in an age of transparency.[15] When governments can control the information people receive, particularly over a long period of time, they can vilify or dehumanize particular groups consistently and without fear of contradiction. Dehumanization is a necessary precondition for killing large numbers of people since making victims seem less than human helps individuals overcome political, social, and cultural constraints against murder.[16] For the killers, dehumanization diminishes "personal responsibility, conscience and ethical norms towards enemies no longer regarded as fellow humans."[17] To build support for violent conflict, leaders throughout history have played up differences between groups of people. However, for any appeal to attack particular groups to be successful, that appeal must find at least some receptive ears. Some proportion of those populations must believe either in their own righteousness or superiority compared to other groups, or that they themselves will be killed if they do not comply. Those beliefs can lead people to harass, oppress, or kill others at least partially because of their nationality, ethnicity, or race. When citizens have access to a wider range of views, they can question whether violence is acceptable in a given situation and ask whether leaders are using hatred toward out-groups to bolster their own political power.[18] They can assess whether stereotypes are true and how real threats from out-groups actually are.

The need to dehumanize enemies in order to justify violence, may explain why societies with free presses do not fight each other. Free presses offer citizens competing interpretations of government policy and humanize the "other." Democracies protect minority rights and typically feature a marketplace of ideas that can refute prejudice. Without these checks, however, governments sometimes can tap into dark but powerful human inclinations.[19] According to Douglas Van Belle, only modest degrees of transparency can tip the balance of power in favor of those who oppose dehumanization. Van Belle argues that "It takes a great deal of information to sway basic opinions, perhaps an overwhelming amount, but it probably does not take much to break that image of dehumanization. If this is the case...challengers just have to find and provide enough information that is considered legitimate to prevent the leader from sufficiently dehumanizing the opponent to justify lethal uses of force."[20] Similarly, because well-informed citizens can make better judgments, some scholars argue that genocide never occurs in pluralistic democracies.[21]

Third, transparency exposes individuals to new ideas and people, which may lead them to change their attitudes and to redefine in-groups and social allegiances in broader and more inclusive ways.[22] People may begin to view themselves as "European" rather than as Belgian, for instance, or as an "Iraqi" rather than as a "Kurd."[23] When communal identification seems less significant as a unifying principle, "It follows that peoples who are distinct at one time may later become virtually indistinguishable from some larger society. The English, for example, no longer make socially meaningful distinctions between Anglo-Saxons and Normans."[24] Similarly, outside of Northern Ireland, the social division between Protestants and Catholics in Western societies have become slowly less relevant.[25] Another possibility is that people will begin to build new social networks and define themselves in categories that are unrelated to ethnicity or country of origin. Information technologies may help to build networks between parents of twins or hobbyists, regardless of their nationality. Transparency, by facilitating the redefinition of social groups in this way, can break down old social loyalties, make the strange familiar, and thereby undermine old conceptions of "the other."

The first of these three arguments focuses on providing people with humanizing information about other groups that they did not have before, while the other two are more complicated and suggest not simply a veil of ignorance being lifted, but a malleability of opinion that can be influenced by information.[26] Greater transparency provides access not just to raw data about tangible, objectively verifiable data such as the number of tanks a country owns but also to beliefs and information specifically framed to persuade people. It provides access to information about social relationships, some of which is information intended to persuade others, and other information that is not. At first glance these two categories of information seem quite different, but in fact the difference is not great. All information must be assessed for credibility, interpreted, and infused with meaning. For instance, as indicated earlier, whether a country's tanks are deemed threatening, depends on the location, quantity, and quality of those tanks. But a determination of threat also depends on the social relationship with the owners of those tanks. If owned by an enemy, more tanks increase the sense of threat; if owned by an ally, they may actually reduce it. Information of all varieties can be used to support particular arguments and to persuade others. It may be framed specifically to achieve a particular goal, whether that goal is to mobilize support for a grassroots campaign against air pollution, or to persuade citizens that a particular group benefits unfairly from international trade rules.

Nonetheless, providers of information do not simply have a "hypodermic" ability to inject audiences with ideas, which they will then simply absorb.[27] Information, however frequent or undisputed, does not alone persuade large groups of people or in extreme circumstances move them to kill members of other groups. Individuals retain free will and bear responsibility for their actions, even in the most politically oppressed societies.[28] This free will extends to both accepting information or choosing to ignore it. Primo Levi argues that during the Holocaust "most Germans didn't know because they didn't want to know. Because, indeed, they wanted *not* to know."[29]

The Complex Effects of Greater Transparency

Unfortunately, greater transparency will not always foster understanding or peace and sometimes will make conflicts worse. When transparency exposes competing values, entrenched hostility, or undermines established social allegiances, the trend toward greater transparency may exacerbate conflicts, particularly in the short term.

Greater transparency increases information about, and contact between, groups, which can help to improve intergroup relations and reduce the chances of conflict.[30] Acquaintance *can* increase positive feelings. But when these circumstances do not exist, transparency can be dangerous. For example, to overcome intergroup suspicion, studies indicate that more contact increases positive feelings toward other groups only under certain conditions, the two most important of which are that the groups have equal status and share common goals. When that is not the case, contact can increase prejudice. If groups interact in stereotyped roles of superiority and subordination, their interaction will reinforce rather than break down stereotypes.[31] Contact also exacerbates hostility when there are significant differences—whether cultural, ethnic, social, or political—between groups or institutionalized preferential treatment for one group over another. If greater transparency exposes these differences, it may increase the likelihood of conflict. According to Yale University law professor Amy Chua, such intergroup differences are particularly likely to create hostility when a minority group controls the vast majority of an area's wealth. This situation can create violent backlash against the minority group, particularly during transitions to democracy and free markets, within a single country or in the global context. Chua believes that hostility toward Chinese in Southeast Asia and Russian Jews is analogous to widespread hatred of Americans, who control a disproportionate share of global wealth.[32]

Greater transparency can either increase or decrease negative feelings toward out-groups depending on what it shows. If it shows carefully balanced, humanizing information that increases true understanding or information about shared values and interests, greater transparency is likely to improve intergroup relations. But if greater transparency provides greater access to negative images, emphasizes differences, or only the virtual equivalent of casual contact, its effects may be neutral or even dangerous.

When negative feelings toward out-groups are widespread, greater transparency can help to legitimize them by showcasing and spreading myths of national or ethnic superiority that exacerbate conflicts and exaggerate differences between groups. The more transparency shows that the general public will accept intolerance, the more transparency will reinforce it.[33] When individuals cannot see that they share common grievances or concerns, it is difficult for them to organize, voice their views, or pressure for change. When the veil between public and private is lifted, it can expose widely held hostility toward out-groups. Because the popularity of an idea also legitimates it to some extent ("how wrong can I be if everyone feels this way?"), this new information can encourage the idea's dissemination and make others unwilling to speak out against it.

There are two key theories about why people form in- and out-groups in the first place. Studies in evolutionary psychology indicate that suspicion toward other groups developed as a cognitive shortcut to reduce uncertainty and to protect people from danger.[34] Social groups have strong incentives to protect and care for each other and for the opportunity to engage in reciprocal behavior (e.g., I share my food today; you share your food tomorrow). These conditions foster trust. Since it is difficult and time-consuming to assess whether any new individual is worthy of trust or not, in order to simplify the world, people began to distrust outsiders especially when they felt threatened. According to Dr. Galen V. Bodenhausen who directs the social psychology program at Northwestern University, "Rational thought is great in a lot of circumstances where you have time and latitude to do it. But emotions provide rapid, immediate guidance, a gut reaction."[35]

In addition to the urge for self-protection, some sociologists and social psychologists argue that the tendency to think in terms of "us" and "them" comes from a universal human desire for self-esteem, which leads people to maximize differences between their own group and other groups in order to promote their own positive social identity.[36] Especially when peoples' values or basic needs are threatened, they may turn to some group for identity. One way of elevating an in-group is to devalue an out-group and blame them for the in-group's problems. This behavior is even more likely in collectivist cultures and when it is exacerbated by fear, contests over power, or perceptions of historical wrongdoing or conflict.[37]

According to the political scientist Jonathan Mercer, "strong in-groups will have equally strong-out-groups." Communities are based on shared traits and on the perceived difference of those traits compared with other groups. Strong in-group identity in those communities leads to sharing, cooperation, perceived mutuality of interests, and a willingness to sacrifice personal interests for group interests. But this has a cost. The more we identify with our group, the more we differentiate our group from other groups. This leads to between-group competition, perceived conflicts of interests, and a preference for relative over absolute gains. This has been dubbed "the double-edged sword of social identity—in-group identity promotes inter-group discrimination."[38]

As discussed earlier, leaders may exploit human inclinations to form in- and out-groups in order to bolster their own political power. By demonizing out-groups, leaders may also build support for using violence against them, especially if they are trusted figures in their societies.[39] Usually, demonizing out-groups entails portraying those groups as a threat to the in-group. The vilification of out-groups gains credence when leaders suggest that people will have a better life once they overcome the threat posed by out-groups.[40]

Animosity towards out-groups can intensify as it evolves. As Ervin Staub writes,

> Individuals and groups change as they harm others. They justify their actions by devaluing their victims more and more. They become desensitized to the suffering of their victims. The standards of acceptable social behavior change, allowing and even encouraging violence.... In the end

there may be a reversal of morality: killing the scapegoat or ideological enemy may become a "higher good."[41]

When a government permits or even encourages this type of behavior, genocide becomes a dangerous but real possibility.

What's for Sale in the Marketplace of Ideas?

Transparency may not discourage ethnic conflicts when the market-place of ideas is selling distortion, bias, and hate and if those hateful words or deeds reflect widespread public sentiment.[42] Racist pamphlets, for instance, may make the beliefs or goals of their publishers more transparent and make other groups more knowledgeable about them, but they are unlikely to reduce tensions.[43] When such pronouncements proliferate and contrary views are pushed out, either by legal restrictions or rhetoric, the marketplace of ideas may no longer promote tolerance and peace.

Why does the marketplace of ideas sometimes promote intolerance of out-groups? Like all markets, a market for ideas is susceptible to collusion and monopoly by those with political, financial, or social power. Even when there is no government monopoly over information, accurate and balanced political information may be a public good that no interest group has an incentive to provide and the potential beneficiaries, that is, the general population, are too disorganized and individually powerless to demand.[44]

Even if information providers respond to citizens' demands for information, they may be overly responsive to majorities and to the politically powerful and underresponsive to minorities and the politically weak.[45] Majorities and powerful elites may monopolize the market and suppress minority views. Certain voices in society, such as media owners, the politically powerful, and speakers favored by advertisers, will have disproportionate access to the public. The marketplace of ideas can also become distorted when rhetoric intimidates those who would otherwise voice unpopular or minority views. For instance, despite a strong bill of rights, many American citizens did not speak up against McCarthyism because they feared being painted as unpatriotic or soft on communism. If current standards of behavior accept or even support such rhetoric, transparency will bring fame, not shame, for those who voice it.

Increasing transparency may raise the awareness of extremist groups and their messages among mass audiences and, possibly, increase the power of those groups.[46] When new political groups are competing for power in a society, growing transparency may encourage groups to stake out more extreme, black-and-white positions that separate them from their opponents. In a fluid and boisterous political climate, transparency may only encourage the press, opposition parties, the government, or civil society to see who can voice their views the loudest, regardless of how hostile they are.[47] In such climates, incomplete transparency may provide exposure for new ideas but not enough information to counter false claims.[48]

Ironically, the very institutions that are supposed to create a balanced and diverse marketplace of ideas sometimes promote intolerant discourse. The media, even free media, can air hatred toward outgroups and legitimate violence—particularly if that sort of coverage has an avid audience and sells newspapers.[49] Democracies and their citizens sometimes embrace prejudice or war. Laws that encourage a marketplace of ideas, such as freedom of speech, can provide "an opening for nationalist mythmakers to hijack public discourse."[50] Civil society can include extremist and terrorist groups as well as groups that advocate civil and human rights. After all, civil society "is not simply a matter of many clamoring voices, but also the set of institutions and social norms that make pluralism a civil process of persuasion and reconciling of differences."[51]

The risk of a distorted marketplace of ideas can be highest in democratizing states, where imperfect institutions may allow threatened elites to exploit their power over the media and generally encourage nationalism and militancy toward out-groups to bolster their own power.[52] Democratization creates a wider spectrum of participants in the political process, some of whom will have incompatible interests. Political institutions may not yet be strong enough to integrate conflicting political beliefs and there may not yet be a political culture in which political opponents engage in a peaceful public debate. Transparency may also open new channels of communication, which increases the number of demands on an overburdened or new government that is ill equipped to handle them.[53] In short, while high levels of domestic transparency and a marketplace of ideas may facilitate peace, getting to that point may be a dangerous process.

The marketplace of ideas analogy suggests that people are shopping for truth.[54] However, if instead they are shopping for self-esteem and view the degradation of out-groups as increasing self-esteem, the marketplace of ideas, sadly, will not function as classical liberals like Mill intended. A marketplace of ideas also may not encourage tolerance if people do not reexamine their views when confronted with evidence that contradicts them.[55] In such circumstances, prejudice is independent of whether negative stereotypes are false.[56] For reasons ranging from self-esteem to human tendency to minimize cognitive dissonance, people may distrust or disregard information that did not fit with their previously held beliefs.[57] For example, after viewing a 2001 videotape of Osama bin Laden in which bin Laden seemed to laugh at the September 11 attacks, some Arabs, convinced that bin Laden is a holy man, argued that the tape was a fake.[58]

A related danger is that the marketplace of ideas produces such a plethora of ideas that citizens pay attention only to information that confirms their existing views, a phenomenon confirmed by empirical evidence.[59] In the information age, people have even more opportunities to pick and choose information that supports their views or find and surround themselves with like-minded people. Hundreds of thousands of groups have their own web pages, blogs, or social networks that are facilitated by the Internet.[60] By protecting themselves from having to defend their views, people can avoid the cognitive discomfort of needing to change their beliefs.

Transparency and Assimilation

Most research on the contact hypothesis focuses more on explaining why the strong correlation between contact and positive intergroup relations varies under different conditions, rather than reexamining the fundamental argument about how that change in perceptions of others takes place. In an interesting departure, H. D. Forbes conducted an extensive survey of the research and concluded that, although increases in contact can reduce animosity under certain conditions, contact does *not* reduce conflict by simply breaking down stereotypes. Instead, contact may encourage a process of homogenization that reduces underlying differences.[61] Groups, Forbes argues, move from contact to competition to accommodation to assimilation.[62] Reducing differences, not reducing stereotypes, may ultimately be what ameliorates conflict. To paraphrase an old saying, to know you is to love you...but only because you are becoming more like me.

If this view is correct, greater transparency can speed up the process of assimilation by providing people with an unprecedented amount of information about how others live and think. When people have access to more ideas, they may find some more appealing than their own. As the adoption of ideas spreads, they become more legitimate, which speeds up their adoption even more. Societies were once more insulated from new ideas and differences. The spread of languages or religions took centuries and only major external shocks, such as war or famine, forced the mass movements of people and made societies cope with the outside world in any sustained way. Now, differences are much more evident and those differences can threaten even friendly relationships.[63]

By speeding up assimilation and social change, the trend toward greater transparency will sometimes create a backlash among those whose power or values are threatened. At a minimum, change can make people feel insecure by threatening their livelihoods, worldviews, and personal identities. The strongest backlash most often comes not from the poorest or most disenfranchised groups, but from what the journalist Thomas Friedman calls the used to be's.[64] This group received substantial benefits from the old system and possesses sufficient power to challenge the new order. When the "used to be's" can draw on the volatile mix of shared grievances (whether real or perceived), a shared group identity, and a common interest, they have a strong foundation for political mobilization.[65]

Yet greater transparency can also help people to resist assimilation by helping them to identify like-minded people and to form social networks of those who share common ideas and values. By forming such networks, people can find the strength to hold certain ideas even if those ideas are not accepted by their local communities. They can share information and strategies with others. This consequence of transparency has both positive and negative implications. On the positive side, human rights advocates receive ideas, logistic support, and moral support through their international networks. On the negative side, terrorists, pedophiles, and other criminals also maintain their own international networks and use some of the same technologies.

Rwanda: A Case Study

Though the vilification of out-groups can occur either within or across societies, the most vivid examples in the last decade were internal conflicts in which the out-groups were ethnic minorities. Examples include violent conflicts in Bosnia, Kosovo, Burundi, Sudan, and Rwanda. All of those conflicts were brutal and tragic, but the latter was the fastest and most deadly. Extremist Hutu and their supporters killed nearly one-tenth of the population in a hundred days, making the Rwandan genocide the "fastest, most efficient killing spree of the twentieth century."[66]

In order to give concrete examples of the dynamics discussed so far, the remainder of this chapter will examine the 1994 Rwandan genocide, a disturbing and extreme example of the intersection of information, group behavior, and violence. Rwanda's genocide occurred not during a period of dictatorship but in a time when Rwanda was democ-ratizing and becoming more open to the world. Though the country was no model democracy, it had an increasingly active civil society, a grow-ing free press, and growing access to communication technologies. Citizens had unprecedented access to information, especially about the ideas of organized nongovernmental groups. Ten years before the geno-cide, a senior scholar of Central African history called Rwanda the best chance for democracy south of the Sahara.[67] Less than one year before the genocide, many observers agreed.

Though no one historical case could adequately illustrate all of the issues discussed in this chapter, a brief overview of Rwanda in the spring of 1994 demonstrates how a campaign of dehumanization against a minority out-group can have particularly dangerous results in a fluid political climate characterized by an opening, but distorted, marketplace of ideas. It demonstrates how increased but still limited transparency will not necessarily show information that humanizes other groups and how transparency sometimes can exacerbate tensions between groups and legitimize the spread of pernicious ideas. Despite increasingly open flows of information, the marketplace of ideas did not refute anti-Tutsi rhetoric; it spread and legitimized it. These ideas encouraged violence, which quickly escalated to genocide.

Between 1991 and the outbreak of the genocide in April 1994 transparency within Rwanda increased along at least two of three dimen-sions.[68] Debate increased with the spread of opposition parties, human rights organizations, and the increased independence of nongovernmen-tal organizations. Control over information diminished with the rise of opposition parties, civil society and a free press. Disclosure of informa-tion increased somewhat due to integration of opposition figures into the government but remained limited.

Some Rwandans had access to ideas from outside Rwanda, but the reach of such ideas was limited. Moreover, because of the political and social upheaval going on, it is not clear whether outside ideas would have garnered much attention or seemed relevant. When societies are in turmoil, they often turn inward. Unless opinion leaders embrace ideas from outside the country, such ideas may have little influence even in an age of transparency.

Rwanda Opens

The early 1990s were a time of profound change in Rwanda. The Hutu-dominated regime was instituting reforms due to pressures from both inside and outside Rwanda. The August 1993 Arusha Accords ended the war between the regime and expatriate rebels from the minority Tutsi group. The accords promised radical reforms, including a transitional government representing two political blocs and the rebel Tutsi Front Patriotique du Rwanda (FPR), free elections within twenty-two months, and integration, disarmament, and demobilization of the military.[69] A new constitution asserted judiciary independence, subordination of the executive to the legislature, legalization of opposition parties, and separation of party and state.[70] The position of president, held by General Juvénal Habyarimana, was transformed into a ceremonial post while the more powerful post of prime minister was held by a member of the Mouvement Démocratique Républicain (MDR), the largest opposition party. The number of opposition parties surpassed ten.

The Habyarimana regime did not embrace reform. After two decades in power, General Habyarimana embarked on reform only after intense pressure from international donors, economic pressures from falling coffee prices (the country's main agricultural product), and gains by the FPR, which was intent on overthrowing the regime. Habyarimana was no democrat. His reign was characterized by corruption, political oppression, and the encouragement of ethnic tensions to support his own power. Only when the pressure was overwhelming did he acquiesce to political change.

As the strength of opposition parties grew, it also threatened groups that prospered under the Habyarimana regime. In the months before the genocide, the Hutu ruling party, the Mouvement Républicain National pour la Démocratie et le Développement (MRNDD), was split between hard-liners and those willing to reform. A clear loser in the redistribution of cabinet seats in the transitional government, the MRNDD's power was declining fast.[71] The more hard-line and racist Coalition pour la Défense de la République (CDR), an ally of the MRNDD, was even more threatened politically and did not receive a single seat in the government. The loss of power by extremists coupled with Habyarimana's reforms seemed to have backed extremist groups into a corner. Hutu extremists had the most to lose from a more truly democratic Rwanda. Faced with the prospect of losing all control and backed by an ideology of racial hatred, the extremists made plans to exterminate the Rwandan Tutsi population as well as the politically moderate Hutu.

Civil society organizations began to take root and voice opinions not previously aired. The Roman Catholic Church, which had previously avoided confrontation with the government, exposed human rights abuses by the government.[72] Several strong and well-organized human rights groups (e.g., the Association Rwandaise pour la Défense de la Personne et des Libertés Publiques, Ligue Chrétienne de Défense des Droits de l'Homme [LICHREDOR], and Association des Volontaires du Progrés, Kanyarwanda) formed a coordination committee called the Comitée de Liaison des Associations de Défense des Droits de l'Homme au Rwanda (CLADHO) and began to report embarrassing details about the human rights situation in Rwanda.

The government's control over information declined. After the end of the government's press monopoly in July 1990, the number of newspapers and journals exploded, though the regime allegedly harassed journalists through the early 1990s.[73] Sixty newspapers and magazines operated by 1992. Some of the new publications, including *Kanguka* and *Kangura*, had strong political leanings and were quite controversial though they had small circulations. The government still controlled the daily bulletin of the *Agence Rwandaise de Presse* and the weekly *Imvaho* (Truth) as well as magazines in both French and Kinyarwanda. Elites listened to short-wave radio broadcasts of Radio France Internationale (RFI), Deutschewelle, BBC World Service, and the Voice of America; most Rwandans did not.[74]

Despite growing press freedom, in a country where only 64% of adult men and 37% of adult women were literate, radio was more effective for reaching the masses than print media.[75] By 1994, Rwanda featured one AM station and two FM stations. The country also had one television station.[76] By 1990, one of every thirteen Rwandans owned a radio, which had been heavily promoted by UNESCO and by other international aid agencies as a development tool.[77] Ownership of radios increased from 65.99 per 1,000 people in 1992, to 83.47 per 1,000 people in 1994.[78] Rwandan political leaders also encouraged radio, seeing it as a useful tool for consolidating public support.

The government and Hutu extremists dominated radio. The government-supported Radio Rwanda reporters began to demonstrate more independence and reported news even if it showed the regime in a less favorable light.[79] However, whereas a healthy marketplace of ideas depends on a pluralism of ideas, most of the commentary did not contradict the government (in addition to being rather formal and bland). Radio-Télévision Libre des Mille Collines (RTLM) was livelier and also more popular. The government granted a license to RTLM, but not to more politically moderate stations.

In terms of communication technology, Rwanda had only one telephone per 1,000 people in 1993 and that telephone system was intended for business and government use, not for the general public. However, in 1993–1994, the African Development Bank and bilateral donors initiated a $30 million project to install 8,000 additional lines as well as cable resources and a satellite receiver.[80] In 1992, France and Belgium contributed about $1 million each for a television station; the government contributed the rest.[81] There were no Internet connections.

During this period of reform, international pressure on the Habyarimana regime continued up to the days, even hours, before the genocide. On April 3, 1994, a group of Western ambassadors met with Habyarimana to insist that he install the transitional institutions outlined in the Arusha Accords. Later that week, at a meeting shortly before his assassination, Habyarimana allegedly consented to a truly broad-based transitional government. The German ambassador remarked, "I personally expect the establishment of the institutions in the course of this week."[82]

The Genocide

On April 6, a plane carrying President Juvénal Habyarimana of Rwanda and President Cyprien Ntaryamina of Burundi crashed after being hit by two ground-to-air missiles. The crash sparked a three-month massacre that killed hundreds of thousands and sent two million refugees into Zaire, Tanzania, and Burundi.[83] The killing ended on July 17 when an FPR victory led to a final retreat of the Hutu extremists. The identity of Habyarimana's assassins remains unknown but American diplomats and intelligence officers identified Habyarimana's own Presidential Guard as the likely culprits.[84] The Presidential Guard included, and was supported by, extremists who likely feared that Habyarimana would implement the Arusha Accords and had the power and organization to carry out the assassination.[85]

The massacre was well organized and planned in advance. Before the genocide, Hutu extremists began arming militia groups with firearms in 1993 and early 1994. After concluding that guns were too expensive, businesspeople close to Habyarimana imported huge shipments of machetes, enough to arm every third Hutu adult male.[86] Lists of "enemies" were developed and distributed before the genocide even began. Though the plane crashed at 8:30 p.m., roadblocks sprang up throughout Kigali and soldiers searched houses by 9:15 p.m.[87] Soldiers and militia killed Tutsi and moderate Hutu political leaders within hours.

According to the nongovernmental organization (NGO) Africa Rights, extremist Hutu quickly eliminated, via assassination or recruitment, nearly all Rwandans who would have provided opposing views. Extremist Hutu also eliminated or distorted all sources of outside information by cutting telephone lines, imposing curfews and roadblocks to limit travel and communication, and expelling foreign journalists.[88] Internal transparency was suddenly limited relative to the pre-genocide period.

Most of the killing was conducted by the Presidential Guard, numbering 700 to 1,500 men; the 50,000 strong Hutu army, comprised mostly of landless peasants and the urban unemployed lured by the promise of food and drink and by the opportunity to loot the belongings of victims; and the 1,700 Interahamwe militia bands that had been trained by Hutu extremists before the genocide.[89] Once the killing started, many thousands of Rwandans joined in. Soldiers and the National Police directed all of the major massacres throughout the country. Usually, the military began the attacks and civilians finished the slaughter of Tutsi and moderate Hutu, mostly by hacking them to death with machetes or beating them with clubs. Though some Rwandans resisted and tried to hide targeted individuals, the danger of such actions quickly became clear. In regions that resisted orders to carry out the genocide, two *préfets* (governors) were killed as were several lower-level officials.[90]

The root cause of the genocide was not simply ethnic differences, but the empowerment of extremists who demonized the Tutsi as a way to defend and bolster their own power. A threatened but politically powerful group of extremist Hutu used the Tutsi minority as a scapegoat and used anti-Tutsi rhetoric to support their goal of stopping political reform. The region's history and the fact that so many Rwandans went along with the killing suggests that ethnic differences were an important context for the genocide. Anti-Tutsi rhetoric was powerful because it played on deep-seated resentment. Beyond pure ethnic hatred, the promise of a better life after the Tutsi were killed must have rung true on some perverse level since Tutsi were far wealthier than their Hutu counterparts. Nonetheless, the fact that so many moderate Hutu were killed makes clear that the motivation of the genocide was political and not purely ethnic in nature.

Observers disagree on the extent to which genocide was embraced by the masses. According to Mahmood Mamdani, the true horror of genocide was that it was embraced by the general public, motivated by fear of, and prejudice against, Tutsi.[91] John Mueller, in contrast, argues that only 2 to 9 percent of the male Hutu population over the age of thirteen was part of the group engaged in hard-core killing—hardly a war of all against all.[92] Mueller's figures are convincing, but the participation of up to 200,000 Rwandans in the massacres is still shockingly high in a country of only 11 million and, in the context of extensive anti-Tutsi propaganda, highlights just how dangerous a campaign of dehumanization can be.

Despite restricted internal transparency, it is likely that most Rwandans had some sense of the extent of the killing. Rwanda is a small and densely populated country. The killings were dispersed throughout the country and the militias ordered citizens to participate in the killings in many circumstances. However, it is likely that there was confusion about the nature of the killing. The RTLM broadcast that more Hutu than Tutsi were killed. In addition, there is evidence that government forces told citizens that they must kill Tutsi in self-defense because Hutu were in grave danger.[93] When the leadership and a popular radio station endorsed the killing, the political culture encouraged people to acquiesce.[94] The killing was justified by support from voices of authority, allegations of Tutsi wrongdoing, and the need for self-defense. Consequently, even if people knew about the killing, they may have interpreted its motivation and purpose in a particular way. How information about the killing was framed and then interpreted was important to the perceived legitimacy of the killings and, presumably, to the willingness of citizens to go along.

Dehumanization and the Genocide

Genocide in Rwanda occurred after a long campaign of anti-Tutsi propaganda.[95] The dehumanization of Tutsi occurred over many years but escalated in the months and days before the genocide began—despite, and perhaps because of, greater flows of information in society. AntiTutsi rhetoric appeared in various pamphlets published by the Kigali magazine *Kangura*, and by other Hutu extremist organizations. A racist pamphlet called "The Ten Commandments of the Hutu," for instance, called anyone who married Tutsi women or engaged in business with Tutsi a traitor and demanded that posts in administration and armed forces be reserved for Hutu.[96] Similar pamphlets argued that Hutu were superior to Tutsi, that the Arusha Accords were a Tutsi plot, that Tutsi had killed and raped Hutu in the past, that Tutsi wanted to exterminate all Hutu, and (a few days before the genocide) that Tutsi had prepared mass graves for Hutu.[97]

The most important media before and during the genocide was radio. Radio, particularly the notorious RTLM, laid the groundwork for, and later expedited, the genocide.[98] Radio Rwanda, though more restrained, also broadcast directives that facilitated the genocide in the early days of April. Launched on July 3, 1993, extremist members of the CDR created RTLM partially in response to an increasingly independent media, especially the FPR's Radio Muhabura.[99] RTLM, which broadcast rowdy banter, pop music, phone-in shows, and interviews, quickly attracted a large following. Transistor radios had become quite cheap and the only other radio station, the government-owned Radio Rwanda, was much more formal and less entertaining.[100] RTLM's main goal, according to analysts, was to demonize Tutsi. Announcers exploited the massacres of Hutu in neighboring Burundi as "evidence" that Tutsi would never peacefully share power with Hutu. They told listeners that Tutsi solders were devils who killed Hutu "by extracting various organs...for example by taking the heart, the liver, the stomach....the cruelty of the *inyenzi* [cockroach] is incurable, the cruelty of the *inyenzi* can only be cured by their total extermination."[101] RTLM told of the Tutsis' allegedly malicious role in Rwandese history, the need for vigilance, that the time would come to reach for the "top part of the house" (where weapons are traditionally kept), and that the Tutsi were evil.[102] Announcers warned Tutsi that "You cockroaches must know you are made of flesh. We won't let you kill, we will kill you."[103]

From April 6, 1994 onward, the RTLM exhorted listeners to exterminate all Tutsi, telling them that "the FPR is coming to kill people; so defend yourselves."[104] Once the killing began, the broadcasts called on Hutu to "go to work," and telling its listeners that "the graves are not yet full."[105] Announcers encouraged listeners to call in and reveal where Tutsi were hiding along with their addresses and license plate numbers. They also asked listeners to resupply weapons to certain areas.[106] According to one police investigator, "There was an FM radio on every roadblock, there were thousands of roadblocks in Rwanda."[107] Tutsi reportedly listened to the broadcasts to see if they were personally targeted.

Before the genocide began, Rwandans chose to listen to RTLM in a relatively open and competitive media environment. After the genocide began, nearly all other media were silenced, which severely curtailed domestic transparency. Some Rwandans with short-wave radios could hear contesting descriptions of events, but RTLM challenged outside sources of information, telling Rwandans to ignore the "biased and ill-informed" reports. C. Kellow and H. Steeves cite the following RTLM announcement broadcast on May 14, 1994:

> This is nothing but propaganda from White people; we are used to it. However, we can still maintain that the *inkotanyi*, wherever they have gone, have massacred the Hutu...after the 200,000 killed, the journalists say that the numbers today rise to 500,000 killed. Where do these other 300,000 come from? These other 300,0000 are without a doubt Hutu....This war that we are fighting is an important one...it is, in fact, a war of extermination, a war started by the *inkotanyi*—because it is they who have started it with the purpose of exterminating the Hutu.[108]

Thus, even if Rwandans had access to other sources of information, RTLM broadcasts may have inspired doubts about their credibility.

The perceived need for self-defense contributed to mass participation. Rwandans were told that Tutsi would kill them and some Hutu were threatened with death if they did not go along. Claims that Tutsi wanted to kill Hutu would not have seemed inconceivable in such a troubled region. As the historian René Lemarchand argues about the neighboring and ethnically similar country of Burundi, "Mythmaking in Burundi is inextricably bound with the experience—real or anticipated—of genocide.... Behind the murders of political opponents, the systematic ethnic cleansing of urban and rural districts, the armed attacks on refugees and internally displaced persons, and the ambushes of civilians lies the conviction held by both Tutsi and Hutu that unless the other's crimes are retaliated against by retribution, planned annihilation will inevitably follow."[109] The combination of illiteracy and the authoritarian tradition meant that many Hutu believed claims by the government and by RTLM that they were in danger.

Experts disagree about how much the Hutu population hated the Tutsi. Some argue that the genocide was embraced by the masses. Others argue that only fanatics demonstrated this level of animosity. Though Tutsi were easily identifiable due to a law requiring all Rwandans to be registered according to ethnic group, Hutu and Tutsi shared a single language and led lives that were closely entwined. A considerable number of Rwandans had both Hutu and Tutsi parents. Differences between Hutu and Tutsi resulted more from social status than from ethnicity, religion, or language. Among ancestors of the modern Hutu and Tutsi, the rich in cattle became known as "Tutsi" while the masses became known as "Hutu." Over time Tutsi and Hutu married within their own group and began to develop common physical features. However, some of those differences disappeared with the increase in mixed marriages after the 1959 revolution. Those in power exploited ethnic tensions in Rwanda. Tutsi held much of the wealth in Rwanda, even if they no longer possessed much political power. And, in neighboring Burundi—a country whose history is closely intertwined with that of Rwanda—Tutsi slaughtered tens of thousands of Hutu in 1972, 1988, and 1991. Some Rwandan Hutu feared that the same might happen in Rwanda if the Tutsi returned to power.[110]

Conclusion

Freer flows of information sometimes can reinforce poisonous views of other groups and, in a few tragic cases, even facilitate violence.

Arguments that a greater availability of information will lead to better relations between groups make assumptions about the content of that information, what information gets attention, and how that information is interpreted. Reality may not always honor those assumptions.

The 1994 genocide in Rwanda shows how a distorted marketplace of ideas and growing, but still restricted, transparency can create a dangerous political environment, especially during a period of major political transition when there is not yet a system of rights and the rule of law to protect minority groups. Before the killing began, the opening of Rwandan society, particularly a freer press and the spread of civil society organizations, empowered those in Rwanda who wanted to persecute the Tutsi minority in order to bolster their own power and identity. What information emerged did little to put Tutsi and Hutu on equal footing. Instead, the media generally highlighted differences, the alleged threat of the Tutsi to the Hutu majority, and reinforced existing in-groups and out-groups despite a long history of contact. To quote a historian of Africa who served as a United Nations monitor in Rwanda, "Multiparty politics, as it took hold in Rwanda, exposed citizens to the open and aggressive promotion of an in-group, as well as, acts of intimidation and violence against those outside the group."[111] Coupled with the spread of communication technology, in this case radio, and a campaign of Tutsi dehumanization, those messages spread all too easily throughout Rwandan society.

The opening marketplace of ideas played a role by creating a climate in which groups across the political spectrum tried to stake out clear identities for themselves and attempted to polarize ethnic groups in society to serve their own political interests.[112] Citizens could access newly available information about human rights abuses and other failings of the government due to the burgeoning free press and the growth of civil society. This information empowered and facilitated the formation of human rights groups and opposition parties, which threatened those in power. At the same time, however, extremist organizations—even those more extreme than the government—also gained power and were able to spread their messages to the masses. The mechanisms that enhance transparency, such as a freer press and civil society, empowered extremist groups, which hijacked these instruments for their own ends. RTLM and other CDR-funded media dehumanized Tutsi and propagated the idea of a Tutsi threat far more than the Habyarimana government ever had. These anti-Tutsi views were more widely available than before and, after years of media dehumanizing Tutsi, seem to have found many sympathetic listeners. Despite the rise of many media outlets, there weren't sufficiently numerous or powerful voices to counter the anti-Tutsi propaganda. As Mark Frohardt and Jonathan Temin wrote in a special report for the United States Institute of Peace, the degree of media plurality "applies not only to the number of outlets but to the number of divergent voices emanating from those outlets. In other words, a multitude of private stations all playing music, or all espousing similar messages, does not constitute plurality."[113]

The case of the 1994 genocide raises the possibility that both very high and very low levels of transparency may reduce conflict, but rapid increases in transparency might distort information flows in uniquely dangerous ways. Greater transparency might have provided more opportunities for moderate voices to refute falsehoods about the Tutsi threat, though that idea presupposes a receptive audience that would reject its prejudices and grievances in the face of humanizing information that disconfirmed their previously held beliefs. If anti-Tutsi sentiment was as strong as some analysts argue, the population may still have tuned their radios to RTLM. In addition, a lack of transparency in the years before the genocide may have so demonized the Tutsi that Hutu would not have trusted contrary information.

Conversely, if the Rwandan government maintained more control over information, the regime may have continued to avoid rhetoric as extreme as that of the CDR and RTLM. It remains unclear how involved the Habyarimana regime was in planning the genocide and whether the regime would have relented to reformists, but the regime had incentives to keep donors like France and the World Bank happy and to rein in extremists. Without such extreme rhetoric over a period of time, the mass acceptance of slaughter might have found less fertile soil. In addition, without the challenge from opposition groups with their own radio station, the CDR might have felt less desperate and may not have resorted to such extreme measures.

After the killing began, a lack of transparency contributed to the genocide by allowing the government and the militias to spread unsubstantiated and unquestioned reports that the FPR would kill Hutu civilians if Hutu did not kill Tutsi first. Extremists hijacked many of the media outlets in the period before the genocide and silenced the rest after the killings started. Some citizens may have been able to access non-Rwandan media sources but the effect of that access was negligible because that access was limited, those sources were discredited, and mostly elites—many of whom were targeted first by the death squads— listened to those reports.

Whether transparency's effects are positive or negative, transparency does seem to encourage either virtuous or vicious circles. In a highly developed and balanced marketplace of ideas, transparency spreads those views and reinforces a political culture in which problems are solved by discourse, not by violence, and minority groups are protected. In a distorted marketplace of ideas characterized by extremism and hate, transparency spreads not only polemical discourse, but also a political culture of intolerance. It can facilitate the dehumanization of perceived enemies and, in extreme cases, mass murder. Transparency spreads "dark norms" and "happy norms" alike. [114]

The classic question regarding conflict is not why leaders lead citizens into violent conflict, but why followers follow.[115] Similarly, in Rwanda and in instances like it, the question is not why some groups tried to persuade others of their superiority over other groups; there are clear material and psychological incentives to do so. The question is why that information was, in the words of communications experts, salient. Why did citizens listen? Why did they actively tune their radios to RTLM before the genocide and why did they not simply disregard the negative information they heard about Tutsi? Most importantly, why did so many Rwandans act on that information and participate in the genocide?

The answers to those questions have little to do with transparency, the mere revelation of information, and the reaction of individuals. What mattered was that in Rwanda, negative information about the Tutsi fell on receptive ears and, in the din of a rapidly opening and changing society, seemed both relevant and meaningful. Believing that information seems to have satisfied not only the interests of Hutu extremists, but also the personal, material, and psychological interests of average citizens. This, the willingness of people to listen to some voices and not to others and find some views credible and not others, is something over which greater transparency has little affect. The content and credibility of information is crucial and, unless greater transparency is accompanied by the widespread availability of certain types of information, transparency may only make matters worse.

Consequently, in cases where international organizations play a strong role in helping a country democratize, a more regulated marketplace of ideas and a more gradual opening up may facilitate a peaceful transition better than an information free-for-all. Institutions that effectively support a truly free marketplace of ideas are a necessary precursor. The efforts of the United Nations Transitional Authority in Cambodia (UNTAC) are instructive. The UNTAC Information/Education Division (Info/Ed) broadcast up to fifteen hours a day of balanced news and other programs, such as roundtable discussions with all twenty political parties, about the upcoming election. UNTAC Radio offered time for each registered political party as well as a guaranteed "right of response" to any political party or candidate that felt that its statements had been mischaracterized. The station also persuaded Cambodians that their votes would be secret. Private Japanese donors contributed 143,000 radios so that these messages could reach a large number of Cambodians.[116] The Information/Education Division also developed print materials, promoted a free and independent press, and developed a professional code of conduct for journalists. Unfortunately, with an overall price tag of $1.6 billion for UNTAC, the Cambodian experiment may not be easily repeated.[117] However, in post-Arusha Rwanda, a similar approach might have saved hundreds of thousands of lives and headed off the need for more military intervention later. Other less elaborate efforts include "Ring around Serbia," a multilateral effort to transmit international programming into Serbia in 1999.[118]

The genocide in Rwanda suggests the need to reexamine several assumptions about the implications of transparency. First, we cannot assume that transparency, by increasing contact with other groups, will necessarily increase positive feelings toward them. Despite a long history of coexistence of Tutsi and Hutu in Rwanda, that close contact did little to improve long-term relations between those groups because that contact exposed political and economic inequalities that could be manipulated and mobilized to support the power of certain individuals or groups. Fewer inequalities probably could have reduced tensions, but more information about existing inequalities did not. When Hutu extremists expressed those grievances in the language of ethnic hatred, they tapped into broad dissatisfaction with the status quo. Academics who research the contact hypothesis will not be surprised by this argument since formal presentations of that hypothesis note that contact only increases positive feelings when the groups are on equal footing.[119] However, that condition often drops out of the popular translation. Second, we cannot make assumptions about what types of information transparency will reveal. Sometimes transparency will reveal information that humanizes other groups, increases positive feelings toward them, and refutes negative stereotypes, but sometimes it will not. Third, we cannot assume that greater transparency will empower democrats, pacifists, and civil society organizations with laudable objectives. Transparency can also empower extremists and those who wish to harm out-groups whether within or outside their country. Fourth, we cannot assume that people will always seek out truth and believe information that disconfirms hateful beliefs. Sometimes they will seek out information that confirms existing views, encourages hostility toward out-groups, or bolsters their own self-esteem. Finally, we should not assume that transparency is irreversible. Transparency in Rwanda was quashed with remarkable speed.

Chapter 4

Transparency and Conflict Intervention

"The whole world will be watching."
—Western diplomat to the Tutsi FPR major general
Paul Kagame after the 1993 Arusha Accords[1]

"In Darfur, my camera was not nearly enough."
—Cease-fire monitor Brian Steidle[2]

The trend toward greater transparency should facilitate earlier and more frequent intervention by third parties who wish to stop violent conflicts in other parts of the world, according to conventional wisdom. Governments have access to more information about foreign disputes, which should help them to identify trouble spots and to intervene before conflicts get out of hand.[3] Such intervention requires political will, which greater transparency can facilitate in two ways. First, information about the human toll of conflict and the threat conflicts pose to nations not directly involved in the fighting can lead nongovernmental organizations (NGOs) to pressure governments or international organizations to intervene. Second, greater transparency lets citizens around the world learn both about foreign conflicts and about their governments' response. When they see human suffering on their television screens, they may pressure their governments to act.[5]

Greater transparency may also help to deter the outbreak of future conflicts if potential combatants see that acts of violence will be stopped and punished. After all, greater transparency makes intervention evident not just to conflict participants and citizens around the world, but also to parties engaged in other foreign disputes. If perpetrators see that violence is not rewarded, the incentive to fight declines and the credibility of future third-party threats to intervene increases. Of course, this view assumes that most perpetrators of violence are rational and weigh the likely costs and benefits of violence before employing it, and studies indicate that perpetrators are indeed rational more often than not.[6]

Nonetheless, greater transparency will not always facilitate conflict intervention by third parties. Despite greater transparency, information about foreign conflicts remains imperfect and media coverage of foreign conflicts, a key source of transparency, is spotty. More importantly, even if information about conflict zones is available and accurate, that information will not necessarily foster the political will necessary to intervene. Many of today's conflicts break out in locations where powerful countries have few national interests at stake and, when conflicts do not threaten the physical security of citizens, energy sources, markets, or transportation routes and the destabilizing effects of conflict are unlikely to reach those with the power to intervene, governments and international organizations may choose to stay out, even when death tolls are high. Leaders of governments and international organizations may hear pleas from NGOs but not act upon them. Publics may see footage of human suffering in the media but not pressure their governments to react.

Greater transparency may sometimes lead to earlier and more frequent conflict intervention but we cannot assume that will be the case. In fact, if greater transparency shows that foreign conflicts will be dangerous and difficult to exit, transparency may have the opposite effect, with citizens pressuring leaders to stay out of conflicts even if those leaders wish to intervene. In ongoing interventions, images of soldiers being killed may lead citizens to pressure leaders to exit countries where the costs appear to exceed the benefits.

Greater transparency also may not illuminate information that will deter future conflicts. Though greater transparency can reveal information that strengthens the credibility of threats to intervene, transparency also makes past idle threats or short-lived interventions widely known. Even if threats are credible, the promise of intervention may only lead perpetrators of violence to speed up their killing to avoid interruption.

For all of these reasons, claims that greater transparency will facilitate intervention to prevent or to end deadly conflict are optimistic, to say the least. During the 1994 Rwandan genocide, numerous powerful governments were aware of the extensive violence but did nothing to stop it. Media coverage and the actions of NGOs did little to change minds until the genocide ended and a massive refugee crisis ensued.

Governments simply lacked the political will to intervene and deliberately chose to stay out. Information did not lead to action.

Transparency and Conflict Intervention: From the Outside Looking In

Protecting civilians from deadly conflict remains a challenge for the international community. Armed conflicts in the 1990s killed 3.6 million people, approximately 90 percent of whom were noncombatants.[7] The threat to noncombatants is particularly high in conflicts within, rather than between, sovereign states, which now account for most of the violent conflicts in the world.[8] In addition to killing civilians, such conflicts confront survivors with abandoned land mines, food shortages, disease, environmental degradation, economic distress, and displacement from their homes. Coalitions of governments do intervene in violent conflicts with increasing frequency, but such intervention ends only some conflicts, and even in those cases, intervention occurs too late to save many innocents.[9]

Experts emphasize the benefits of intervening before violence escalates since resolving conflicts early is both easier and cheaper.[4] After violence spreads, positions harden and intervention by third parties becomes both more difficult and more expensive. The strategy of preventive action—alternate formulas of which are known as preventive diplomacy and coercive prevention—is defined as efforts to "prevent disputes from arising between parties, to prevent existing disputes from escalating into conflicts, and to limit the spread of the latter when they occur."[10] Early interventions have been rewarded in practice. For instance, in the mid-1990s the United Nations Preventive Deployment Force helped to stop the spread of violence from Bosnia and Croatia into the former Yugoslav Republic of Macedonia.[11]

Some advocates of early action emphasize the moral duty of the international community to stop conflicts that threaten civilians. The "responsibility to protect" appears to be a growing international norm, in tension with, or even outweighing traditional norms of sovereignty in some circumstances. Others focus on how conflict intervention, especially early in the conflict cycle, serves national interests. According to Bruce Jentleson, when we "seek to do as little as we can, or at least avoid squarely facing up to the issues until they press themselves upon us so intensely as to be undeniable...[w]e then end up with commitments that last much longer, cost much more, and accomplish much less than promised...the interests at stake and the costs of inaction are too great."[12]

Whatever their justifications, those who want the international community to do more to stop deadly conflicts, especially in their earliest stages, confront three major obstacles. The first is informational. Preventing deadly conflicts before they break out requires detailed information about, and analysis of, the internal politics of foreign countries. The second is organizational. Individuals who collect and analyze warning signs must be able to convey that information to governments and organizations with the capacity to stop conflicts quickly.[13] The third is political. Conflict intervention is expensive and difficult, so there must be sufficient political will to support efforts to end foreign conflicts. In democracies the public ultimately must support those efforts.

The trend toward greater transparency can help the international community overcome two of those three obstacles: informational obstacles and political obstacles.[14] News about foreign disputes is more accessible in an age of transparency. The media documents events in conflict zones and disseminates that information around the world. NGOs monitor disputes and publicize their findings. International organizations send observers and fact-finding missions to collect information about regions in turmoil. Individuals in conflict zones use information technologies like the Internet or video cameras to call attention to their situation easily and inexpensively. The decentralization of information also facilitates good analysis of that information because it allows for multiple, independent assessments that serve as a check on each other. This information and analysis provides the opportunity to head off conflicts before they erupt and to respond effectively later in a conflict.

Because of its reach, the media is the information source that is most likely to generate public pressure for intervention in foreign conflicts. Broadcast media in particular tends to produce a public reaction due to its ability to capture a story in pictures and to evoke an emotional response to the human costs of conflict. Citizens who see graphic footage of human suffering on their television screens, the argument goes, then will pressure their governments to "do something." Dubbed the "CNN effect," this phenomenon is credited with encouraging the American intervention in Somalia and, ultimately, in Bosnia. Substantial anecdotal evidence suggests that media reports and the public pressure they generate lead governments to focus on particular areas of the world more than they otherwise might. For instance, according to one American official, the West took months to act in Kosovo, and NATO intervened only after "The massacres put it very graphically on the front pages in Europe and America and it is hard for our administration or any government to ignore it."[15] Others argue that the substantial global efforts to respond to famines in Africa in the 1980s and 1990s resulted from media coverage.

Although transparency can help remove both informational and political obstacles to earlier and more frequent intervention in foreign conflicts, that will not necessarily be the case. Greater transparency will not necessarily make publics and even leaders better informed about foreign conflicts nor is it the only obstacle to earlier and more frequent intervention. In some circumstances, greater transparency can make conflict intervention less likely.

Despite greater transparency, particularly when it is facilitated by the global media, citizens have only imperfect information about foreign conflicts. The American journalist Walter Lippmann once wrote that the press is like the "beam of a searchlight that moves restlessly about, bringing one episode and then another out of darkness and into vision."[16] However, to the extent that this effect is real, the media may be as powerful for the crises it keeps in darkness as for the crises it brings into light. Most internal conflicts languish in obscurity despite twenty-four-hour news broadcasters like the BBC and CNN.[17] As one senior British official put it, "We are under no pressure to do something about crises that are not on TV."[18] In the 1990s, the media largely overlooked conflicts in Angola, southern Sudan, Armenia, and Afghanistan and paid only sporadic attention to conflicts in Liberia, Nagorno-Karabakh, Kashmir, Angola, Georgia, East Timor, and Tajikistan. Only six months before the genocide in Rwanda, massacres in Burundi claimed 35,000-50,000 lives but received little attention.[19] In March 1994, the world focused on responding to violence in Sarajevo and Bosnia. However, at approximately the same time, extremists murdered more than 1,000 people in Burundi over the course of just two days but received little notice. Sudan coped with a humanitarian crisis more desperate than the one in Somalia but received little international aid. One American diplomat described the situation in Sudan as "Somalia without CNN."[20] Though 500,000 people died from famine in Sudan in 1992, roughly the same number as in Somalia, Sudan received far less media attention.[21]

Many factors explain the limited coverage of international conflicts.[22] The physical safety of journalists is one explanation. Tragically, in 2001 and 2002, eighty-two foreign journalists were killed, and such dangerous conditions reduce in-depth coverage of foreign conflicts. Geography also affects coverage. The famine in Somalia was concentrated in a relatively accessible area, whereas suffering in Sudan was spread over great distances, making coverage logistically difficult.[23] Similarly, because journalists could access it, the siege of Sarajevo was covered rather than the siege of Mostar, for instance, even though the situation in Mostar was far worse.[24] Some conflicts are not deemed newsworthy since they drag on for a long period of time with no significant change in status.[25] Financial constraints are also a serious impediment since overseas coverage is extremely expensive. News organizations seeking to cover the 2001 U.S. attack on the Taliban regime of Afghanistan, for example, faced very high costs. Business class airfare from New York to Islamabad was $3,133 on Pakistan International Airways. Shipping and setup costs for satellite communications equipment ran between $50,000 and $70,000 for each up link and could cost at least that much to maintain each week. Broadcasting from remote areas led to satellite transmission fees costing up to $2,000 for fifteen minutes. In addition, media organizations expended significant sums on transportation, bribes, and translation.[26] Even publicly funded news organizations like the BBC, do not need to turn a profit, but they still must make difficult choices about where to spend scarce resources, especially when budgets are tight. Moreover, news organizations prefer to focus on one major crisis at a time, but world events do not always cooperate.[27] According to one study, between 1978 and 1985, there were an average of 5 complex humanitarian emergencies each year. In 1989, that number grew to 14. In 1994, the number grew to 20.[28] A *Christian Science Monitor* cartoon illustrated this point by depicting an editor announcing, "Tadjikistan? Sorry we've already got an ethnic war story."[29] Other factors affecting coverage include time, decisions by editors, and lack of direct national involvement.[30]

Spotty coverage of foreign conflicts by the media and by NGOs would be less worrying if the most deadly conflicts or meritorious causes received the most attention. However, as the political scientist Clifford Bob argues, attention (not to mention money) does not always go to the most deserving recipients.[31] Bob asks why, for instance, Tibetans and their cause have received such extensive coverage, while the Uighurs in China's northwest Xinjiang Province have not. Both have fought a long struggle for independence from China, but the Uighurs have failed to inspire support anywhere close to support for Tibetans. According to Bob, "marketing trumps justice" and even the most deserving causes face long odds as they compete for the world's attention and support.[32]

Nor does greater transparency mean that we will assess information about foreign disputes accurately. The volume and variety of information not only overwhelms us, but also impairs our ability to process it. Humans rely on cognitive shortcuts to cope with large amounts of information and those shortcuts make it possible to operate effectively in an information-rich environment. However, cognitive shortcuts can mislead us as well. People may fail to interpret information correctly or understand its implications. We may fail to recognize important information embedded in streams of data, that is, the ability to sort signals of future events from "noise."[33] We tend to interpret new information in the context of existing beliefs and values, which may change slowly even when new information disconfirms those beliefs. We may see what we want to see. As David Rawson, the U.S. ambassador to Rwanda before and during the genocide, observed, "We were looking for the hopeful signs, not the dark signs. In fact we were looking away from the dark signs...."[34]

Arguments that more information about foreign conflicts will lead to earlier or more frequent conflict intervention often assume that information about atrocities will produce a certain response—namely, that NGOs and citizens will react by clamoring for governments to do something and that reluctant leaders will comply. However, that is not always the case. Though greater transparency allows NGOs to mobilize information strategically to pressure governments and international organizations to act, their power is limited. Since NGOs do not typically have much operational capacity, particularly military capacity, for preventing violence compared to major governments or international organizations, to be successful NGOs generally must persuade other groups—the disputing parties themselves, governments, or international organizations—to play a role they cannot. Effectively making a case for intervention amid the din of international politics in the information age is a challenge for NGOs. There are so many issues and so many voices advocating them that calls for intervention may simply get lost in the clamor. Moreover, leaders may not heed calls for intervention by NGOs until there is overwhelming evidence of atrocities. Taking early warnings seriously is difficult because signals are rarely clear. Moreover, NGOs sometimes will be wrong about which potential conflicts will escalate and which conflicts will not be resolved without the help of outsiders. Leaders may then fail to listen because they think NGOs are "crying wolf."[35]

Citizens may also fail to lobby successfully for intervention to stop deadly conflicts. The so-called CNN effect is real but weak.[36] Though the media inevitably influences the views of citizens, studies indicate that television images, even dramatic ones, ultimately lead to policy change only when government positions are weak or fluctuating and when there is little public support for them.[37] The media steps into the vacuum if governments cannot articulate and defend their policies.[38] When governments have clearly defined goals, intervention is unlikely unless conflicts threaten national interests.[39] At least in the United States, public support for intervention in conflicts is influenced far more by casualties and by the duration of a conflict than by television images.[40] Though the Korean War received little television coverage, and the Vietnam War was, at that time, the most televised war in American history, support for the Vietnam War did not drop below the level of support for the Korean War until the war dragged on and the casualties grew.[41]

In many instances, the media helps governments to persuade the public, not the other way around.[42] Public opinion is malleable and leaders can convince citizens that intervention in foreign conflicts is necessary.[43] For instance, according to Peter Feaver and Christopher Gelpi, two political scientists serving as consultants to President George W. Bush, the key to maintaining public support for military intervention is persuading people that the mission will succeed. The president must project confidence. By disseminating this sense of confidence, therefore, the media plays a critical role in sustaining public support for war.[44]

Sometimes leaders would like to intervene but reluctant publics constrain them. As with most aspects of transparency, the response to conflicts covered by the international media depends on what that coverage shows. Greater transparency can reduce support for preventive action and military conflict intervention when it gives groups information that politicizes even small acts of preventive diplomacy or if it shows that conflict intervention is likely to be dangerous, costly, and possibly ineffective. Sometimes the sheer number and scope of conflicts is overwhelming, and near constant footage of conflict zones seems to induce "compassion fatigue" among viewers.[45] People only seem to be able to process so much suffering at a time so pictures have less and less impact.[46] Limiting intervention or showing the potentially high costs of intervention may not necessarily be negative, of course. If transparency helps leaders and citizens make better-informed decisions, transparency would play a positive role. The risk is that transparency will not just inform, but also distort, civic discourse about preventive action or conflict intervention and overemphasize the short-term costs of intervening over the long-term costs of not intervening. Despite the logic of early action, governments may find it difficult to convince publics to intervene early in a crisis when the costs are low but the need seems less pressing, and easier later on when there is a more compelling need to intervene, but the costs are far higher. Greater transparency may do little to change that.

Transparency and Conflict Intervention: From the Inside Looking Out

The effects of transparency on violence depend on what transparency shows and how actors respond to that information. Transparency encourages violence if it shows that outside intervention is not likely or that threats to intervene are not credible. If the potential intervener's history, political climate, and public opinion indicate that support for intervention will be weak, perpetrators will not view threats as credible. Greater transparency makes outsiders ever more aware of these factors and that knowledge can empower perpetrators of violence. For instance, Mohamed Farah Aideed, who led a Somali faction that attacked American soldiers, told U.S. ambassador Robert Oakley, "We have studied Vietnam and Lebanon and know how to get rid of Americans, by killing them so that public opinion will put an end to things."[47] Aideed's assessment was correct. The United States withdrew from Somalia after rebels killed eighteen American soldiers and dragged them through the streets of Mogadishu. That episode, plus ensuing discussion about how the United States should avoid "nation building," sent a clear message heard around the world. Similarly, during the Rwandan genocide, Hutu extremists had reason to believe that the world would sit idly by while they tried to exterminate the Tutsi. In late 1993, the international community failed to act when Hutu in Burundi slaughtered thousands of Tutsi, and Tutsi soldiers killed thousands of Hutu civilians. According to Alison Des Forges, "organizers of the Rwandan genocide felt encouraged to believe that even larger scale slaughter of civilians would be tolerated."[48] Even if the international community intervened, its staying power was not likely to be great. Hutu extremists undoubtedly watched how quickly the United States pulled out of Somalia. Such lessons are learned quickly in an age of transparency.

Of course, transparency does not mean that outsiders will assess the credibility of threats accurately. Outsiders can misread the credibility of even the most open governments and transparency may only confuse political signals. Democracies in particular are deceptively difficult to read because they are politically decentralized and send multiple and even conflicting signals. Competing political messages can lead adversaries to question a government's resolve and can make the mistake of interpreting divided opinion as weakness.[49] For example, before the 1991 Gulf War, there is evidence that Saddam Hussein doubted President Bush's threat to forcefully repel Iraqi troops from Kuwait if Saddam did not withdraw by the UN mandated deadline. Between sometimes obstreperous opposition in Congress as well as polls showing flagging public support, Saddam became convinced that, as he told the American ambassador to Iraq, April Glaspie, the United States did not have "the stomach" for a costly war.[50] Of course, Saddam was wrong. A divided Congress does not necessarily constrain presidential action and public opinion historically rallies behind the president once troops have been sent.

Arguments that intervention will deter violence contain the hidden assumption that perpetrators will be cowed by the prospect of foreign intervention, an assumption that may or may not be correct. Sometimes information that outsiders will intervene makes combatants fight all the harder so that they may achieve their objectives before they are stopped. It is important to note that credible threats of third-party intervention sometimes increase violence in the short term. For perpetrators of violence who are truly intent on killing, announcing a future intervention may only speed up their work and encourage them to create a fait accompli. Some analysts claim that announcing a broader role for peacekeepers or deploying additional troops would have stopped the killing in Rwanda because extremists and their supporters would have stopped in order to avoid being caught and punished. But others claim that the extremists would have tried to finish the job and kill witnesses while they still had the chance. According to Alan J. Kuperman,

> Hutu militias attempted to wipe out remaining Tutsi before the rebels arrived. During the genocide, the ringleaders even trumpeted false reports of an impending Western intervention to help motivate Hutu to complete the killings. Although the Hutu generally held back from mass killing at sites guarded by foreigners to avoid provoking Western intervention, they would have lost this incentive for restraint had such an intervention been announced.[51]

Similarly, in the Darfur crisis, the possibility of foreign intervention led the Sudanese government and Janjaweed militia to launch a major offensive before the window of opportunity closed.[52]

Parties to foreign conflicts may also escalate violence when intervention is not imminent in order to attract international attention and to broadcast a political message.[53] As Bob observes, simply posting information on a web site is insufficient to attract external attention and support since there may be dozens, if not hundreds of such sites. A better tactic is to attract global media attention, and the best way to attract media attention is through some dramatic act.[54] Unfortunately, violence is dramatic.

Transparency and Intervention in Rwanda

The empirical record supports the idea that transparency will not necessarily lead to earlier and more frequent conflict intervention by the international community. Turning again to the case of the Rwandan genocide (discussed first in chapter 3), we now have ample evidence that the international community had the information it needed to recognize and stop the genocide in Rwanda—if it wanted to do so. The real issue was not a lack of information, as some policy makers argued at the time, but one of political will, which transparency did little to build.[55] Though the situation on the ground was confusing, the international community had sufficient information to recognize that Rwandans were systematically slaughtering Tutsi, even if they could not predict the full scope of the genocide.

Before discussing the role of transparency, it is necessary to review a brief chronology of international intervention in Rwanda. A small UN peacekeeping force known as UNAMIR (United Nations Assistance Mission in Rwanda) was on the ground in Rwanda in December 1993 in order to support the Arusha Accords, which ended the civil war between the Hutu regime and Tutsi rebels and that laid out a framework for political reform. UNAMIR remained in Rwanda during the genocide. However, with only a little over two thousand soldiers, it was too small to respond effectively, nor did it have a mandate to do so.

Though the genocide began on April 6, 1994, the UN Security Council did not authorize a second peacekeeping force to protect Rwandan civilians and to ensure access to humanitarian aid until May 17. Even then, the United States delayed implementation of the decision while it sought guarantees that the operation would conform to the recently established Presidential Decision Directive 25 (PDD 25), regarding American support for peacekeeping forces.[56] The United States insisted that the mandate to use force not be expanded to stop the genocide and stalled the eventual troop deployment by seven weeks while it negotiated contracts for equipment.[57] Other governments also failed to act. Few nations wanted to contribute without American leadership or a forceful mandate from the Security Council.[58]

After weeks of inaction, on June 15, France offered to lead a multinational operation into Rwanda. Because of France's close ties to the Hutu regime, the Front Patriotique du Rwanda (FPR) opposed French intervention. Other members of the security council authorized the mission but questioned France's ability to be a neutral broker. The Security Council warned that "the strictly humanitarian character of this operation...shall be conducted in an impartial and neutral fashion, and shall not constitute an interposition force between the parties."[59] Nearly a month later, on July 9, France established a "humanitarian safe zone," which protected displaced persons but attracted criticism for also protecting known perpetrators of the genocide.

On July 18, the last Hutu stronghold fell to rebel Tutsi forces and the FPR swore in a new government the next day. Five days later, a new contingent of international troops arrived in Zaire to help the more than

2 million refugees fleeing to countries bordering Rwanda. Despite the UN resolution and, by now, extensive information regarding the extent of the genocide, only 550 of the 5,500 UN peacekeeping troops authorized, were actually on the ground before July 23. President Bill Clinton ultimately committed a total of 4,000 troops to aid humanitarian relief efforts but no troops for peacekeeping.[60]

Mass publics may not have been fully aware of the crisis in Rwanda, but foreign policy elites certainly were. Though there was little television coverage of Rwanda between the start of the genocide in April and late July when the international community intervened to cope with the ensuing refugee crisis, there was significant print media coverage throughout the genocide. The French newspapers *Libération* and *Le Monde* reported on April 11 and 12, respectively, on the atrocities and on the fact that victims were mostly Tutsi. The *New York Times* printed 145 articles on Rwanda between April 7 and May 31, and the *Washington Post* printed 77. Twenty-five and fourteen of those stories, respectively, were on the front page. The articles regularly contained estimates of the level of killing in Rwanda. To give just one example, the *New York Times* reported on May 14 that a recent rampage by Hutu extremists against Tutsi and moderate Hutu "adds weight to relief agencies' estimates that at least 200,000 have died in this country."[61]

NGOs warned the international community about events in Rwanda both before and during the genocide. Thirty-eight NGOs operated in Rwanda in 1993 and monitored the situation there.[62] The NGO Africa Watch claimed evidence of mass graves in two areas, Gisenyi and Ruhengeri, before the genocide. In 1993, the International Committee of the Red Cross expressed extreme concern about the plight of refugees in southern camps, a concern echoed by the World Health Organization, and indicated that the situation was worse only in Bosnia and Somalia.[63] In January 1993, an International Commission comprised of representatives from Human Rights Watch, the International Federation of Human Rights Leagues, the International Center for Human Rights and Democratic Development, and the InterAfrican Union of Human and Peoples' Rights led an inquiry to Rwanda and condemned the Habyarimana regime for massacres in Bugusera as well as for other human rights abuses. The commission report documented systemic killings directed against Tutsi and the commission used the term *genocide* to describe the killing of 2,000 Rwandans between 1990 and 1992. It also noted the increasing levels of hate propaganda on Rwandan radio.[64] Published on March 8, 1993, the report was widely distributed to donor nations such as the United States, Belgium, Canada, and France.

NGOs also sounded the alarm after the killing started. As early as April 11, the International Red Cross estimated that there were some 20,000 dead in four days of killing, about half of them in areas removed from any battle zone.[65] On April 19, Human Rights Watch reported that the number of dead had reached 100,000 and used the term *genocide*. On April 28, the British NGO Oxfam issued a press release indicating that it feared that there was a genocide going on in Rwanda.

International organizations, particularly the UN, had reason to suspect that a serious ethnic conflict would erupt even if they did not suspect genocide.[66] As Astri Suhrke and Bruce Jones conclude, "The striking fact of the Rwandan genocide is that it was devised, planned, publicly broadcast, and ultimately conducted in view of a UN peacekeeping force."[67] Before the genocide, the United Nations Commission on Human Rights documented massacres of Tutsi as early as 1990. Later, the UN was actively engaged in the transition and authorized UNAMIR on October 5, 1993. The first UNAMIR peacekeeping troops, led by Canadian general Roméo Dallaire, arrived in early November. In January 1994, General Dallaire informed his superiors at the UN and the ambassadors of the United States, France, and Belgium, that he had received details of preparations for systematically eliminating Tutsi from Rwanda. In February, UNAMIR officials protested the existence of training camps and the distribution of arms to civilians at a time when the government and the FPR were supposed to be demobilizing.[68] General Dallaire reported that groups of militia were ready to attack the capital and to kill up to 1,000 Tutsi in twenty minutes.[69] In early 1994, UNAMIR was aware of the fact that the Rwandan government continued to receive planeloads of weapons in violation of the Arusha Accords. Dallaire requested more troops and a stronger mandate six times.[70] In addition, his requests to confiscate stocks of arms and to protect his informant were refused. At the urging of NGOs, shortly before the genocide the UN's special rapporteur B. W. Ndiaye visited Rwanda and presented a report to the International Commission of Inquiry on Human Rights. The report described politically motivated attacks by militias and stated that Radio Rwanda instigated the massacres. The report also referred to articles of the Genocide Convention to describe activities in Rwanda.[71]

The political scientist Michael Barnett provides evidence that the UN Secretariat, the body of civil servants headed by the secretary general, and Secretary General Boutros Boutros-Ghali himself, had credible information that a genocide or at least ethnic cleansing was going on well before that information was brought to the Security Council's attention. Barnett speculates that the delay in sharing this information was politically motivated since it would have bolstered voices in favor of intervention and pressured the UN to intervene more assertively in Rwanda, despite the reluctance of some of the Security Council's most powerful members. Members of the UN Secretariat had organizational interests *not* to intervene in Rwanda since they feared that another failure could diminish the organization's power and effectiveness.[72]

National governments also had reasons to suspect trouble due to ample evidence from their own intelligence and diplomatic agencies. In 1991, French intelligence reported that a powerful inner circle was using ethnic hatred to resist democracy and to increase its power. In 1992, the Belgium ambassador reported to Brussels that secret groups planned to exterminate the Tutsi and to resolve the ethnic problem "once and for all."[73] In mid-March 1993, the Belgian minister of defense proposed strengthening the peacekeepers' mandate because Kigali was "awash with weapons." Belgian intelligence reported to Belgium and the UN about secret meetings to plan the massacres.[74]

Embassy staff in Rwanda must have suspected that ethnically motivated violence was a possibility.[75] According to Suhrke and Jones, the "UN Secretariat and the French, U.S. and Belgian diplomatic missions in Rwanda received clear warnings that the closer the Arusha Accords came to being implemented, the more the extremists were prepared to unleash a death campaign against supporters of the accords and the entire Tutsi community."[76] Members of the diplomatic community jointly told President Habyarimana on April 3, 1994, that hate radio broadcasts (by the notorious station Radio-Television Libre des Mille Collihes [RTLM] were undermining the peace accords.[77] Diplomats stationed in Rwanda certainly knew about human rights abuses and that militia groups were forming and training in several locations.[78] After the killing of hundreds of Tutsi in Bugesera on March 4-9, 1992, five human rights groups revealed that local officials determined to ruin "the new politics," had organized massacres in northern Rwanda. The human rights groups linked the officials to broadcasts on Radio Rwanda that urged the killing of prominent Hutu and encouraged people to "clear the bush" and "clear their hill of Tutsi."[79] In addition to the RTLM broadcasts, the anti-Tutsi political party known as the Coalition pour la Défense de la République (CDR), issued a press release in November 1993 that called on the "majority population" to be "ready to neutralize by all means its enemies and their accomplices." The bishop of Nyundo in northwestern Rwanda issued a press release in December 1993, asking for an explanation of why firearms were being distributed to civilians.

Though many American policymakers claimed that genocide in Rwanda was unthinkable or defied imagination, analysts in the U.S. government predicted extensive ethnic violence. A CIA analysis in January 1994 completed a worst-case projection of violence leading to half a million casualties.[80] Moreover, declassified government documents reveal that American officials anticipated as early as April 11, 1994, and probably earlier, that "a massive bloodbath (hundreds of thousands of deaths) will ensue."[81] Declassified American documents also indicate that the federal government was well aware of the fact that the army was "pursuing a policy of genocide to destroy the leadership of the Tutsi community."[82] On April 28, State Department spokesperson Christine Shelly announced that 100,000 civilians had been killed. A May 18, 1994 memo indicated that between "200,000 and 500,000 are dead."[83] However, Secretary of State Warren Christopher did not authorize officials to use the term *genocide* until May 21 and, even then, American officials waited three more weeks before using the term in public for fear of incurring obligations to act under the 1948 Genocide Convention.

The history of the region also makes it hard to believe that officials in the United States and elsewhere could not imagine that a genocide was taking place in Rwanda. Earlier massacres took 20,000 lives in Rwanda in 1963, 100,000-300,000 in Burundi in 1972, 25,000 in just one day of clashes in Burundi in 1988, and another 50,000-100,000 in Burundi in 1993–1994.[84] In the 1972 crisis, the U.S. State Department estimated that Tutsi had tried to kill every Hutu male over the age of 14.[85] In the 1993 crisis in Burundi, 150,000 Tutsi fled to army-controlled towns and another 300,000 Hutu fled across borders, mostly to Rwanda.

American officials knew who was leading the genocide and told Rwandan leaders privately that the killings were unacceptable.[86] However, public statements condemning the killing were limited and the United States lobbied for a reduction in UNAMIR's troop strength to 270 men. National Security Adviser Anthony Lake's statement asking Rwandan military leaders to "do everything in their power to end the violence immediately," was the sole public rebuke of the Rwandan regime during the genocide. When alerted to that fact by an interviewer, Lake remarked, "That is truly pathetic."[87]

Knowledge Amid Confusion

Though we now have evidence that officials in both governments and international organizations were aware of the genocide earlier than they originally admitted, there *was* some confusion about what was actually happening on the ground. Confusion came from several sources. The foreign media wrongly interpreted the violence as part of a civil war. The Rwandan government, which maintained a seat on the Security Council throughout the crisis, attempted to mischaracterize the genocide. And, the sheer volume of information available before and at the beginning of the crisis led analysts to draw faulty conclusions.

One of the primary reasons for the lack of wider public knowledge about the genocide was not a lack of information per se, but inaccurately interpreted information.[88] Though reports of killings in Rwanda circulated widely in the media only hours after the genocide began, even journalists from the most respected newspapers reported that the killings were not well-organized murders intended to exterminate an ethnic group, but a continuation of a civil war and an instance of tribal warfare between ethnic groups motivated by "ancient hatreds." As indicated earlier, journalists did submit reports throughout the crisis, but they were slow to recognize the big story, namely that a genocide raged in Rwanda. Media coverage, especially television coverage, did ultimately help to convince the world that something must be done, but substantial broadcast coverage only appeared once the killing was over and the story had turned into a refugee crisis.[89] Even after the media arrived, many journalists portrayed the mainly Hutu refugees in the camps as victims even though many participated in the killing.[90]

Some information coming out of Rwanda was misleading or just plain wrong. Although the *New York Times* estimated 8,000 to tens of thousands of deaths three days into the killing, estimates by the *Times* or by any other major newspaper did not rise until Human Rights Watch reported on April 20 that as many as 100,000 people died and the Red Cross estimated perhaps hundreds of thousands. In addition, most reporting in April focused on the capital and did not focus on violence in the rest of the country.[91]

Officials in the U.S. government and in the UN also mischaracterized the conflict in ways that mitigated against intervention. As Barnett summarizes, officials interpreted the violence in Rwanda as a return to civil war.

> The accepted script was [that] the UNAMIR was to oversee a cease-fire and resolve a civil war between contending ethnic groups....The [Security] Council was well aware of the obscenely high civilian death toll and the gruesome conditions on the ground. But because they predicted that sustained violence would be connected to a civil war, that is what they saw.[92]

According to Barnett, the notion that violence in Rwanda was a civil war supported the perceived need for only a small peacekeeping force since that would be all that was necessary to negotiate a cease-fire.

Hutu extremists made accurate interpretation of the genocide more difficult by actively trying to hide the genocide from the international community. At sites where Red Cross aid workers or UN troops stood guard, the pace of killing was much slower.[93] At the Hotel des Mille Collines, for example, ten peacekeepers and four UN military observers protected several hundred civilians for the duration of the crisis.[94]

Adding to the confusion was the sheer volume of information coming out of Rwanda. According to Alan J. Kuperman, during the first week of the genocide, officials in Washington received as many as a thousand separate intelligence reports on Rwanda per day. One way to cope with such information overload is simply to disregard the most extreme or unsubstantiated accounts. This led executive branch officials to disregard Defense Intelligence Agency (DIA) accounts, which ultimately were the most accurate.[95]

Transparency and Intervention

There were many reasons for American reluctance to intervene but ignorance that ethnically motivated killing was going on, was not among them. American officials decided to stay out of Rwanda as a matter of policy. American reluctance had broad implications since other governments waited for American leadership on the issue. In this climate NGOs called attention to the genocide in vain while the general population did not feel compelled to press for action until they saw dramatic footage of the refugee crisis on television. Print media coverage did little to encourage public cries for intervention.

Why did the U.S. government fail to intervene earlier in the crisis? In short, the U.S. government lacked the political will to intervene because leaders believed that national interests were not at stake or because they believed that members of Congress held that belief and therefore would not support intervention. The United States had no strategic interests or significant investments in Rwanda in 1994. For similar reasons, the United States stood by when 40,000 people were killed in Burundi in 1993, and African experts in the American government expected the violence in Rwanda to similarly flare up and then die out without any wider repercussions. American policy makers also feared a "repeat of Somalia," the 1993 peacekeeping operation that ended with the death of eighteen American soldiers and the televised dragging of an American corpse through the streets of Mogadishu, and the withdrawal of all forces within six months.[96] After the incident, policy makers decided that the United States should avoid risky and distant peacekeeping operations, especially in Africa. The murder of ten Belgian peacekeepers in Rwanda early in the crisis only confirmed the sense that this was Somalia all over again and could end with similarly devastating results. For this reason, administration officials believed that the

Republican majority in Congress would never allow the United States to intervene in Rwanda militarily even if the White House wanted to do so. Senator Robert Dole reflected the sentiments of many other members of Congress when he remarked on the television show *Face the Nation* in April 1994, "I don't think we have any national interest here....I hope we don't get involved there. I don't think we will. The Americans are out. As far as I'm concerned in Rwanda, that ought to be the end of it."[97] Finally, the Clinton administration was distracted by events in Bosnia and Haiti where it thought more pressing national interests were at stake. Consequently, Rwanda simply did not get the attention it would have if it were the only conflict ongoing at the time.

Transparency and Accountability in Rwanda

Even if greater transparency did not speed up efforts by the international community to end the genocide, information made available through greater transparency held decision makers on all sides accountable for that decision—if accountability means having to answer for actions rather than for any sort of formal sanction. The United States was quickly called to task by nongovernmental organizations, the media, and scholars. Freedom of Information Act (FOIA) requests provided documentary evidence of the American decision-making process and led to an exposé in a major American magazine.[98] Scholars published and continue to publish, critical accounts of the decision not to intervene in Rwanda. Former government officials have publicly second-guessed their decisions about Rwanda. President Clinton visited Rwanda in 1998 and publicly criticized the response of the international community and his own government for failing to intervene earlier. In so doing, the president's speech contradicted accounts of American decision making at the time, which had since been proved false by groups outside of government.

The French government also came under heavy criticism for its role in the genocide.[99] The French newspapers *Le Monde* and *Le Figaro* charged that the French government foresaw the genocide in Rwanda and did almost nothing to stop it.[100] Others charged that French arms traders violated the arms embargo and supplied weapons to the Rwandan government even while the military was conducting the genocide.[101] A panel assembled by the Organization of African Unity singled out France as a country that not only could have stopped the genocide, but could have prevented it as well. Ambassador Stephen Lewis, a Canadian member of that commission, stated that

> We repudiate the position of the government of France, the position that asserts they had no responsibility. They were closer in every way to the

Habyarimana regime than any other government. They could have stopped the genocide before it began. They knew exactly what was happening.... There is almost no redemptive feature to the conduct of the government of France.[102]

Ambassador Lewis also claimed that the French peacekeeping mission allowed a huge number of Hutu war criminals to flee the country.

An unprecedented parliamentary commission in December 1998 exonerated the French government from blame in the 1994 Rwandan genocide, but criticized the government for failing to anticipate the killings and for responding inadequately.[103] There were some limited political consequences. Though France has continued to intervene militarily in Africa, most notably in Côte d'Ivoire, the French government decided to reduce its engagement in francophone Africa, recognizing that it could no longer afford such frequent intervention. France closed two military bases in the Central African Republic, reduced its standing force in Africa from 8,500 to 6,300, and cut its financial aid to African militaries from 803 million francs in 1997 to 780 million francs in 1998.[104]

International organizations, scholars, and NGO analysts criticized the UN for its failure to act more decisively in Rwanda. Even an independent inquiry commissioned by the UN itself, condemned the UN Secretariat, the Secretary General, responsible officials within the UN Department of Peacekeeping Operations, the UN Security Council, and member governments of the UN for failing to prevent and end the genocide. Secretary General Kofi Annan, after reviewing the report issued by the independent commission, stated that "On behalf of the United Nations, I acknowledge this failure and express my deep remorse."[105] The international panel assembled by the Organization of African Unity identified the United States, France, Belgium, the UN, and the Roman Catholic and Anglican churches as those most guilty of not doing enough to stop the genocide and asked that those governments and organizations pay reparations to help rebuild Rwanda—a request that was unsuccessful.

This outcome clearly shows that transparency empowered the media, NGOs, scholars, and others to criticize and hold individuals, organizations, and governments accountable for their actions. Increasingly, leaders and their organizations must answer to the public, the media, or to highly knowledgeable NGOs, a possibility that can have a powerful influence on leaders' behavior, particularly in democracies where leaders need political support in order to maintain positions of power. Whether transparency and criticism alone—as opposed to the loss of jobs or political office, or payment of reparations—are sufficient to encourage better policy is a separate and more complicated matter.

Conclusion

Despite hopes to the contrary, greater transparency will not necessarily lead to earlier or more frequent intervention to prevent or to end deadly conflicts. More often than not, it has little effect on the political will of governments and, in the absence of a UN rapid reaction force that can be sent to stabilize crises, governments are the only viable source of troops for peacekeeping operations. When powerful governments lack the political will to intervene, there is no one to step in and end even a genocide of shocking proportions. Greater transparency may alert NGOs and publics to conflicts, but they will not always press governments to act.

In Rwanda, information about the genocide was imperfect but ignorance of the situation does not sufficiently explain the failure to intervene. Governments chose not to intervene and the availability of information regarding the genocide did little to change those decisions. NGOs repeatedly sounded the alarm but governments and international organizations did not answer. Citizens were able to access significant coverage of the crisis in the print media but did not call for their governments to intervene until they saw televised images of the refugee crisis well after the height of the genocide. In short, transparency did not unleash forces to stop the killing.

Though governments have intervened more actively in the Darfur crisis in Sudan—where 300,000 people have been killed and approximately 2,000,000 have been displaced by the government-backed Arab Janjaweed militia—transparency has not motivated any large-scale intervention by foreign governments despite being called a genocide by Secretary of State Colin Powell in September 2004.[106] There have been some tangible steps by the international community. For instance, the UN Security Council passed an historic resolution calling for war criminals to be referred to the International Criminal Court, instituted and extended an arms embargo, and established a mission in Sudan. The African Union has played a useful peacekeeping role and governments such as the United States have carefully monitored and condemned the humanitarian crisis. However, powerful international actors have been slow to make more aggressive efforts to end the crisis and the UN resolutions had not begun to be implemented four months after being passed. That is not to say that transparency has played no role in this case. Governments have been quicker to recognize the severity of the crisis than they were in Rwanda, thanks in part to media coverage, publicized reports by NGOs like Amnesty International, international organizations like the UN and the African Union, and actions by foreign governments. The United States, for example, publicly used high-resolution satellite images to refute the Sudanese government's positions and to demonstrate the extent of destruction and displacement.[107] These actions have all helped to generate interest by politicians and undoubtedly contribute to the high public support for a strong American role in Darfur, short of deploying troops.[108] Nonetheless, in Darfur as in Rwanda, there is clearly no direct link between transparency and conflict intervention or resolution.

In the future, the effects of transparency on conflict intervention will continue to vary. Though greater transparency sometimes will create sufficient political pressure to force governments to respond, the trend toward greater transparency sometimes may constrain governments from acting even when leaders feel that intervention is justified. In other words, in addition to a CNN effect, we may also see a "reverse CNN effect." If publics are informed but feel that the price of intervention outweighs the benefits, they may tell their leaders to stay out of foreign disputes. An essay about the 2003 Iraq War articulated this viewpoint, arguing that "Americans' attitude toward war in general and this war in particular would change drastically if the censor's veil were lifted and the public got a sustained, close look at the agonizing bloodshed and other horrors that continue unabated in Iraq. If that happened, support for any war that wasn't an absolute necessity would plummet."[109]

Greater transparency also affects the dynamics of conflicts themselves depending on what it shows about the likelihood of possible intervention and how the parties react. After all, it is not just potential intervenors, NGOs, and publics that have access to more information; participants in conflicts have unprecedented access to information as well and react in ways that advance their own objectives. Sometimes the prospect of intervention means that killers will be deterred from further action. Sometimes they will just kill all the faster. We should not assume that fighters will always respond to information about impending intervention in a particular way.

What transparency does most effectively is help the international community to hold governments, international organizations, and individuals accountable for their involvement (or lack thereof) in conflicts. Though there are indeed limits to the actual sanctions that guilty individuals will face—and especially individuals guilty of inaction rather than those guilty of war crimes—leaders can at least be sanctioned in the court of public opinion. Holding people accountable for actions falls short of what many optimists would hope for in a world of greater transparency. However, unless governments muster the political will to intervene in foreign conflicts more frequently or to create new mechanisms to do so, this may be the most positive role transparency can play. Greater transparency alone will not lead the international community to prevent or to end wars.

Chapter 5

Transparency and Governance

"Authoritarian regimes that had successfully controlled their own communications networks have grown powerless to stop the flow of information through satellite dishes and faxes."
—John Hopkins University professor Lester M. Salamon[1]

"The world sees you."
—Chant at riot police during 1989 Velvet Revolution in Czechoslovakia[2]

Greater transparency is a boon for democracy and good governance, according to most observers. The trend toward greater transparency diffuses control over information and, in so doing, takes power from the strong and gives it to the weak and disenfranchised. This reallocation of power occurs within states, allowing citizens to challenge or even topple authoritarian regimes.[3] Greater transparency also strengthens transnational civil society and increases the influence of nongovernmental organizations (NGOs) vis-à-vis national governments. Transparency empowers the weak by giving them access to politically sensitive information, which can be wielded to encourage political change. Tactics include exposure ("Look at this!"), the threat of exposure ("I'm going to tell unless..."), and shame ("You're going to be embarrassed when everyone sees this"). These "shame-throwers" operate either domestically or internationally and may or may not have their own bases of political power, for instance, the ability to mobilize voters. When they do not have this power, the ability to share important information with citizens, legislatures, law enforcement agencies, foreign governments, or international organizations can be sufficient to provoke change.

The conventional wisdom is that this decentralization of power is inevitable.[4] Governments that try to control information are fighting a losing battle and, if they bother trying, will face exorbitant costs.[5] Some analysts argue that the price of opacity is so high that "radical transparency" will emerge, making abuses of power almost impossible to hide. "No contentious action would go unnoticed and unpublicized," writes Allen Hammond. "The Internet has already begun to make censorship virtually impossible, as governments around the world are discovering."[6] Innovations in information and communication technologies facilitate the decentralization of global power and, once invented, such innovations can be difficult to control.[7] As MIT professor Nicholas Negroponte pithily remarked, "If someone tells you that you can [control cyberspace], they are probably smoking pot."[8]

Most observers also see the decentralization of international power as desirable, a boost for the "good guys" in international politics and a force for freedom and justice.[9] Transparency, the argument goes, is fundamentally linked with democratization and good governance.[10] It gives citizens and civil society organizations the ability to monitor the powerful and to expose corruption and abuse.[11] It helps people to hold their leaders accountable. It gives them political power and new tools with which to fight oppression. It increases the reach and potential impact of even small organizations. The big losers, according to this view, are sovereign states, which have become "little more than bit actors" and an "artifact of the 18th and 19th centuries."[12]

These predictions range from deficient to wrong. Much to the chagrin of democrats, transparency is not inevitable nor will it reliably lead to democratic change. Skillful states can control the flow of information in their societies and, at least sometimes, they do so with the support of their citizens. Though the trend toward greater transparency does decentralize power, we should not assume that all NGOs have admirable intentions or that popular revolutions will always install democratic governments that respect human rights.[13] We should not assume that sovereign states will become weaker or that weaker states are always desirable. Sometimes more decentralized power will lead to more responsive, representative government or more just policies, but that will not always be the case.

Though opacity has a price, governments can control information and still be well integrated into the international community and into the global economy. It is impossible to be completely closed and still maintain extensive international links, yet there is a large range of options between the relative openness of the United States and fortress-like North Korea. Where a given state lies on that continuum is a matter of political choice at least to some extent. True transparency is more than a "resigned surrender to the technologically facilitated intrusiveness of the information age. It is a choice, a potential standard for the way powerful institutions ought to behave."[14]

This chapter argues that greater transparency is not inevitable, inevitably good, or a unambiguous force for democracy and good governance. It examines the case of Singapore, which illustrates how a government can control information successfully by using "soft" methods and by weakening the link between information flows and political change. The difficulties for other governments to replicate Singapore's example successfully should not be understated. Singapore's government is neither incompetent nor corrupt, two all-too-common pitfalls of secretive governments. Nonetheless, Singapore's open but illiberal society offers a cautionary tale for those who equate openness with democracy and for those who hope to see the power of sovereign states decline in an age of transparency.

The Decentralizing Power of Transparency

Transparency decentralizes power by breaking monopolies over information. [15] When information flows freely,

> Hierarchies of all sorts, whether political or corporate, come under pressure and begin to crumble. . . . Large, rigid bureaucracies, which sought to control everything in their domain through rules, regulations, and coercion, have been undermined by the shift to a knowledge-based economy, which serves to "empower" individuals by giving them access to information. Just as rigid corporate bureaucracies like the old IBM and AT&T gave way to smaller, flatter, more participatory competitors, so too did the Soviet Union and East Germany fall apart from their inability to control and harness the knowledge of their own citizens.[16]

Politicians across the political spectrum agree that the free flow of information, so necessary for economic success, can revolutionize political control. President Ronald Reagan declared in 1989 that "the Goliath of totalitarian control will rapidly be brought down by the David of the microchip."[17] Regarding China's attempt to control the Internet, President Bill Clinton declared: "Good luck! That's sort of like trying to nail Jello to the wall. . . . In the knowledge economy, economic innovation and political empowerment, whether anyone likes it or not, will inevitably go hand in hand."[18] President George W. Bush proclaimed that "When the Internet takes hold in China, freedom's genie is out of the bottle."[19]

When citizens can evade government controls, they can collect and disseminate information in ways that give them political power.[20] Domestically, shame-throwers can become powerful enough to bring down authoritarian governments, particularly if they can expose large gaps between government rhetoric and reality."[21] As the scholar Ithiel de Sola Pool observes of totalitarian systems, "the state is inherently fragile and will quickly collapse if information flows freely."[22] The 1989 revolutions in Eastern Europe are the classic example of this phenomenon. When populations realized that their governments' performance was much poorer than previously imagined and that their quality of life was substantially lower than comparable societies, they used that information to mobilize political support for change.[23]

Greater transparency not only makes citizens aware of the freedoms they lack, but it also allows them to see that their dislike for the current regime is shared by a broad spectrum of society. This information, in turn, further legitimizes dissenters' views and may encourage citizens to demand change from, or even overthrow, their regime.[24] As Charles Lipson observes,

> Secrecy and the suppression of public discourse help nondemocratic regimes maintain their political power because they block groups (inside the government and outside) from discovering their common grievances and organizing around them. Secrecy divides and isolates. It keeps information fragmented and opens a chasm between private preferences and their public expression.[25]

Similarly, if publics see that popular protests bring political change in neighboring countries, transparency may create a contagion effect in which methods employed in one country are copied in another. The Rose and Orange revolutions in Georgia (2003) and in Ukraine (2004) are examples of this dynamic—and those revolutions were quickly copied in Kyrgyzstan.

Information and communication technologies increase transparency and, in so doing, facilitate political mobilization beyond the reach of governments. In the spring of 2005, Lebanese citizens used mobile phone text messages to organize grassroots anti-Syrian protests, some of which drew one million demonstrators.[26] Video equipment donated by the NGO Global Witness allows human rights groups to document abuses and prevents governments from denying such abuses. According to its cofounder, Peter Gabriel, "a camera in the right hands at the right time can be more powerful than tanks or guns. Let truth do the fighting."[27]

The Internet, with its core technical property of distributed connectivity can be particularly well suited to evading government controls.[28] The experience of Serbian activists in 1996 seemed to validate this perspective. After Slobodan Milosevic nullified local elections that put democratic reformers into power, an independent radio station called Radio B92 broadcast information about the resulting protests and mobilized support for the newly elected government. Milosevic quickly shut down the radio station, but B92 rerouted programming to the Internet, making the station's broadcasts—and information about the plight of one small town in one small country—available worldwide. Listeners around the world flooded email boxes with news of the shutdown and sparked protests around the world. Two days later, Milosevic succumbed to international pressure and let the station back on the air.[29]

Even relatively unsophisticated information technologies can help to mobilize political resistance. Cassette tapes helped to spread the Ayatollah Khomeini's message through bazaars and religious meetings and gave Iranians a sense of how many others shared their political views. Greater transparency first eroded the legitimacy of the government and then empowered those who sought revolution by allowing them to recognize widespread support for their agenda in Iranian society. Of course, this example also shows how greater transparency can facilitate types of popular revolutions other than democratic revolutions.[30]

The trend toward greater transparency empowers not only activists within states but also transnational NGOs that employ "information politics, the ability to quickly and credibly generate politically usable information and move it to where it will have the most impact...and accountability politics, or the effort to hold powerful actors to their previously stated policies or principles."[31] NGOs often wield shame as their weapon of choice.[32] Transparency gives NGOs both access to shameful information and an audience with which to share it.[33] The power of shame varies depending on the issue, the target, and the identity of the shame-thrower.[34] But in all cases, the power of transnational NGOs comes from being known as an independent provider of credible information that either will embarrass governments into changing their behavior, or lead other governments to press for change.[35] To give just one example, the NGO Transparency International's efforts have led to indigenous anticorruption campaigns in eighty countries and an international treaty against corruption signed by thirty-five countries.[36] Most importantly, Transparency International is credited with changing attitudes about what types of behavior are tolerable.

As they attempt to promote change, NGOs use a variety of tactics. They can use information to pressure governments directly; give domestic groups access to information that will encourage them to pressure their own governments; or share information with governments, NGOs, or citizens worldwide that will exert pressure for change. Domestic activists can challenge their government directly or use so-called boomerang strategies to encourage foreign governments or NGOs to pressure the government for change.[37] Examples of boomerang strategies can be seen in China where international NGOs like Human Rights Watch, Human Rights in China, and the Committee to Protect Journalists work with Chinese citizens to collect information regarding human rights abuses. These non-Chinese groups then use that information to pressure both the Chinese government and foreign governments that could pressure the Chinese government in turn. They also post information on the Internet where it can be accessed by dissidents and political activists based in China.[38]

The Complexity of Transparency and Power

Though greater transparency decentralizes power and gives the weak new sources of power over the strong, citizens and transnational NGOs confront significant limits to their influence. Greater transparency often strengthens the strong as well as the weak and even may give the strong new sources of power. Though transparency may indeed help "good guys," as just discussed, it may also strengthen terrorists, nondemocratic popular movements, and oppressive governments. Greater transparency will not automatically promote democracy or good governance.

Regrettably, greater transparency may even strengthen illiberal regimes if it shows that they are competent and not corrupt.[47] This is particularly true in semi-authoritarian regimes in which the government and other major organizations are relatively transparent, the economy is fairly open, and the government is perceived as legitimate.[48] Greater transparency helps governments that are legitimate and politically powerful, to spread their message to their own people, to other states, and to the global community whether they are democratic or not.[49]

Although it is harder and harder for governments to control the flow of information and keep secrets, governments *can* control information at least for a while. Governments have proven to be resourceful at managing information flows and—more significantly—controlling the environment in which information is exchanged. Controlling information may be costly, difficult, and sometimes unsuccessful but it is possible nonetheless. Even cyberspace is not outside the control of governments. "The Internet is wildly misunderstood," observes Cambridge Internet analyst Rafal Rohozinki, "It is built around very specific chokepoints" that can be controlled.[50]

Sometimes government controls over information find popular support. This fact may disturb civil libertarians, but citizens may deem controls on the Internet and other sources of information as legitimate, particularly when those controls can be justified by some internal or external threat, and willingly accept restrictions on their rights. Citizens also may accept government controls if they protect widely held values in the society or if they are part of a political bargain in which citizens acquiesce to political repression in return for stability and economic rewards.[51] Sustaining the legitimacy of government control is a major challenge since it is effective only as long as the threat remains credible.[52] Nonetheless, oppressive governments could sustain their legitimacy for a very long time under certain circumstances.

Economic dynamism and a competitive market economy seem to make a population more willing to accept government controls over information. That assertion may seem to be counterintuitive since the conventional wisdom is that economic and political openness are entwined. However, if the personal well-being of citizens is improving and if the government runs efficiently, citizens may be politically apathetic, more trusting of the government, and uninterested in political change.[53] The combination of economic prosperity and good governance is more likely in a democracy, but highly centralized, nonrepresentative governments can also be successful at fostering economic development.[54] China, for instance, has emerged as a country that so far is successfully balancing economic modernization, controls over information, and nonrepresentative government.

Governments have at their disposal many potentially effective mechanisms with which to control information. One of the most frequently discussed ways in which modern governments restrict information is censoring, monitoring, filtering, or restricting access to the Internet or to certain Internet sites. Although the Internet was initially heralded as being outside the reach of sovereign states, governments can control the Internet because the network is comprised of data inside computers that are located within the physical territory of sovereign states and, hence, are subject to local laws.[55] States also can centralize the hardware of the Internet. For instance, all Chinese Internet Service Providers (known as ISPs) must go through the Ministry of Posts and Telecommunications.[56] The knowledge that governments monitor Internet traffic stifles discussion even when offenders are not punished. The mere idea that one is being monitored can encourage self-censorship by users. Saudi Internet users who try to access forbidden websites receive a message that all attempts to access such websites are logged. Though there is no evidence that anyone has been punished for trying to access sites that are off-limits, such messages are sure to chill Saudi enthusiasm for finding alternate viewpoints on the web.[57]

Some of the same technologies that enhance transparency also give governments more power to monitor, influence, and control activities within their borders. Especially in large and geographically dispersed countries like China and Russia, information technologies create more transparency at the regional level and allow the central government to exercise more control. China's investment in telecommunication infra-structure gives citizens in distant provinces more access to information, but also ties those regions closer to the center. Access to satellite imagery, likewise, decentralizes control over information but also empowers national governments. In 1997, for instance, the Chinese gov-ernment learned that it had 20 to 25% more land under cultivation than it realized. Thanks to Beijing's access to high-resolution satellite imagery, the government is now able to more easily identify provincial tax dodgers who understate their property holdings.[58]

New trends in technology are giving governments even more power. One example is "geolocation" technology, which can pinpoint a web surfer's country of origin 70 to 90% of the time. Countries can use this technology to help them enforce laws in cyberspace. In November 2000, a French judge ordered the Internet company, Yahoo! to prohibit French Internet users from buying Nazi memorabilia from any of its sites, even those located outside of France.[59]

Governments use legal means to control information such as laws that effectively criminalize dissent or so called "slander" of the govern-ment. Just a few well-publicized arrests or crackdowns can discourage thousands of potential "violations" by citizens who stay quiet in order to avoid the risk of punishment.[60] Furthermore, punishing the conduits of information such as Internet service providers—the equivalent of charging a phone company for conversations that take place over its lines—is often effective and constitutes a serious impediment to free expression. Other effective measures for stifling transparency include restrictions on the media (one of the most effective ways of releasing more information about government actions to the mass public); limiting civil society; and erecting barriers to opposition parties, which have a strong incentive to bring government missteps to the public's attention.

Governments also use more subtle (and often more effective) "soft" measures to control information. Creating a culture of surveil-lance leads people to censor themselves. When journalists, civil society leaders, and opposition party members modify their views for public presentation, the culture of self-censorship reinforces itself further and the availability of certain types of information declines.

With respect to the power of NGOs, states still retain considerable power and are likely to remain powerful for the foreseeable future. They retain a monopoly on the legitimate use of force as well as on the ability to tax their citizens. They control physical territory and can limit the ability of NGOs to operate within their borders. They have infrastructures through which to process information and organize action. They can summon the power of patriotism or nationalism. States also have an advantage in the marketplace of ideas. Unlike non-state groups that must clamor for attention from the media and from an information-saturated public, governments generally are better positioned to attract listeners when they talk.

States also tend to have more resources, which helps them to capitalize on greater transparency. Greater transparency makes access to information easier and cheaper than ever, but it also bombards organizations with information. Making the best use of that information often requires significant resources and wealthy governments have the resources to collect, analyze, and disseminate information—to a degree that few corporations, NGOs, or individuals can replicate.[39] Customized software, elaborate databases, expensive computing equipment, attention-grabbing graphics, and huge staffs, are luxuries that many NGOs, not to mention many governments, simply cannot afford.

Compared with states, NGOs have a limited arsenal. For most NGOs, power depends on the ability to shame, cajole, and organize political resistance. But these tactics have limits. Though resources vary widely among states, only the most powerful NGOs have the resources to rival even the weakest of states and then often require the support or at least tacit cooperation of states. To have real power, organizations must be able to translate information into political change. That is a tough challenge for organizations that usually have no formal role in governments' decision making. NGOs can try to frame debates about government policy, pressure governments to change their behavior, or mobilize those who do have influence over the government, but ultimately most NGOs rely on governments or on intergovernmental organizations to implement change. That does not mean that NGOs cannot wield significant power at times, but it does mean that they are far from being able to usurp substantial power from sovereign states.[40]

Because NGOs typically have less power than national governments, they often are most effective when they ally with governments. The story of the International Campaign to Ban Landmines (ICBL), an oft-told tale of the rising power of NGOs, is an interesting example. Though usually told as an uplifting tale about the power of the seemingly powerless, the ICBL is also a story about the limits of NGO power. Literally hundreds of NGOs lobbied governments, staged public awareness campaigns, and bombarded the media with horror stories about land mines. However, in the end, they depended on the willingness of governments to develop an effective ban. A conference in 1995 stalled because governments disagreed about the legitimacy of using land mines as a weapon and whether the use of "smart" mines was an acceptable compromise. Only when Lloyd Axworthy, the Canadian foreign minister, decided to champion the cause, did the ban become a realistic possibility and, in 1997, led to the signing of the Convention on the Prohibition of the Use, Stockpiling, Production and Transfer of Anti-Personnel Mines and on Their Destruction. Though some 147 countries have signed the treaty, some key countries such as the United States, Russia, China, and Israel did not. The convention's effectiveness will depend on the willingness of states to live up to their obligations.[41] Transparency can help NGOs hold governments accountable to their publics if they do not uphold the treaty, but that will be effective only if publics care. Ultimately, the success of the convention depends on national governments, no matter how much NGOs lobby, argue, wheedle, and shame.

Though many NGOs promote noble causes, there are reasons to be grateful that the power of NGOs does not rival sovereign states. First, while governments may be accountable to civil society in many countries, NGOs are frequently accountable to no one. Though many NGOs themselves are transparent and accountable to their members and to the global public, many are not and there is no watchdog or international organization to force them to be transparent and accountable. Unlike the politicians who serve the citizens of democracies, employees of NGOs were not elected to serve the common good. They may claim to represent a large number of supporters, but they are vested with no real authority to do so.

Second, while civil society organizations can contribute significantly to good governance, they do not always play that role. Civil society, both international and domestic, can weaken governments and overwhelm them with an impossible agenda of demands.[42] A world of strong NGOs and weak states, consequently, could create what Jessica Mathews calls "excessive pluralism."[43] Transparency may only showcase this cacophony of voices and lead to paralysis of decision making by governments and by NGOs. It may lead to "more conflict and less problem-solving."[44] NGOs also tend to represent either a single issue or a narrow range of issues and do not provide comprehensive leadership.

Third, though greater transparency helps good people promote good causes, not all NGOs are noble. To the extent that transparency does decentralize power, it aids good and bad causes indiscriminately. Open societies give publics information about nuclear power plants, which helps citizens monitor potential abuses and public health risks but also aids terrorists whose only goal is to harm. Open societies also give terrorists publicity. Terrorism, as Susan Carruthers observes, is "armed propaganda" that seeks to influence an audience far beyond the immediate victims of violence.[45] Terrorists seek to change behavior by spreading fear and greater transparency helps them to do that.[46] The media instantly shines a spotlight on terrorist activities while Internet chat rooms and radio talk shows allow citizens to voice their fears about terrorists to a mass audience. Finally, the same technologies that help citizens organize to promote democracy and good causes also help terrorists. Al-Qaeda uses mobile communication and Internet technologies to recruit supporters, disseminate its message, and organize attacks.

A Case Study of Singapore

The example of Singapore demonstrates the continuing ability of states to control information and shows that increasing transparency and democratization need not necessarily go hand in hand. As long as there is little gap between government rhetoric and reality, there may be few pressures for political reform. As long as there are obstacles to organizing political opposition, transparency need not promote political pluralism. As long as companies and investors feel informed about the economic environment, benefit from a clear and effective legal system, and enjoy a climate of political stability, they have no incentive to press for greater political openness. In short, if states can manage the task of being economically open, politically stable, and administratively efficient, the price of controlling information may be relatively low. Monitoring this mixture of political and economic openness may be difficult since the risks of abuse and mismanagement in a politically closed system are high. Politically closed systems may tempt elites to hijack the economy for their own interests rather than maintain a competitive open economy.

Singapore is a fascinating model of a relatively open but illiberal society. Citizens have almost unlimited access to alternative viewpoints and information from outside the city-state. On a per capita basis, access to information technologies is among the highest in the world.

Citizens can express opposing viewpoints and many of those views are aired in the media. In some areas, the government is both transparent and responsive.

Nonetheless, the link between openness and the potential for political change in Singapore is quite weak. There are significant constraints on the ability to use information in order to apply political pressure or to organize opposition to government policies. Cultural, political, and technical conditions encourage citizens to censor themselves. And, most importantly, the government argues that controls are necessary in order to protect the stability, security, and prosperity of Singapore. So far, most Singaporeans seem to agree.

As noted in chapter 3, transparency within a society can be measured along three dimensions: debate, control, and disclosure. Debate refers to the level of societal competition over ideas and the incentives faced by the government and by other actors to disclose information about government decision making and actions. Control refers to the degree to which a government can control the flow of information in a society and the potential for groups to disseminate information that is contrary to the official government position. Disclosure refers to the degree to which the government actively and intentionally releases information to the public.[61]

By these measures, Singapore is not a particularly transparent society—but it is also not as authoritarian as some caricatures suggest. Singapore has one of world's most competitive economies and is well integrated into the international economy. Sixty-five percent of Singaporean homes have Internet access and 99 percent of Singapore's homes, offices, and schools can connect to the Singapore ONE broadband network. Ninety-one percent of the population subscribes to mobile services.[62] The country is a major hub for media companies in the Asia Pacific region, with more than 30 companies maintaining headquarters or bureaus there including Reuters, the *Economist*, the *International Herald Tribune*, and *Asahi Shimbun*.[63] According to Singapore's Ministry of Information and the Arts, there are approximately 5,500 newspapers and magazines circulating in Singapore.[64] Singapore has open borders and citizens travel freely. A high percentage of Singapore's population, nearly one in five people, is comprised of foreigners.[65] To protect its interests, Singapore is active in international organizations like the United Nations that encourage the disclosure of various types of information. Indeed, a recent report by AT Kearney and *Foreign Policy* magazine named Singapore the most globalized society on earth.[66]

Despite being firmly embedded in a global system characterized by rising transparency and decentralization, Singapore's government is far from transparent and there are significant controls on the ability of citizens to wield information to mobilize political power. The government controls information in a variety of ways. First, there is no viable opposition to the dominant People's Action Party (PAP).[67] The lack of a competitive party system inhibits the release of more information into the public domain, since competing parties have an incentive to illuminate rivals' mistakes and their own strengths. Despite free elections and the existence of 22 registered opposition parties, the PAP held 82 of 84 elected parliamentary seats and all ministerial positions in 2001.[68] Since 1966, only 2 of the 22 opposition parties have won parliamentary seats. This situation is unlikely to change anytime soon due to the many obstacles that opposition parties face.[69] A major hurdle is the government's propaganda advantage since the domestic media is owned and controlled by the government and the government maintains a right to respond to any critical article in the press, guaranteeing it the last word on any issue.[70] Another major hurdle is the fear of persecution. This persecution includes not only the loss of business or other career opportunities in a society dominated by the PAP, but also the fear of lawsuits. Former prime minister Lee Kuan Yew has personally sued at least 13 people for libel and such suits are not uncommon. A highly publicized case in 1997 left an opposition leader with fines of over $5 million.[71] The Public Entertainment Act prohibits public speech or entertainment without a permit. In September 2000, police denied such a permit to an opposition member of parliament to speak at a dinner organized by his party.[72] Finally, opposition parties suffer from their own internal weakness. For a variety of reasons, they have failed to consistently attract strong candidates and to mount a credible alternative to the PAP.

Second, Singapore features few nongovernmental organizations and a relatively inactive civil society due to legal limitations on assembly and due to the PAP's success in channeling dissent and discussions through state-controlled institutions.[73] Though the government is becoming more tolerant, the prevailing sentiment until recently is summed up by Minister for Communications and Information Won Kan Seng: "Public policy is the domain of the government. It isn't the playground of those who have no responsibility to the people, and who aren't answerable for the livelihood or survival of Singaporeans."[74]

Civil society groups in Singapore face numerous obstacles. The 1967 Societies Act virtually outlawed pressure groups by barring political engagement by organizations not registered for that purpose.[75] Since July 2002, the Public Entertainment Act requires organizations to submit an application for assembly to a sub-unit of the police known as the Public Entertainment Licensing Unit, or PELU. Activists claim that receiving such licenses often takes weeks and appeals take still longer. Though the act has recently been relaxed—it no longer applies to garden parties or charity sales—activists complain that there is little transparency in the process. As one activist puts it, "You hand in your form. And then you wait blindly. There's no acknowledgement that they've got your form. Who decides on your application? How do they do it? It's not clear what is or is not allowed."[76] The need for such licenses is taken seriously since the law *is* enforced. An opposition politician named Chee Soon Juan was jailed for more than a week in 1999 for speaking in public without a permit after he refused to pay an $827 fine.[77]

Third, despite widespread access to the Internet, Singapore's government imposes controls on information technology.[78] Satellite dishes are illegal and information on the Internet is controlled using the same legal infrastructure as that applied to other media.[79] This creates pressure for self-censorship among Internet Service Providers since under the Newspaper and Printing Presses Act, the distributor and publisher, not just the author of objectionable material, is legally liable. Though Singapore does not require its citizens to clear the content of web pages with the government, Internet content providers need to register with the Singapore Broadcasting Authority (SBA), a statutory board under the Ministry of Information and the Art (MITA), if their pages are "primarily set up to promote political or religious causes."[80] Registration does not mean that these providers cannot post political or religious content. However, it does ensure that content providers are responsible for the content of their web sites and may be sued under Singapore's relatively stringent antidefamation laws. According to the Singapore Broadcasting Authority Act, the SBA's duty is to "ensure that nothing is included in any broadcasting service which is against public interest or order, national harmony or which offends against good taste or decency."[81] The SBA argues that, although it does block access to sites it finds objectionable, these sites are mainly pornographic or racist.[82] Monitoring the Internet is not easy work, the Ministry of Information and the Arts acknowledges. However, MITA minister George Yeo stated that "Censorship can no longer be one hundred percent effective, but even if it is only twenty percent effective, we should not stop censoring."[83]

Singapore has embarked on a major state-led initiative to become an information technology hub in the Asia Pacific region and to give its entire population high-speed access to the Internet. However, some analysts surmise that "Singapore's authoritarian leaders have no intention of surrendering political control in the process" and have displayed adeptness at reconciling tensions between their economic and political objectives.[84]

Fourth, Singapore continues to "restrict freedom of speech and press significantly."[85] The media and other forms of expression are controlled by the Internal Security Act (ISA), which gives the government the power to restrict or to place conditions on media that incite violence; counsel disobedience to the law; risk arousing tensions among different segments of multi-ethnic population; or threaten the national interest, national security, and national order. Undesirable material or publications may be censored by invoking either the ISA or the Undesirable Publications Act. Due to the risk of lawsuits, some journalists allegedly engage in self-censorship.

Singapore's government can also exercise control over the media using its ties to media companies. Singapore Press Holdings Ltd., a private holding company with close ties to the government, owns all widely circulated newspapers in Singapore. The government approves and can remove holders of the company's management shares, who have the power to hire and fire staff. Singapore International Media Pte Lte holds a near monopoly on radio and television broadcasting and is subsidized by the government. An exception is a completely independent radio station operated by the British Broadcasting Corporation.

Control over the media extends to foreign news sources as well. The Newspaper Printing and Presses Act enables Singapore's minister of communications and information to restrict the circulation of foreign publications in Singapore that are deemed to be engaging in domestic politics. The *International Herald Tribune* paid over $600,000 in fines in 1994 for two articles regarding Singaporean politics, and in 2004 *The Economist* paid a fine of $125,800 for an article on the appointment of Prime Minister Lee's wife to head the government's investment arm.[86] In theory, this restriction extends to the Internet as well, though in practice the law is not commonly enforced in this realm.[87] The import of some newspapers from Malaysia is not permitted and there are restrictions on other publications. However, Internet access to these publications is not blocked.

The main newspaper, the *Straits Times*, regularly publishes critiques of the government. However, critiques only go so far and there is sometimes an observable willingness to avoid sensitive topics. For instance, a February 27, 2000 article on the annual human rights report issued by the U.S. State Department, noted some questionable behaviors on the part of the government, such as probing ISP customer files to see if they were infected with a computer virus, but it generally noted areas where Singapore had shown progress. There was no mention of the report's extensive discussion on limited freedoms of press, speech, and assembly.[88]

Why Has Singapore's System Endured?

Why has Singapore been able to control information to such a surprising degree? There are three convincing answers. First, Singapore's security and survival are persistent concerns. Second, Singapore's economic success is extraordinary by all accounts, which legitimates the government and its policies in the eyes of the Singaporean people. Third, the PAP justifies its continued dominance with a general lack of corruption, administrative effectiveness, and a coherent ideology.

Security Concerns. Singapore is a country of extreme vulnerability though it has never been attacked militarily.[89] This vulnerability has many sources. The most obvious is that Singapore is a country of only 622 square kilometers, and 4 million people, located on a strategic archipelago near larger, stronger, potentially unstable, and potentially aggressive countries. Access to Singapore by sea and air requires passage through Indonesian and Malaysian sea and air space and Malaysia has occasionally denied that access.[90] Singapore's history enhances this sense of vulnerability. Japan invaded Singapore in World War II and a largely Muslim region has long been suspicious of Singapore's ethnic Chinese population. Most significantly, the creation of Singapore as a sovereign nation came when the country was expelled from the Malaysian Federation in 1965 against its will.

Economically, Singapore's position is also precarious. The country lacks natural resources and sufficient food supplies. The supply of potable water is always a concern, since half of Singapore's water supply is provided by Malaysia via pipeline.[91] The economy is heavily dependent on international trade, with 2004 exports totaling $185 billion, and imports comprising $169 billion.[92]

Though relations with Malaysia have improved since Malaysian prime minister Mahathir Mohamad stepped down, security concerns are not a matter of the distant past. A maritime boundary agreement was not concluded with Malaysia until 1995.[93] In November 2000, Indonesia's president publicly criticized Singapore and suggested that Indonesia and Malaysia should "teach a lesson" to Singapore by cutting off its water supply.[94] In addition, fear of domestic threats is rising. Singaporean authorities foiled terrorist attacks in 2002 and arrested twenty-one persons suspected of trying to establish a single regional Islamic state—a state with no room for a multi-ethnic, secular government like Singapore's.[95] Because of this enduring threat, Singapore maintains a defense budget of $5.8 billion, approximately 5 percent of gross domestic product (GDP), in 2006.[96]

This vulnerability has spawned a highly interventionist government with a broad definition of security.[97] This definition includes not just military defense capabilities, good diplomatic relations with neighbors, and a strong economy, but also "internal stability," which the government defines as "working toward and maintaining social cohesion, harmony and tolerance. The result is a stable society where there is unity of purpose between leaders and people."[98]

Economic Success. A longtime trading post, Singapore has tried to make up for its lack of political and military might with economic power. This strategy has paid off and Singapore's economic and diplomatic power now far outstrips its size. In 2004, Singapore boasted a per capita GDP of $27,800—higher than Italy, Spain, or New Zealand.[99] Despite political controls, Singapore maintains an extremely open and competitive economy, ranked seventh in the world in the 2004-2005 World Economic Forum Global Competitiveness Report, and third in the Institute for International Management's 2005 World Competitiveness Yearbook.[100] In 2005, the unemployment rate was 3 percent.[101]

Singapore maintains the world's largest port in terms of tonnage, with ships arriving or departing every two to three seconds.[102] It is a major hub for international finance and for communications in the Asia Pacific and is home to more than 130 banks. Heavily dependent on international trade, the country suffered a recession after the 1997 Asian financial crisis, and another downturn after the 2003 Severe Acute Respiratory Syndrome (SARS) crisis, but quickly rebounded with economic growth of 5.4% in 1999, 10.1% in 2000, and 8-9% in 2004.[103]

Singapore's economic success is related to the country's political openness in several ways. First, in Singapore, economic success is a matter of fundamental security. In a 1972 speech, Foreign Minister Sinnathamby Rajaratnam argued, "We draw sustenance not only from the region but also from the international economic system to which we as a Global City belong and which will be the final arbiter of whether we prosper or decline."[104] Second, many believe that the country's economic success has not come in spite of the government's controlling tendencies, but because of them.[105] Goh Keng Swee, Singapore's principal economic architect, argues that rapid economic growth demands a sacrifice that people would not accept in a democracy, even if it guaranteed long-term prosperity.[106] Third, the government is credited with the economy's success, which is so essential to the nation's well-being and security. This success legitimates both the government and its policies and weakens the opposition. Why would anyone vote against the PAP, some argue, if it has been so beneficial for the country?

Political Success. The PAP enjoys apparently widespread political legitimacy in Singapore, winning 75.3% of the vote in 2001. Up from a 65% share of the vote in 1997, the win was the PAP's third best showing in its history.[107]

The most persuasive explanation for the PAP's continued power is the party's own success. By most accounts, the PAP has protected Singapore's security interests, brought extraordinary economic success, avoided corruption, maneuvered deftly in the world of diplomacy, improved the education and public housing systems, and generally made life better for most Singaporeans. This recognition is shared by foreigners as well as by citizens; Singapore ranks high on numerous external assessments.[108]

The PAP's legitimacy is enhanced by a mixture of democratic and authoritarian institutions, which enhance the PAP's hold on power on one hand, but give Singaporeans significant freedoms on the other hand. This blend of democracy and authoritarianism has been characterized as "illiberal democracy," a form of government which, by some estimates, is spreading.[109] Elections, far from presenting a threat to the PAP, actually enhance the PAP's legitimacy by demonstrating public support for the party and its policies and by giving the government significant freedom of maneuver in between elections.[110] As Christopher Tremewan puts it, "The ideological effect of voting on Singaporean voters is that they have consented either to the government in power, or the whole system of governance, or both."[111]

Government leaders, especially Lee Kuan Yew, have been able to justify their policies to voters with a coherent and articulate, if undemocratic, ideology. They argue that a communitarian model is more suitable for East Asian societies and that Singaporeans prefer to trade greater freedom for stability, avoiding the social problems endured by Western democracies like the United States.[112] In the words of Lee Kuan Yew, "In the East the main object is to have a well-ordered society so that everybody can have maximum enjoyment of his freedoms. This freedom can only exist in an ordered state and not in a natural state of contention and anarchy."[113] Greater freedoms of assembly and expression allegedly threaten that order. To quote Lee again, "The top three to five percent of a society can handle this free-for-all, this clash of ideas." For the rest of the population, the free exchange of ideas on the Internet is likely to have destabilizing social and political effects.[114]

This ideology seems to cohere with that of most Singaporeans. According to a Channel NewsAsia/Gallup poll taken in November 1999, 82% are satisfied with the overall level of censorship in Singapore. Of those who felt that censorship should be relaxed, most felt that it should be relaxed for material containing sexual or violent content. Only 11% felt that it should be relaxed for material related to politics.[115]

Dissent is channeled away from opposition politics and toward formal mechanisms of consultation with the government. Critiques of the government are openly aired in the media and elsewhere. However, the government guarantees itself the last word and has the legal mechanisms to limit such critiques. Singaporeans are free to travel, communicate with foreigners and each other, and engage in economic activity, all of which give them a sense that they—and not the government—exercise control over their lives.

Some observers argue that the government and the PAP cannot maintain this control indefinitely, that it is only a matter of time before Singapore becomes a liberal democracy in the Western sense. *New York Times* columnist Thomas Friedman argues, "It is not an accident that every country with a per capita income above $15,000 is a liberal democracy, except Singapore, which is a city-state and almost certainly will become a liberal democracy once there is a generational change."[116] This view is shared by others like Hussin Mutalib, who writes, "It is in the nature of mature and developed societies that citizens will demand greater political pluralism and more political space for their views to the heard, if not considered, in the formulation and implementation of government policies."[117] This is particularly true for young people, argues Mutalib, since they are more likely to be exposed to alternative sources of information via the Internet, travel and tourists, and Western ideas of democracy. Some Singaporeans agree that the PAP's monopoly on information cannot last. According to a Channel NewsAsia/Gallup Poll, 66 percent of Singaporeans believe that technologies such as the Internet and satellite technology will make censorship irrelevant in the future.[118]

However, the evidence for this position is ambiguous. Indeed, an examination of why Singapore has been able to control information in the past indicates that, under the right circumstances, Singapore and other countries as well, may be able to limit transparency and de-link information and political change for a long time or even indefinitely.

Pressures for Change. Singapore *is* changing and there are signs that the PAP is easing its monopoly on information. This change is PAP-driven and motivated by a concern for Singapore's continued economic competitiveness and security. Specifically, many opinion leaders in the government believe that Singaporean society must become freer if it is to encourage the sort of innovative, entrepreneurial thinking that is rewarded by the global economy. In addition, leaders fear that a lack of public engagement has depoliticized Singaporean society and weakened support for the government, particularly among young people.[119] Singapore's weak hold on its citizens was evidenced by a 1997 Mastercard survey, indicating that one in five Singaporeans wanted to emigrate.[120]

In a 1997 speech before Parliament, former prime minister Goh Chok Tong worried aloud that this lack of popular support could ultimately threaten Singapore's security.

> But what if we should suffer an external shock and run into economic difficulties?...What will hold Singaporeans here? Affluence and prosperity cannot be the only glue holding us together. If Singaporeans are just economic animals, materialistic with no sense of belonging, they will be like migratory birds, seeking their fortunes in other lands when the season changes....If it ever comes to this, Singapore will not survive as a sovereign nation. To meet this problem, and other challenges now unknown, it will not do just to make minor course corrections, small improvements to a generally working model. We need a new vision for Singapore....We need to move beyond material progress, to a society which places people at its very center.[121]

At the 2004 swearing in ceremony of Prime Minister Lee Hsien Loong, the son of former prime minister Lee Kwan Yew, the former indicated that he had "no doubt that our society must open up further."[122]

This concern spawned Singapore 21, a plan to encourage greater public participation in government as well as other initiatives to increase political openness.[123] On August 10, 2000, the government introduced a speaker's corner modeled on the forum by the same name in London. However, the popular response has been underwhelming. Some supporters claim that the lack of interest reflects satisfaction with the government. More critical observers argue that numerous restrictions on speaking on the corner discourage wider participation: speakers must be citizens, show identification, and register with the police their intention to speak thirty days in advance.

There are additional signs of increasing openness. Internet chat rooms feature vibrant discussions. The government is considering competition in the media, an industry in which one company currently has effective control of print media and another controls broadcast media.[124] There are signs of life in civil society and a few nongovernmental organizations, such as the Association of Women for Action and Research (AWARE), Nature Society of Singapore (NSS), and Action for AIDS, have become active. In 2001, the government allowed the first legal political rally by a nonparty organization in support of one of three opposition Members of Parliament.[125] And, whereas the government had previously prevented visits from Amnesty International, in 1997 and

1999, both Amnesty and the International Commission of Jurists were allowed to observe legal proceedings against two opposition politicians. Critiques of these cases were reported in Singapore's press along with government responses.[126] Many observers see fewer restrictions on artistic expression.[127] And, licenses are no longer needed for indoor lectures—though that change does not extend to talks concerning race or religion.[128]

   Singapore's Future. Despite these changes, there are also reasons to be skeptical that Singapore will become an open, liberal democracy in which the government relinquishes significant control over information. As indicated earlier, the PAP maintains a formidable capacity to challenge opponents and there is no viable opposition in the foreseeable future.[129] Furthermore, though civil society is being encouraged by the Singapore 21 plan, activities of NGOs, particularly those dealing with political or religious issues, are still subject to strict controls. Some analysts even believe that Singapore 21 will limit true public debate rather than open it up. In the swearing in ceremony just discussed, Prime Minister Lee indicated that he would not tolerate "criticism that scores political points and undermines government's standing" or "crusading journalism."[130] According to Garry Rodan, the PAP is reaching out to sectional interests in order to divert their disaffection from the realm of politics and to keep them from joining the opposition.
   Whether the PAP has loosened its control over society in some ways, it has tightened it in other ways. In 2000, the government passed the Political Donations Act, which requires anyone contributing more than $3,300 to a political campaign to be identified publicly. Though this sort of sunshine law is seen as a positive step toward exposing the sources of political influence and strengthening democratic governance in many countries, openness in the Singaporean context has interesting but distinctive political implications. Opposition groups worry that sunshine laws will further restrict their already limited funding, since only supporters of opposition groups will object to being identified.[131]
   As for the media, partial press freedoms continue to limit the spread of transparency in Singapore. There is no tradition of investigative journalism, and formidable legal barriers stand in the way of a truly free press.[132]
   Finally, and most importantly, the PAP maintains a monopoly on information in Singapore because it has been able to convince Singaporeans that greater openness is not in their interest and could threaten their security, political stability in a multi-ethnic society, and economic success. The PAP has established a record of protecting those

interests and has avoided many—though not all—of the corruptive temptations of secrecy.

Change may indeed come to Singapore, but it is not inevitable. In the wake of the 1997 Asian financial crisis, erratic relations with unstable neighbors like Malaysia and Indonesia, the 2001 economic recession, and especially the growing threat of terrorism, it is conceivable that there will always be a new crisis to justify the PAP's tight rein. The American war on terrorism is likely to only increase the sense of vulnerability for this American friend and largely Chinese society in a region surrounded by Muslim countries, which contain Al-Qaeda sympathizers and even training camps. If Singapore's economy continues to thrive, citizens may be wary of handing the reins to another party. And, if Singapore's government continues to deliver security, stability, and economic success, its political legitimacy could endure even in the information age.

Conclusion

This chapter challenges the conventional wisdom about the impact of transparency on democratization and on the power of global civil society. Many observers believe that transparency and a free flow of information will empower transnational NGOs that promote noble causes, increase public participation in international governance, erode the power of authoritarian regimes, and lead citizens to challenge their governments' authority.[133] That prediction sometimes may be accurate, but democracy and good governance are not the inevitable results of greater transparency. By decentralizing power, greater transparency may empower NGOs with nefarious objectives as well good ones. And it may not empower citizens to create democratic institutions.

NGOs and citizen movements of all varieties face significant limits to their influence. Though greater transparency gives domestic and international civil society new instruments of power, governments retain significant control even in an age of transparency. The case of Singapore indicates the possibility for a successful and advanced country to maintain an open but illiberal system that is integrated into the world economy. Though change may indeed come to Singapore if certain conditions prevail, the city-state's semi-authoritarian system could endure indefinitely. Singapore's government seems to have discovered a formula for sustaining a minimally transparent system: a blend of significant individual freedoms; open but controlled dissent; partial press freedom; and strong disincentives for opposition parties, civil society, and more aggressive media.

It is tempting to conclude that Singapore is exceptional. Singapore is one of the tiniest countries in the world. It is remarkably vulnerable and located in a region of instability. It maintains a unique combination of economic and political freedoms. Singapore also has a distinctive nanny-state culture that is legendary for its government campaigns against gum-chewing, poor grammar, rudeness, and other social ills.

Yet Singapore is not unique when it comes to controlling information. Forty-five countries currently restrict Internet access, and twenty of those countries filter that access heavily.[134] Though the wealthy and technically able can often circumvent these controls, most citizens do not fit that description, making governments surprisingly adept at limiting mass access to the Internet. The Internet is only one aspect of transparency, but policy toward the Internet—an instrument often characterized as outside government control—provides a useful metric of a government's commitment to openness.[135] Another metric is the existence of freedom of information acts, which allow citizens to access classified government documents. Fifty countries currently have such provisions and many of those are quite recent.[136]

Notably, other countries are watching Singapore closely and experimenting with their own variations to this formula. Former Chinese premier Deng Xioaping visited Singapore in 1978 seeking a model for economic growth with tight central government control. Now China is among the most sophisticated managers of domestic communication in the world, successfully balancing economic modernization and political control.[137] For instance, China is currently the world's largest user of mobile telephones with a market of 350 million and Internet users numbering approximately 100 million, with an annual growth rate of 30 percent. However, China reportedly maintains a staff of as many as 50,000 "Internet police," and sophisticated filtering technologies. These resources are primarily directed at the Internet right now, but "there are things the bureaucracy could do" if the government decided that text messages were a threat to its control.[138]

Saudi Arabia, one of the world's least transparent states, has opened up access to the Internet though its contents are heavily censored. Saudi Arabian leaders are also discussing the possibility of limited elections to the king's 120-member advisory council. However, as in Singapore, elections may be controlled so as to increase support for the government, not create viable opposition to the government or to its policies. As Prince Walid bin Talal, a member of Saudi Arabia's royal family told the *New York Times*, "If people speak more freely and get involved more in the political process, you can really contain them and make them part of the process."[139]

The notion that governments can control information does not detract from the administrative skills necessary to do so successfully. Limiting transparency at an acceptable cost is quite difficult. But, not all countries care about the cost and can maintain their system if they have the will and resources to be sufficiently oppressive. The major risk of limiting transparency is that a government will become corrupt, unaccountable, distrusted, poorly managed, and illegitimate in the eyes of its people. Historically, the ability to operate outside the purview of public scrutiny breeds inefficiency, contempt for the law, and abuse. Public scrutiny also ensures that policies are carefully considered, which is likely to improve their quality. A lack of transparency in the economic realm discourages investment since investors usually want to be well informed about the risks of their investment. Moreover, a lack of transparency, especially in the areas of science and technology, may discourage innovation.[140]

Though this assessment of enduring state power may depress those who hope that transparency will promote democratic revolutions, well-intentioned NGOs, and the demise of sovereign states, the enduring power of states has some benefits. The experience of the post-Cold War era suggests that weak governments are often far bigger threats to human security and well-being that even the most oppressive governments. In the Congo, Sudan, and in parts of central Asia, areas outside the reaches of governments are by far more miserable than the oppressive regimes of Iran, Libya, or Iraq under Saddam Hussein. A total lack of governance usually harms average citizens even more than bad governance. And, at least for the time being, governments are still the best providers of governance. Weakening state power may be extremely positive if it helps citizens free themselves from oppressive governments, but for citizens on the ground, this change may make life worse.

The good news is that transparency tends to reward the type of governance that most citizens of democracies would prefer. Greater transparency is often a first step to more accountability by governments, since it gives third parties—or even parties in other parts of the government—the ability to monitor performance. Transparency rewards governments that are legitimate and perform well since, if people can see credible evidence of good performance, they are more likely to support that government. Finally, when governments are performing poorly, the information available through greater transparency gives activists more tools to pressure for change. The bad news, at least for democrats, is that openness and illiberal government is a possible—if difficult to balance—combination. Transparency can be both controlled and reversed.

Chapter 6

Global Implications of Growing Transparency

"In the context of international relations, transparency means that the chances of misinterpretation, whether deliberate or inadvertent, are reduced to a minimum."
—Pervaiz Iqbal Cheema[1]

"Everyone looking at everyone else. Everyone seeing something different."
—Quoted from the play, *Democracy*, by Michael Frayn[2]

This book challenges the conventional wisdom regarding transparency and argues that it is not an unmitigated good. If the trend toward greater transparency continues, it *will* transform international politics by reducing uncertainty, helping people know each other better, and decentralizing power—but the implications of those developments are complex. Less uncertainty can both encourage and discourage international conflict, and increase and decrease international cooperation. More information about other peoples and cultures can promote or diminish tolerance and the likelihood of violence between groups. Widely available information about foreign conflicts makes third parties either more or less likely to intervene and to stop deadly violence, depending on what transparency shows. More decentralized power gives the weak more influence over the strong and strengthens advocates of democracy but it also empowers terrorists and gives authoritarian governments new instruments of power. Transparency has a dark side.

Most predictions about the effects of greater transparency rely on unanalyzed assumptions, usually that transparency will reveal harmony rather than conflict, and tolerance rather than hate. Greater transparency may indeed reveal harmony and tolerance, but analysts rarely warn us that their predictions are conditional. This book disentangles predictions about greater transparency from the assumptions on which they are based and argues that the effects of greater transparency depend largely on what transparency shows, how people interpret the information they receive in a more transparent international society, and how people react to that information. They depend on who wins from greater transparency and the goals of those winners.

Though this book strips predictions about transparency from value-laden assumptions, values and ideas are critical to predicting the effects of greater transparency. Ideas and values influence where people seek information and how people interpret and act on that information. They influence whom people view as a friend or enemy, whether actions seem benign or threatening, whether they feel morally obligated to protect citizens in distant countries, and whether others seem worthy of trust. They affect whether citizens find controls over information legitimate and the conditions under which they will object. Consequently, the effects of transparency will change over time because ideas and values are *variables*; they evolve.

Greater transparency presents governments, nongovernmental organizations (NGOs), and even individuals with the opportunity to influence the relationship between people and information. Groups can marshal evidence and persuade people to change their minds. They can influence what people think is right or good and what sorts of behavior are appropriate.[3] Because ideas and values are so powerful, the ability to convince others to share one's ideas and values—what Joseph S. Nye, Jr. calls "soft power"—conveys remarkable influence. When others share your ideas and "want what you want," they are likely to cooperate easily when they agree on an issue and tolerate disagreement without conflict when they do not.[4] Achieving goals is easier and successes are more durable. Force, when exercised, is more effective and typically less necessary in the first place. In an age of transparency, any organization or individual that can command broad attention and support has the potential to acquire soft power. Nonetheless, governments, especially legitimate governments that speak for their people, retain an advantage and legitimate governments that are also strong will find that the combination of soft and hard power—the ability to persuade the many and force the few—gives them extraordinary influence over world events.

What Transparency Reveals

The effects of transparency depend on what it reveals. That point seems obvious, but it is one frequently missed by a wide spectrum of scholars, analysts, and politicians. As just indicated, the idea that transparency can solve a host of global problems is based largely on unspoken assumptions that transparency will illuminate cooperation, friendship, and support for democratic ideals and, when it does not, offenders will readily change their behaviors in shame. However, as indicated throughout this book, transparency will not always illuminate positive information or encourage desirable behavior.

This conclusion has many implications. For instance, an important area of political science scholarship argues that uncertainty about the intentions of other governments leads cautious nations to assume that others wish to harm them. This uncertainty leads them to take steps, like building up arms, which ultimately make them less secure. Knowledge that others do not intend to harm them—transparency of intentions—would help governments avoid counterproductive behavior and make their citizens more secure. That insight is important and valid—if, and only if, transparency lets governments see that others are not aggressive and unprepared to attack. But if transparency shows that other states are aggressive, building up their military capabilities, or not committed to avoiding violent conflict, the effects of transparency will not create the peaceful relations these analysts predict. In fact, transparency of intentions in that circumstance can encourage arms races and spirals of aggressive rhetoric if not war.

With respect to military capabilities, the effects of transparency once again depend on what transparency reveals. Advocates of arms transparency, the sharing of information regarding military capabilities, assume that transparency will reduce misperceptions and help countries avoid war. That view may be true, as long as transparency reveals stability or that the costs of war are unacceptably high.[5] However, if transparency of military capabilities exposes vulnerability, it can undermine deterrence and invite aggression by the strong against the weak.[6] When using force seems easy, strong states have more incentives to use it in order to achieve their goals. Less uncertainty about military capabilities makes strong states more confident of success in war and removes the strategic ambiguity that protects the weak.

Turning to the social dynamics of conflict, greater transparency can reduce intergroup hostility by helping people to know each other better, disconfirming stereotypes, and humanizing other groups—*if* the information available is credible, does not reinforce existing stereotypes, and actually increases positive feelings toward other groups. If transparency only provides access to superficial or biased information or that information demonizes other groups, however, it may actually make intergroup relations worse. Some analysts argue that greater transparency will reduce intergroup conflicts since monopolies over information are necessary in order to dehumanize groups sufficiently to justify violence against them. A free marketplace of ideas, they argue, has a "self-righting tendency to correct errors and biases." Unfortunately it is not at all clear that greater transparency will always give people access to information that humanizes others since, like all markets, marketplaces of ideas can become distorted.[7] The media, even free media, can and does, spread hatred of other nations or ethnic groups—particularly if that sort of coverage has an avid audience and sells newspapers. Well-intentioned laws protecting freedom of speech and press can provide "an opening for nationalist mythmakers to hijack public discourse."[8] Civil society can include extremist and nationalist groups as well as groups advocating respect for human rights. Citizens sometimes embrace prejudice or war, even in well-developed democracies, especially if trusted leaders begin to advocate extremist views.[9]

Early democratic thinkers recognized the potential for majorities to abuse minorities even in an open marketplace of ideas.[10] The Federalist Papers, for instance, note that there are times when the public will be "stimulated by some irregular passion, or some illicit advantage, or misled by the artful misrepresentations of interested men" into advocating unfortunate policies.[11] This sort of tyranny of the masses can be more dangerous to minorities than political oppression by the government. Consequently, societies should adopt laws that protect the rights of minorities and encourage dissent. As Jack Snyder and Karen Ballentine observe in their study of ethnic conflict, "Just as economic competition produces socially beneficial results only in a well-institutionalized marketplace . . . so too increased debate in the political marketplace leads to better outcomes only when there are mechanisms to correct market imperfections."[12] Openness alone offers insufficient protections.

When armed conflicts do break out between groups, the trend toward greater transparency can either encourage or discourage intervention by the international community. Sometimes greater transparency can facilitate preventive diplomacy and conflict intervention by providing better and more widely accessible information about foreign conflicts. Specialists (increasingly found outside of government thanks to more decentralized flows of information) alert the media, governments, and international organizations when disputes escalate to violence and then pressure those with power to respond. Average citizens who see human suffering on their television screens launch grassroots campaigns to encourage their governments to act. However, greater transparency also can discourage conflict intervention, depending on what transparency reveals and preexisting values about when foreign conflicts warrant the costs of intervention. If transparency shows that conflicts will be difficult to resolve or that their continuation will not threaten vital national interests, transparency actually may discourage third parties from helping. Greater transparency may assist people in overcoming informational and political obstacles to preventive diplomacy and earlier conflict intervention, but that is not necessarily the case.

Greater transparency amplifies trends whether they are negative or positive and, for this reason, encourages both virtuous and vicious circles. If a government is genuinely peaceful, for instance, greater transparency makes others aware of this fact and gives them confidence in that assessment. That knowledge can lead those governments to reciprocate, which makes the first government more secure and reinforces efforts to improve relations on both sides. Evidence that peaceful gestures are productive, strengthens politicians who support such steps and encourages them to make further peaceful gestures. Because transparency can encourage virtuous circles of cooperation, deliberate acts of transparency can be effective confidence and security-building measures (CSBMs) when countries or groups are actively trying to improve their relations. However, aggressive actions or words can fuel vicious circles of confrontation and conflict if transparency shows ill will, a failure to comply with international agreements, arms buildups, aggressive rhetoric, or a willingness to use force. Such acts will be evident and create pressure to reciprocate, fueling a vicious circle of distrust that can lead to violence if unchecked. Because of this risk, when groups or governments are just starting to mend their relations, transparency measures may not be a good way to start conflict resolution since reluctance and steps backward will be all the more evident and encourage reciprocal acts of retreat.

Transparency also can create virtuous or vicious circles with respect to the spread of ideas and values. It makes ideas and values more widely accessible and, in so doing, may encourage collective action by letting people see how widely a particular sentiment, whether dissatisfaction with an oppressive government or hatred toward a particular ethnic group, is shared. Evidence that ideas and values are shared widely, legitimizes those ideas and values and encourages their further dissemination, regardless of their content. Transparency is indiscriminate. When ideas— whether democratic revolution or ethnic cleansing—gain legitimacy and spread, they allow people to justify behaviors such as civil disobedience or violence in which they did not previously engage. Evidence of mass support for an idea can also intimidate dissenters into silence even if there are no formal penalties for speaking up. People may not be brave enough to distance themselves from the majority. They may fear social penalties. They may question whether they are right if so many others disagree. Or, they may feel their cause is hopeless given the depth of popular support and therefore not worth advocating.

In the Eye of the Beholder

The implications of greater transparency depend not just on what it shows, but also how information revealed by transparency is interpreted. What information people pay attention to and the meaning they draw from that information depends on preexisting ideas and values that can change slowly even when new information calls those views into question. To cope with the volume of information received each day, people tend to interpret new information in the context of existing views and values and discard contradictory data.[13] As the weight of contradictory evidence grows, most people will adjust their views accordingly. However, information is rarely so clear-cut and people are not quick to change.[14] The implication is that the marginal increase of information we gain from increased transparency may have limited meaning in the short term. Greater transparency eventually may help us to know others better, but not soon.

People are more likely to change their minds if new information comes from a trusted source. At a time when people are overwhelmed with information, sources considered credible have tremendous power because people will turn to them and ignore many others. How do people determine if sources are trustworthy? One way is through an individual's or organization's reputation for being an unbiased, accurate source. Consumers of information may trust the *New York Times* or the *Economist* as information providers because they have a reputation for sound reporting and analysis. Or, they may consider the source of information credible because it coheres with their own worldviews. People might seek information from Fox News or *Mother Jones*, for example, because those information providers report the type of information in which they are interested and in a way that reflects their values. In the British context, where objectivity means making a political bias explicit, a person might choose *The Guardian* or *The Independent* as a daily newspaper depending on their political views.

People assess not only the credibility of the source of information, but also the identities and reputations of the people or groups involved.[15] People are more likely to interpret favorably information about groups they like or trust and discount positive or ambiguous information about groups they distrust. Because people tend to use new information to confirm existing beliefs, negative views of others may be slow to change, even in the face of information that disconfirms negative stereotypes. People also rely on the identities and reputations of others to give them cues about future behavior. Though we may have no information about how France is going to react on a particular issue, we know who the actor involved is, and that information alone gives us a strong basis for prediction. We know France's history, the nature of French democracy, and the values the French embrace. Greater transparency helps to illuminate this information of course, but access to that sort of information is not new.

The role of trust and identity affects not only how people interpret news about people or groups where there is clearly a social relationship, but also how they interpret "tangible" data. The meaning of information, and therefore how people ought to respond to it, depends heavily on existing views about what is right and wrong, what actions are threatening or benign, who is an enemy or a friend, or who is part of an in-group and who is not. Information is viewed through the lens of preexisting values. For instance, though interpreting information regarding military capabilities seems concrete, it is deceptively complicated. Transparency can let us see how many aircraft carriers a country owns. It cannot tell us definitively whether those aircraft carriers are a threat. That assessment depends on how we assess the intentions of the owner as well as the owner's identity. If the owner is considered a friend, people are less likely to interpret the aircraft carrier as a threat, but if the owner is an enemy, even a single aircraft carrier may seem dangerous. Turning to a different example, most societies view killing as generally wrong, but acceptable for particular reasons such as self-defense. Therefore, people need to apply values about right and wrong to draw meaning from information as straightforward as the fact that Person A killed Person B. [16]

The importance of social relationships in interpreting information means that governments may change their interpretation of an enemy's behavior reluctantly even when there is substantial information that a long-standing enemy's intentions have become conciliatory. In the language of political science, mistrust as well as uncertainty drives the security dilemma. To give an example, after the former Soviet Union signed the 1987 *Intermediate-Range Nuclear Forces* Treaty (INF

Treaty), withdrew forces from Afghanistan in 1988, announced conventional force reductions in Europe, and acquiesced to the 1989 revolutions in Eastern Europe, some American policy makers still questioned Soviet motives.[17] Six months before the Berlin Wall fell, Secretary of State James Baker praised the Soviets for releasing political prisoners and for reforming emigration policies but said, "We must all, I think, face the fact that the Soviets continue to pose a significant military threat.... For all the talk of 'defensive defense,' Soviet military exercises still continue to show a marked inclination for taking the offensive. For the all the talk of openness, the Soviets have yet to publish a real defense budget."[18] It took the extremely costly signal of acquiescing to the 1989 revolutions in Eastern Europe to convince American leaders that the former Soviet Union had changed truly and irreversibly.[19]

Information and Action

The implications of greater transparency also depend on how actors respond to information and here too, ideas and values come into play. Governments (and other organizations and groups) usually have a range of policy tools to choose from and what they choose is influenced by what policies they think are effective and legitimate. As apparent in changing views regarding assassination and the use of unilateral economic sanctions, these values and ideas change over time—and sometimes change back. To give an example, there are many possible responses if a government has credible information that a neighbor is building up its arms and interprets that buildup as a threat. Which is appropriate? Even if we assume that the government merely wishes to protect its national security, a government still could respond in various ways. If leaders believe that arms buildups are a precursor to attack, they could launch a preemptive strike. The government could build up its own arms so as to deter aggression. The government could attempt to negotiate a bilateral treaty to reduce arms. It could use diplomatic or other measures to pressure that government to reduce its arms. It could unilaterally reduce its own arms in order to signal that it is not a threat and make the other side appear the clear aggressor if it does not do likewise. It could turn to international organizations or allies for assistance.

Many disagreements between the United States and Europe are about what measures are appropriate responses to threats. Consider the 2003 war in Iraq. Before the war, the United States and its allies generally agreed that Saddam Hussein was obstructing efforts to inspect Iraq's weapons facilities and most agreed that Saddam probably had weapons of mass destruction. However, there was major disagreement about how to respond to that threat. The U.S. government believed that Saddam had been given too many chances to evade inspections and that a military response was necessary immediately. The governments of France and Germany, in contrast, argued that the United Nations should insist on further inspections rather than attack. Turning to intergroup relations, how people act on information depends on values and ideas regarding what types of behavior are considered acceptable or necessary. For instance, the mere existence of prejudice or hate does not mean that genocide is imminent. Some societies and regions witness intergroup hostility for decades without that hostility erupting into violence. But ideas about what sorts of actions are appropriate and legitimate can change. In the former Yugoslavia hostility erupted where once there was tolerance.

Transparency helps to spread norms about what types of actions are acceptable and appropriate and, when those norms clash with the values of others, makes those differences more evident. When values clash, people are more likely to confront differences and, ultimately, one set of values may "win." Compared with previous decades, for instance, few people now advocate slavery or centrally planned economies.

Widespread awareness of clashing values also may intensify support for those values precisely because they seem threatened. Whether domestically or internationally, as information about clashing values becomes more widespread it can deepen divides between, and strengthen the cohesiveness of, in- and out-groups. It can create intolerance for others and for their way of life. Clashes may remain rhetorical or escalate to violence, depending on the nature of the clash, values about how best to resolve conflicts, and the costs of war. The idea that more information about others can highlight clashing values casts doubt on optimistic assessments that more knowledge of others will lead to peace and tolerance. Though that may indeed occur if transparency shows shared values, evidence of clashing values may have the opposite effect.

Winners and Losers in the Age of Transparency

Greater transparency decentralizes control over information, which empowers nongovernmental organizations and helps them reach mass publics with their message. Governments retain substantial power, but NGOs of all varieties—as well as individuals—are significantly more influential than in the past. With governments' monopoly on controls of information broken, such groups have more access to information, more ability to share that information with others, and more ability to spread their own views and values. That power can help individuals to join together, overthrow their governments, or lobby groups outside their countries to pressure their governments to change.

Most analysts of this trend treat the decentralization of information as positive, without acknowledging underlying assumptions about who will benefit from increased transparency and the goals of those beneficiaries. Often, the winners will indeed be "good guys"—citizens and NGOs that advocate noble causes, fight oppression, and shine a spotlight on wrongdoing or abuses of power.[20] But that will not always be the case. Transparency decentralizes power indiscriminately and we should not make assumptions about the implications of greater transparency without considering the nature of groups that it empowers.[21] Those seeking to overthrow secular democratic governments or foment ethnic conflict benefit, as well as those seeking to overthrow dictatorships. Terrorist networks gain as well as advocates of environmental protection. Whether greater transparency will be negative or positive, therefore, depends on the identities of the winners and the nature of their goals.

Most observers view the weakness of states vis-à-vis governments as not only desirable but also inevitable. Yet the implications of greater transparency are more complex than this characterization suggests. The trend toward greater transparency both strengthens and weakens states—and it does not only strengthen democracies and weaken dictatorships. Indeed, by increasing the ability of governments to monitor their people and by giving them new tools to spread their message, greater transparency can strengthen authoritarian and especially semi-authoritarian regimes. When transparency weakens states, we should not assume that there is only one outcome, namely, the fall of repressive governments and the rise of democracies. Sometimes, weak regimes get weaker but persist to the benefit of criminals and warlords.

The city-state of Singapore provides an example of how governments can manage a system of limited transparency successfully and de-link access to information from the power to promote political change. Transparency undermines the legitimacy of governments if it exposes gaps between rhetoric and reality, widely held values, and the actions of government. In Singapore, however, transparency generally shows citizens that their government is performing effectively and acting in-line with the values held by the society. The government has persuaded Singaporeans that controls over political dissent and assembly are necessary in order to protect their security in a dangerous region and their domestic stability in a multi-ethnic society. Consequently, limited transparency and access to information are not politically damaging since they currently expose no gap that will serve as the basis of a more powerful political opposition. If the values held by Singaporeans and their government diverge, however, transparency may no longer legitimize the illiberal regime.

To the extent that greater transparency strengthens states, it tends to strengthen the strongest states of all. Although greater transparency makes access to information easier and cheaper than ever, the ability to use that information effectively often requires significant resources. Governments, like most organizations, are bombarded by information. But wealthy governments have the resources to collect, analyze, and disseminate information to a degree that few corporations, NGOs, or individuals can replicate.[22] Customized software, elaborate databases, expensive computing equipment, attention-grabbing graphics, and huge staffs are luxuries that many NGOs, not to mention many governments, simply cannot afford. Powerful states can also deny access to information to others. For instance, the U.S. government if it sees fit, can jam radio broadcasts, destroy satellites, or simply exercise "checkbook shutter control" and purchase all satellite time over sensitive sites.[23]

What's Left of the Conventional Wisdom?

This book refutes common views regarding the trend toward greater transparency and illustrates that many hopes regarding transparency are either overly optimistic or ill-founded. This conclusion begs the following question; if greater transparency is not always good, are there still reasons to cheer it? The answer is yes, for four reasons.

First, transparency is morally right. Citizens deserve to know how their governments are spending their tax dollars, why they are sending their citizens to fight, and how well they are performing. Secrecy breeds abuses of power.

Second, many of the arguments refuted in this book may indeed be accurate under certain circumstances. Transparency *can* reinforce deterrence, prevent war, facilitate conflict resolution, encourage international cooperation, and help make the strong accountable to the weak. It can reinforce positive trends, disseminate friendly intentions, and spread new norms of behavior. Yet these outcomes will be reached only in certain cases and must be much more actively worked on than some advocates of transparency suggest. Greater transparency is no magic bullet.

Third, because a commitment to transparency itself is a value, deliberate acts of transparency sometimes are more revealing than the specific information they reveal. Intentional acts of openness can be a political signal about a government's stand on a particular issue (e.g. that it adheres to particular international agreements); its relationship with a particular country or group (e.g., that Slovenia is "European" and embraces the values of the European Union); or its general orientation toward the international community (e.g., that a country is part of the "West"). Intentional openness sends a message about what sorts of values a government embraces and who its friends are. At least in the current international environment, deliberate transparency is perceived as a signal of intentions, identity, and trust.[24] Governments, like individuals, are more open with friends and more secretive with those they doubt. Consequently, sharing information signals friendship and that a government has nothing to hide whereas secrecy signals distrust.[25] Deliberate acts by Libya to share information about its nuclear weapons program, for instance, sent a clear political signal about a change in policy and the regime's political orientation.

The very act of secrecy signals that a government has something to hide. Consider Iraq under Saddam Hussein in the early twenty-first century. The most sophisticated intelligence agencies in the world believed, apparently falsely, that Saddam possessed weapons of mass destruction. Due largely to Saddam's refusal to allow international inspections, they interpreted ambiguous pieces of evidence to support this hypothesis. In fact, Saddam seems to have been hiding the fact that he did not have weapons of mass destruction, but his secretive instincts themselves led others to draw conclusions about Saddam's intentions and capabilities.[26]

Though this discussion concerns voluntary, deliberate acts of transparency, transparency is not always deliberate. Much of the global transparency in the world comes from the cumulative effects of small decisions—by individuals, by opposition parties, by NGOs, or by individual media or information technology companies—and those acts may occur against the will (and outside the control) of many governments. Will involuntary transparency have the same effects as the careful and deliberate acts of transparency that are intended to signal political intent? With all likelihood the answer is no. Involuntary transparency can be highly useful for revealing injustice or corruption and for holding powerful organizations accountable. However, it is not likely that it will demonstrate reliably the sorts of peaceful intentions, tolerance of others, and shared interests that make deliberate acts of transparency such a promising foundation for future cooperation and peace. Involuntary transparency is more likely to produce the negative scenarios discussed throughout this book.

Fourth, transparency helps publics to hold authorities accountable for their actions and discourages corruption and other illegal activities. In 2003, for instance, the United Kingdom launched the Extractive Industries Transparency Initiative, which requests voluntary publication of revenue data by governments and corporations. The hope is that publication of such data will prevent corrupt officials from selling the natural resources of developing countries and diverting the profits away from citizens in need. Though this initiative has met with limited success so far, there is no good argument against such initiatives. Citizens are robbed when officials exploit national resources to line their own pockets and deserve access to such information.[27] To give another example, video records of the murder of Bosnian Muslims by a Serbian paramilitary force in Srebrenica, a small part of a massacre that claimed the lives of seven thousand Muslim men and boys, will keep government officials from denying that such killings occurred and perhaps help to bring the perpetrators of that violence to justice.[28] And, surveillance footage helped British police to quickly identify the suicide bombers in the July 2005 attacks on the London transit system. Unfortunately, transparency tends to be more useful for punishing crimes after the fact, rather than preventing them in the first place.

Diplomacy in an Age of Transparency

Transparency complicates diplomacy. Governments once had more control over what information was available to the public and derived influence from that control. Now governments must compete with more and more independent sources of information and are less in control of their message. Saying different things to domestic and international audiences undetected is becoming harder as news organizations, NGOs, and individuals disseminate that information worldwide. People around the globe are better able to identify policies they do not like, share their outrage with others, and organize political opposition or violence. Hypocrisy, saying one thing and doing another, can not only be detected, but also publicized and used by political opponents to mobilize support.

Though governments must now compete with other sources of information, they retain substantial influence in the age of transparency. Governments still typically have the most resources within their countries and, through their embassies, they maintain a local presence in most foreign countries of the world. Governments retain a natural link to the media and are able to marshal attention far more than other groups, even though they cannot control this attention completely. As other types of organizations, all clamoring for a voice, proliferate in societies, there is still only one government. Governments can "set the agenda" and influence what issues people think are important. They can frame information so that people are more likely to interpret it in a desired way.[29] Finally, especially in democracies, governments can claim to speak for the people in a way that no other organization can. They therefore have a platform and a legitimacy that no other organization can match.

Despite these sources of strength, governments must work harder to explain and justify their policies to foreign governments and to their citizens. In the past, governments focused on disseminating information through press releases, interviews with foreign media, and speeches. Now, governments wishing to convey their message successfully must also focus on convincing others to seek out certain information sources, persuading others to view information differently, creating a climate of trust and goodwill in which others interpret information, and trying to influence what sorts of reactions people will find acceptable. To do this effectively they must not only take advantage of their unprecedented ability to reach foreign publics directly, but also use their unprecedented ability to listen to what average citizens are thinking. More than ever before, they must win hearts and minds through the power of persuasion.[30]

Why should governments care how they are perceived and spend resources trying to convince others they are justified? Governments, particularly democracies, are obligated to protect the interests of their own citizens. If they do that, popularity contests held by foreigners are irrelevant. Nonetheless, negative perceptions by foreigners can threaten real national interests and empower enemies. How a government or a nation is perceived by others, affects significantly whether their actions will be considered threatening or not and, as a result, how others will react. How a people are perceived affects whether others will attack or cooperate with them. The ability to influence how information is interpreted and the norms others hold, is an important element of power.

The act of informing, engaging, and persuading foreign publics (as opposed to traditional methods of diplomacy that target government officials) is known as public diplomacy and it is critically important in an age of transparency. In an age of clamoring voices accessible via a range of different information technologies, governments must define their message or others will do so for them. If the image of a country becomes negative, foreign publics may object to cooperating with that country, even when that country is an ally, as the Turkish population did when it prevented its government from assisting the 2003 American invasion of Iraq. They may reject policies regardless of their content. They may distrust information, even if it is true, because of the messenger. As publics gain more power vis-à-vis their governments, negative images held by publics will increasingly constrain leaders.

The analysis in this book suggests several rules for public diplomacy. First, governments must be credible sources of information, interpreting and explaining their policies to their foreign publics lest others do that for them. In the marketplace of ideas, they need to articulate their position effectively. Second, public diplomacy must try to influence where people get their information. If governments broadcast their views on the radio, but most people get their information from television, their efforts to sway opinion will fail. Third, public diplomacy must find credible messengers. If a government is not deemed trustworthy, they must find messengers who are. Fourth, governments must try to persuade, to marshal evidence in order to influence opinion. Fifth, governments can listen to others so they understand objections to policies and present policies in a way that is sensitive to others, even if the content of the policy remains the same.[31] Sixth, governments can foster trust, respect, and a climate of goodwill in which information is interpreted. They can provide humanizing information about their people and ideas to encourage empathy. Finally, even if there is disagreement about particular policies, they can highlight what values and interests they do share in common and encourage foreigners to see disagreements in the context of a larger and more complex relationship. Importantly, in an age of transparency, such relationships cannot be built on a lie. Foreign governments and publics will know if rhetoric and action do not match or if there is a fundamental clash of interests. Kind words alone are insufficient to improving relationships.

Governments must also carefully match statements, actions, and policies. In an age when every act or word may be scrutinized and weighed for consistency, discrepancies between action and stated intent, and reality and rhetoric, create distrust. Governments can lose credibility quickly when hypocrisy is readily detectable. As discussed throughout this book, losing credibility means that others will interpret a government's acts in a negative light and distrust even accurate information about policies and intentions. When a government loses credibility, others will no longer turn to it for information in which case the government will lose a valuable platform to influence the ideas and values of others.

Other Policy Implications

This book suggests other lessons for policymakers as well. In the area of arms control, it suggests that voluntary disclosure of data regarding military balances can send signals regarding intent. However, it also suggests that policy makers should place little faith in transparency regimes alone as a way of constraining state behavior. In the area of conflict resolution,

Table 6.1. Diplomacy in the Age of Transparency

Rules of Engagement

1. Assume that whatever you say and do will become public, everywhere.

2. Recognize that hypocrisy undermines credibility and losing credibility has a cost.

3. Expect others to notice inconsistencies—and to use them to their advantage.

4. Don't let others define your message.

5. Find credible messengers.

6. Talk to publics not just elites.

7. Create a climate of trust and goodwill.

8. Find and highlight common values.

9. To understand the views of others, analyze where they get their information and the roots of their values.

it suggests that international organizations and third parties should not press transparency measures on conflict participants unless those participants are truly committed to ending their dispute. In postconflict scenarios, it suggests following the model of Cambodia and creating the infrastructure for a truly balanced marketplace of ideas in which pluralistic opinions are granted equal time and majorities respect minorities. It underscores the importance of a transparent and enforced set of laws. The book suggests that governments can convince publics to intervene in foreign conflicts but also that leaders should expect constraints if intervention does not go well. Finally, it suggests that transparency alone will not lead to democracy. Consequently, governments interested in democratization around the world must look for other benchmarks of democracy—such as political participation, the protection of civil rights, and opportunities for dissent—beyond openness.

Conclusion

Greater transparency is not an antidote to the world's problems. Unfortunately, greater transparency will not lead inevitably to greater peace, cooperation, tolerance, and democracy. It may support those goals in many circumstances, but it sometimes will undermine them as well. Transparency is a complex phenomenon with effects that are both good and bad.

To the extent that the international community values peace and democracy, it must work toward those goals in the context of greater transparency. Those efforts will be difficult, but transparency can facilitate virtuous circles if governments and their citizens work to start them. Coping with the implications of greater transparency is likely to be more difficult in the short term as governments, transnational organizations, and citizens adjust to what is a profound change in the international system. Over time, people will find new ways of coping with the volumes of information produced by transparency, the speed of change it encourages, and the political implications of decentralized information. But, especially in the short term, greater transparency may lead to errors, misunderstandings, and conflicts. Governments must manage those risks in the short term and develop new strategies, tactics, and institutions for managing those risks in the long term.

To cope with transparency effectively, leaders must change the way in which they think about information and its influence on politics. Governments still have significant power to influence what greater transparency will reveal, even if that power is not absolute. That power presents an opportunity for governments to influence how they are perceived and to strengthen their relationships with other societies. Leaders must learn to recognize transparency's effects and integrate that understanding into policymaking and analysis. They must also learn how to conduct more effective public diplomacy, not only to explain policies better to foreign audiences, but also to create a climate in which information is interpreted in a more positive light.

Keeping information from the public is often morally unacceptable and, in the medium- to long-term, unwise for those who seek good governance. Secrecy, particularly in democracies, is destructive.[32] It hides abuses of power, robs citizens of their chance to have a voice in governance, and prevents policymakers from having to defend their policies. It shields policy makers from other, potentially more valid, points of view and allows those in power to get away with acts of injustice. It prevents citizens from punishing their leaders for decisions they don't like. During the spring of 2004, the newspapers were full of photos capturing the abuse of Iraqi prisoners at the hands of American soldiers. They, and the values they reflect, are abhorrent. They are also a reminder that even a great democracy like the United States is not immune to abuses of power and that secrecy allows such abuses to continue. Power can corrupt even the well intentioned and, for that reason, the powerful require scrutiny, and the most powerful require the most scrutiny of all.

The 2004 Abu Ghraib prison scandal is an endorsement of transparency. Without publicized inquiries by NGOs like the International Committee of the Red Cross, the media, and Congress, these or similar abuses could have persisted. Without transparency, the executive branch would not need to defend its policies and the nation would not be having a public debate about the proper treatment of prisoners in times of war. Greater transparency also meant that citizens worldwide viewed, and were horrified by, the photos of abuse at Abu Ghraib. Some will translate their disgust into anti-Americanism, which will make American objectives harder to attain. That is a price that the United States must pay for the illumination of acts that violated our most cherished values. Transparency is worth that price.

Greater transparency may not provide easy solutions to persistent global problems of conflict, hate, and political oppression, but as a principle of governance it is both just and morally right. Though transparency is a condition of relative openness that governments can control only partially, a *commitment* to transparency is a value, and governments worldwide should embrace it. Transparency ensures that abuses of power will be discovered, that those with peaceful intentions will be recognized, that fruitful efforts at cooperation may be realized, that positive ideas and values may spread, and that oppressive governments cannot derive their power from a lie. Consequently, we should advocate transparency even as we protect against its more negative effects. Transparency holds perils, but also promise.

Notes

Chapter 1

1. Jamie Metzl, "The International Politics of Openness," *Washington Quarterly* (Summer 1999), p. 11. Microsoft CEO Bill Gates echoed this statement: "Keeping information out of a country is getting harder and harder." See Gates, *The Road Ahead,* 2d ed. (London: Penguin, 1996), p. 310.

2. Christopher Dunkley, "Far Too Much Information," *Financial Times* (November 7, 2001), p. 18.

3. China had more than 3,000 reported cases of SARS, more than any other country. "China to Be transparent, Honest in Reporting of any SARS Cases—Minister, AFX News (April 23, 2004). See also, "China Lags in Sharing SARS Clues, Officials Say," *New York Times* (August 5, 2003), p. F1.

4. "New Media Mobilizing China's Masses," *BBC Monitoring Asia Pacific* (June 28, 2005). Lara Wozniak, "Rumour Mills," *Far Eastern Economic Review* (April 23, 2003), p. 29. It is worth noting that ridiculous cures for the disease spread just as quickly. Text messages and the Internet remained important sources of news throughout the crisis. One search engine reported that SARS was the most popular search string, generating 30,000 entries per day and news about personal experiences with SARS was reported in blogs. Michael Jen-Siu, "Net Used to Spread News on Virus," *South China Morning Post* (May 20, 2003), p. 7; and Henry L. Davis, "Blogs Offer Personal Accounts of Life with SARS," *Buffalo News* (May 19, 2003), p. H1.

5. The government fired high-level officials for not fighting the disease more effectively and for allowing the media to cover the SARS crisis. John Pomfret, "China Broadens Effort against SARS," *Washington Post* (April 28, 2003), p. A1. See also, "China Finds it Difficult to Hide Big News Like SARS," *Pittsburgh Post-Gazette* (April 27, 2003), p. A4.

6. Later, when China accurately reported that the number of SARS cases was declining, the WHO gave those statements credibility by confirming that China's estimates seemed accurate. "Kathy Chien, "China Is as Good at Fighting SARS as at Hiding It," *Wall Street Journal* (June 4, 2003).

7. Henry Hoenig, "China Turns on those Who Spread the News of SARS," *Pittsburgh Post-Gazette* (June 29, 2003), p. A10. After the crisis ended, the Chinese government ultimately arrested numerous individuals who spread

news about the SARS virus and cracked down on certain media outlets. See John Pomfret, "China Closes Beijing Newspaper in Media Crackdown," *Washington Post* (June 19, 2003).

8. Pamela Hess, "Cause and Effect—Another look at Newsweek," *UPI* (May 16, 2005).

9. Katharine Q. Seelye and Neil A. Lewis, "Newsweek Says it Is Retracting Koran Report," *New York Times* (May 17, 2005), p. A1.

10. Incidents of desecration of the Koran have been reported by the *Washington Post*, the *Guardian*, MSNBC, *Al Jazeera*, the *Daily Mirror*, the *New York Times*, BBC, Reuters, and *Harper's* between March 2003 and May 2005. Whether the single incident involving a toilet actually took place remains unproven. For a discussion, see James C. Goodale, "Communications and Media Law: Newsweek and CBS Got It Basically Right," *New York Law Journal* (June 3, 2005), p. 3.

11. Mary Graham, "Regulation by Shaming," *Atlantic Monthly* (April 2000), p. 36.

12. The implications of the "age of transparency" are apparently a subject with global appeal. See, for example, Uwe Buse, "Der wahre Big Brother," *Der Spiegel* (January 30, 2001).

13. Some commentators noted how far the United States went out of its way to protect the Koran. See, for instance, John Hinderaker, "Study in Abuse: The Media Ignores the Facts about the Koran Abuse and Piles on the Army," *Weekly Standard* (June 6, 2005). See www.weeklystandard.com/Iutilities/printer_preveiw.asp?idArticle =5698&R=C5B114. Accessed June 9, 2005.

14. See "Freedom in the World" (Washington, DC: Freedom House, 2004), available at http://www.freedomhouse.org/research/survey2004.htm. Note that not all democracies have equivalent levels of freedom.

15. See Bernard I. Finel and Kristin M. Lord, eds. *Power and Conflict in the Age of Transparency* (New York: St. Martin's Palgrave Macmillan, 2000). This definition is similar to that offered by Antonia Handler Chayes and Abram Chayes in their work on international regimes. "Transparency is the availability and accessibility of knowledge and information" regarding international regimes, their policies, and the activities of their parties. See Chayes and Chayes, "Regimes Architecture: Elements and Principles," in Janne E. Nolan, ed., *Global Engagement: Cooperation and Security in the 21st Century* (Washington, DC: Brookings, 1994), p. 81.

16. It is worth noting that the term *transparency* comes loaded with normative baggage. Like *security*, it is hard to be against transparency. Who is in favor of concealment or censorship?

17. For a discussion, see Alexandru Grigorescu, "International Organizations and Government Transparency," *International Studies Quarterly* (December 2003).

18. See "Democracy's Century: A Survey of Global Political Change in the 20th Century" (Washington, DC: Freedom House, 1999), available at www.freedomhouse.org/reports/century.htm.

19. Quoted in Mirslav Nincic, *Democracy and Foreign Policy: The Fallacy of Political Realism* (New York: Columbia University Press, 1992), p. 129.

20. For a discussion, see Ann Florini, ed., *The Third Force* (Washington, DC: Carnegie Endowment for International Peace, 2000), pp. 19–20.

21. On the institutional pressures for democracies to reveal information through elections, see Anthony Downs, *An Economic Theory of Democracy* (New York: Harper, 1957); and Kenneth A. Shepsle and Barry R. Weingast, eds., *Positive Theories of Congressional Institutions* (Ann Arbor: University of Michigan Press, 1995).

22. Wendy J. Williams, "The CNN Effect: The First 24-Hour News Channel Has Reshaped the TV Landscape," *Boston Herald* (May 28, 2000), p. 6.

23. For a critical review of the CNN Effect, see Steven Livingston and Todd Eachus, "Humanitarian Crises and U.S. Foreign Policy: Somalia and the CNN Effect Reconsidered," *Political Communications* 12 (1995); and Jonathan Mermin, "Television News and American Intervention in Somalia: The Myth of a Media-Driven Foreign Policy," *Political Sciences Quarterly* 112:3 (1997).

24. Quoted in Williams, "CNN Effect," p. 6.

25. See interviews with government officials in Warren P. Strobel, "The CNN Effect," *American Journalism Review* (May 1996).

26. Quoted in Florini, *Third Force*. See also, Margaret E. Keck and Kathryn Sikkink, *Activists beyond Borders* (Ithaca: Cornell University Press, 1998).

27. An excellent example is the Human Rights Watch report, "Massacres of Hazaras in Afghanistan" (February 19, 2001).

28. On the pipeline deal, see Douglas Farah and David B. Ottaway, "Watchdog Groups Rein in Government in Chad Oil Deal," *Washington Post* (January 4, 2001), p. A14.

29. International organizations and regimes monitor compliance with international agreements. When monitoring compliance, these regimes identify cheaters publicly and sometimes even punish them. Even when the regimes cannot punish cheaters, governments that violate disclosure requirements can come under fire from other governments as well as from interest groups domestically and around the world. See Chayes and Chayes, "Regimes Architecture," in *Global Engagement*, p. 83.

30. To give another example, in the Strategic Arms Limitations Treaty (SALT II), the United States and the former Soviet Union were required to self-report the number of strategic weapons each party deployed in categories covered by the proposed treaty. When the Soviet negotiator complied, he remarked,

"You realize, you have just repealed 900 years of Russian history." Quoted in ibid, p. 84.

31. See Alexandru Grigorescu, "Transferring Transparency: The Impact of European Institutions on East and Central Europe," in R. Linden, ed., *Norms and Nannies: The Impact of International Organizations on the Central and East European States* (Boulder: Rowman and Littlefield, 2002).

32. See http://global-reach.biz/globstats/.

33. Computer Industry Almanac, www.c-i-a.com.

34. Ibid.

35. Florini, *Third Force*, p. 21.

36. "World Development Indicators 2000" (Washington, DC: World Bank, 2000). Data on radio penetration is compiled by UNESCO. Data on television penetration is compiled by the International Telecommunication Union.

37. "Global Mobile Markets," report by the high-tech research firm, Ovum. Excerpts available at www.ovum.com.

38. "Space Imaging Awarded License to Provide Half-Meter Resolution Commercial Satellite Imagery." News release from Space Imaging, Denver (January 19, 2001).

39. Thomas Friedman, *The Lexus and the Olive Tree* (New York: Farrar, 1999).

40. Florini, "The End of Secrecy," in *Power and Conflict in the Age of Transparency*, p. 52.

41. Press Conference, President George W. Bush, April 13, 2004. Accessed April 14, 2004 on www.washingtonpost.com/wp-dyn/articles/A9488-2004Apr13_2.html.

42. Dennis F. Thompson, "Democratic Secrecy," *Political Science Quarterly* 114. 2 (Summer 1999), p. 181.

43. Daniel G. Dupont and Richard Lardner, "The Culture of Secrecy," *Government Executive* (June 1995), p. 36. See also, "Report of the Commission on Protecting and Reducing Government Secrecy," Senate Document 105-2, 103rd Cong. (Washington, DC, 1997), p. 58. Note that the figures regarding employees do not include the intelligence agencies because those numbers are classified. A 1994 survey sponsored by the U.S. Defense Department indicated that a majority of Americans think that the government keeps too much information secret. "Public Attitudes Towards Security and Counter-Espionage Matters in the Post Cold War Period," Department of Defense Personnel Security Research Center (Monterey: November 1994). Analysts familiar with the Freedom of Information Act (FOIA) call the act "profoundly dysfunctional"—offices are understaffed and underfunded, there are often delays, and agencies regularly wield nine exemptions (e.g., for law enforcement, and to protect national defense and foreign policy). Kate Doyle, "The End of Secrecy: U.S.

National Security and the Imperative for Openness," *World Policy Journal* (Spring 1999), p. 35.

44. For examples, see Glasgow University Media Group, *War and Peace News* (Milton Keynes, PA: Open University Press, 1985); Susan L. Carruthers, *The Media at War: Communication and Conflict in the Twentieth Century* (New York: St. Martin's, 2000); and Haynes Johnson, "The Irreconcilable Conflict between Press and Government: Whose Side Are You On?" in Thomas M. Franck and Edward Weisband, *Secrecy and Foreign Policy* (New York: Oxford University Press, 1974), p. 165.

45. Clifford Bob, "Merchants of Morality," *Foreign Policy* (March/April 2002), pp. 1–2.

46. Darin Barney, *Prometheus Wired: The Hope for Democracy in the Age of Network Technology* (Chicago: University of Chicago Press, 2000), p. 58.

47. Analysis of Iraqi intentions differed within the intelligence and diplomatic communities.

> Even the Kuwaitis at first believed Hussein was merely bluffing to gain economic concessions. Analysts tracking the situation within both the Central Intelligence Agency (CIA) and the Defense Intelligence Agency (DIA) eventually concluded (by July 25 and July 30 respectively) that Iraq intended to invade Kuwait. Even at this late date, however, high-ranking officials in the intelligence and military communities remained skeptical of the invasion analysis, believing instead that Iraq was likely to make only a limited border crossing.

Alexander L. George and Jane E. Holl, "The Warning-Response Problem and Missed Opportunities in Preventive Diplomacy," in Bruce W. Jentleson, ed., *Opportunities Missed, Opportunities Seized: Preventive Diplomacy in the Post-Cold War World* (New York: Carnegie Commission on Preventing Deadly Conflict, 2000), p. 27.

48. See Herbert A. Simon, "Information 101: It's Not What You Know, It's How You Know It," *Journal for Quality and Participation* (July/August 1998).

49. Alexander L. George and Jane E. Holl, "The Warning-Response Problem and Missed Opportunities in Preventive Diplomacy," in *Opportunities Missed*, p. 24.

50. Ibid., pp. 23–24.

51. See Colin Kahl, "Constructing a Separate Peace: Constructivism, Collective Liberal Identity, and the Democratic Peace," *Security Studies* 8:2 (Fall 1998).

52. Ted Hopf, "The Promise of Constructivism in International Relations Theory," *International Security* 23: 1 (Summer 1998), p. 178.

53. Benjamin Frankel, "Notes on the Nuclear Underworld," *National Interest* (Fall 1987), p. 124.

54. My thanks to Marty Finnemore for her thoughts on this point.

55. Our discussion bears on numerous policy questions as well. How effective should we expect formal transparency regimes, such as arms registers, to be? Should governments and international organizations actively promote transparency in conflict zones? Should governments promote transparency as a means to bring down oppressive governments?

56. Transparency can also prevent conflict by keeping efforts at cooperation from breaking down. Robert Jervis, "From Balance to Concert: A Study of International Security Cooperation," in Kenneth A. Oye, ed., *Cooperation under Anarchy* (Princeton: Princeton University Press, 1986).

57. In his classic study of the causes of war, the historian Geoffrey Blainey argues that wars occur most often when states disagree about their relative power. To the extent that transparency illuminates relative capabilities, it might be expected to prevent this sort of war. See Blainey, *The Causes of War*, 3d ed. (New York: Free Press 1988), p. 293.

58. This phenomenon is also known as the "spiral model" because it leads other states to take similar defensive steps and can spiral into an arms race, conflict, or even war. The concept of the security dilemma is usually credited to Robert Jervis, "Cooperation under the Security Dilemma," *World Politics* 30:2 (January 1978), but also is attributed to John H. Herz, *Political Realism and Political Idealism: A Study in Theories and Realities* (Chicago: Chicago University Press, 1951); Herz, "Idealist Internationalism and the Security Dilemma," *World Politics* 2 (January 1950); Herbert Butterfield, *History and Human Relations* (London: Collins, 1951); and Thucydides, *The Peloponnesian War* (New York: Random, 1982). For a more recent discussion of the security dilemma's role in international politics, see Charles L. Glaser, "The Security Dilemma Revisited," *World Politics* 50 (October 1997).

59. See Michael Spiertas, "A House Divided: Tragedy and Evil in Realist Theory," *Security Studies* 5:3 (Spring 1996). See also Jervis, *Perception and Misperception in International Politics* (Princeton: Princeton University Press, 1976), p. 64.

60. This view can be observed in the literature on cooperative and defensive security, the offense/defense balance, reassurance, and confidence- and security-building measures. On cooperative and defensive security, see Janne E. Nolan, ed., *Global Engagement*; on reassurance, see Andrew Kydd, "Sheep in Sheep's Clothing: Why Security Seekers Do Not Fight Each Other," *Security Studies* 7:1 (Autumn 1997); and Kydd, "Trust, Reassurance and Cooperation."

61. See Michael Dertouzos, *What Will Be: How the New World of Information Will Change our Lives* (New York: HarperCollins, 1997), p. 218. Similarly, Nicholas Negroponte argues, "Digital technology can be a natural force drawing people into greater world harmony." See Negroponte, *Being Digital* (New York: Vintage Books, 1995), p. 230.

62. An extreme example of how media broadcasts are used to prepare a society for genocide is this statement from Rwandan radio: "[The Tutsi] cruelly

kill mankind...they kill by dissecting Hutus...by extracting the various organs from the bodies of Hutus...for example, by taking the heart, the liver, the stomach...the [Tutsi] eat men." Broadcast on Radio-Television Libre des Mille Collines. Quoted in Neil Munro, "Inducting Information," *National Journal* (March 27, 1999). This sort of propaganda is deemed so necessary to the success of ethnic cleansing campaigns that the (now defunct) United States Information Agency implemented procedures for countering hate propaganda around the world.

63. See Douglas A. Van Belle, *Press Freedom and Global Politics* (Westport, CT: Praeger, 2000); Van Belle, "Press Freedom and Peace," in *Power and Conflict in the Age of Transparency*; Rafael Moses, "On Dehumanizing the Enemy," in Vamik Volkan, Demetrious Julius, and Joseph Montville, eds., *The Psychodynamics of International Relationships,* Vol. 1, *Concepts and Theories* (Lexington, MA: Lexington Books, 1991); and Eric Staub, "The Evolution of Bystanders: German Psychoanalysts and Lessons for Today," *Political Psychology* 10 (1989).

64. See Susan L. Woodward, *Balkan Tragedy: Chaos and Dissolution after the Cold War* (Washington, DC: Brookings, 1995); and John Mueller, "The Banality of Ethnic War," *International Security* 25:1 (Summer 2000).

65. The idea that control over information is necessary to prop up dictatorships is very popular. See, for example, Blaine Harden, "How to Commit the Perfect Dictatorship," *New York Times* (November 26, 2000).

66. See Walter Wriston, "Bits, Bytes, and Diplomacy," *Foreign Affairs* (September/October 1997).

67. Ibid.

68. Elizabeth Rosenthal, "Web Sites Bloom in China, and Are Weeded," *New York Times* (December 23, 1999), p. A1.

69. Speech by William J. Clinton, May 2000. David E. Sanger, "Yes, Trade Brings Freedom. Except When It Doesn't," *New York Times* (May 28, 2000), p. D4.

70. For a discussion of assumptions that there is an underlying harmony of interests among nations, see Jonathan Mercer, "Anarchy and Identity," *International Organization* (Spring 1995), p. 235. See also Kenneth N. Waltz, *Man, The State, and War* (New York: Columbia University Press, 1954). As Edward Hallett Carr writes, "To make the harmonization of interests the goal of political action is not the same thing as to postulate that a natural harmony of interests exists." See Carr, *The Twenty Years' Crisis*, 2d ed. (New York: Harper Torchbooks, 1946), p. 51.

71. An irreconcilable clash of values and interests led to the Civil War, which President Abraham Lincoln eloquently captured in his second inaugural address. In Lincoln's words, "Both parties deprecated war, but one of them would *make* war rather than let the nation survive, and the other would *accept*

war rather than let it perish, and the war came." No amount of transparency could have resolved this fundamental disagreement. See Lincoln, "Second Inaugural Address" (March 4, 1865).

72. Ann Florini, *The Coming Democracy: New Rules for Running a New World* (Washington, DC: United States Island Press, 2003), p. 32: "Transparency means deliberately revealing one's actions so that outsiders can scrutinize them."

73. See Joseph S. Nye Jr. *Soft Power: The Means to Success in World Politics* (New York: Public Affairs, 2004).

Chapter 2

1. Andrew Kydd, "Sheep in Sheep's Clothing: Why Security Seekers Do Not Fight Each Other," *Security Studies* 7:1 (Autumn 1997), pp. 125 and 119.

2. Quoted in Rob Stein, "Fear of the Unknown," *Washington Post* (June 9, 2003), p. A.8.

3. A state is defined as a political entity with sovereign authority over a space within geographically defined borders. A government is the law-making, judicial, administrative, and enforcement apparatus of a state. Definitions are based on definitions offered in Paul R. Viotti and Mark V. Kauppi, *International Relations Theory* (New York: Macmillan, 1987), pp. 591-598.

4. For a discussion of the international system as a self-help system, see Kenneth N. Waltz, *Theory of International Politics* (New York: McGraw-Hill, 1979), p. 111.

5. For a discussion of how the security dilemma operates in domestic ethnic conflicts, see Barry R. Posen, "The Security Dilemma and Ethnic Conflict," *Survival* 35:1 (Spring 1993).

6. Michael Spirtas, "A House Divided: Tragedy and Evil in Realist Theory," *Security Studies* 5:3 (Spring 1996).

7. Bruce Bueno de Mesquita and David Lalman, *War and Reason* (New Haven: Yale University Press, 1992).

8. According to the political scientist Jack Levy, the two forms of misperception most central to the study of war are misperceptions about capabilities and misperceptions about intentions. See Levy, "Misperception and the Causes of War: Theoretical Linkages and Analytical Problems," *World Politics* 36:76-99 (October 1983).

9. See Geoffrey Blainey, *The Causes of War* (New York: Free Press, 1973). See also, Richard Ned Lebow, *Between Peace and War* (Baltimore: Johns Hopkins, 1981). According to Levy, there are numerous examples of wars caused by the "erroneous expectation of victory." These include the Russo-Japanese War, World War I, Hitler's war against Russia, and the Korean War. See Levy, *Misperceptions and the Causes of War*, p. 84.

10. Caveats to this argument are discussed later in this chapter.

11. Blainey, *Causes of War*, p. 145.

12. See de Mesquita and Lalman, *War and Reason*, chap. 3; and Robert Powell, *In the Shadow of Power: States and Strategies in International Politics* (Princeton: Princeton University Press, 1999), chap. 3. For a discussion of the effects of private information on conflict, see James D. Fearon, "Rationalist Explanations for War," *International Organization* (Summer 1995). See also Fearon, "Bargaining, Enforcement, and International Cooperation," *International Organization* (Spring 1998); James D. Morrow, "Capabilities, Uncertainty and Resolve: A Limited Information Model of Crisis Bargain," *American Journal of Political Science* 33:4 (November 1989); and Kydd, "Sheep in Sheep's Clothing."

13. For a discussion of the role of information in determining the occurrence, fighting, and ending of wars, see R. Harrison Wagner, "Bargaining and War," *American Journal of Political Science* 44:3 (July 2000).

14. Powell, *In the Shadow of Power*, p. 83. Though this is a theoretical proposition, a world in which there is more information about government intentions and preferences should move reality closer to theory. It is not fair to criticize theories, which intentionally simplify reality in order to highlight key relationships, for failing to mirror that reality exactly. However, it is fair to expect that real outcomes will move toward predicted outcomes as real conditions move toward theorized conditions.

15. Kenneth A. Schultz, *Democracy and Coercive Diplomacy* (Cambridge, MA: Cambridge University Press, 2001), p. 4.

16. Kim Il-Sung made a similar mistake. Alexander L. George and Jane E. Holl argue that "the North Koreans acted as they did on the mistaken notion that the United States would not intervene militarily on behalf of South Korea. Thus, the Korean War, with all of its fateful consequences, qualifies as a genuine example of war-through-miscalculation. It was a war that might well have been avoided had Washington been more receptive to warning and acted on it." George and Holl, "The Warning-Response Problem and Missed Opportunities in Preventive Diplomacy," in Bruce W. Jentleson, ed., *Opportunities Missed, Opportunities Seized: Preventive Diplomacy in the Post-Cold War World* (New York: Carnegie Commission on the Preventing Deadly Conflict, 2000), p. 25. See also, Burton I. Kaufman, *The Korean War* (New York: Knopf, 1986), p. 33.

17. For a discussion of how fears of relative gains prevent cooperation even when cooperation would benefit all parties to an agreement, see Joseph M. Grieco, "Anarchy and the Limits of Cooperation: A Realist Critique of the Newest Liberal Institutionalism," in David A. Baldwin, ed., *Neorealism and Neoliberalism: The Contemporary Debate* (New York: Columbia University Press, 1993).

18. A good example of a collective action problem is proposals to place embargoes on exporters of small arms. With more than sixty states known to

manufacture small arms that must agree, and heavy pressure for overseas sales, the incentive to cheat is high—especially if violators are not detected. For a discussion, see Joanna Spear, "Arms Limitations, Confidence-Building Measures, and Internal Conflict," in Michael E. Brown, ed., *The International Dimensions of Internal Conflict* (Cambridge: MIT Press, 1996).

19. See Kenneth A. Oye, ed., *Cooperation under Anarchy* (Princeton: Princeton University Press, 1986). See also, John Steinbruner, "Renovating Arms Control through Reassurance," *Washington Quarterly* (Spring 2000), p. 200. For a good summary of this perspective, see Ted Hopf, "The Promise of Constructivism in International Relations Theory," *International Security* 23:1 (Summer 1998), p. 190. For elaboration on market failure logic, see Robert Keohane, *After Hegemony: Cooperation and Discord in the World Political Economy* (Princeton: Princeton University Press, 1984); and Mancur Olsen, *Logic of Collective Action: Public Goods and the Theory of Groups* (Cambridge: Harvard University Press, 1971). For a critique of that logic, see Stephen Krasner, *International Regimes* (Ithaca: Cornell University Press, 1983).

20. Antonia Handler Chayes and Abram Chayes, "The UN Register, Transparency, and Cooperative Security," in Malcolm Chalmers, Mitsuro Donowaki, and Owen Greene, eds., *Developing Arms Transparency: The Future of the United Nations Register*, Bradford Arms Register Studies, no. 7 (University of Bradford and Center for the Promotion of Disarmament and Non-Proliferation, and Japan Institute for International Affairs, 1997), p. 207. See also, Elinor Ostrom, *Governing the Commons* (Cambridge, MA: Cambridge University Press); Thomas C. Schelling, *Strategy of Conflict* (Cambridge: Harvard University Press, 1960); and Robert O. Keohane, "Reciprocity in International Relations," *International Organization* 40:1 (Winter 1986). For a discussion of verification in arms control agreements, see Bhupendra Jasani and Frank Barnaby, *Verification Technologies: The Case for Surveillance by Consent* (Dover, NH: Berg Publishers, 1984).

21. Jonathan Alford, "The Usefulness and Limitations of CSBMs," in William Epstein and Bernard T. Feld, eds., *New Directions in Disarmament* (New York: Praeger, 1981), p. 135, quoted in Marie-France Desjardins, "Rethinking Confidence-Building Measures," *Adelphi Paper* 307 (London: Institute for International and Strategic Studies, 1996), p. 8.

22. See Schelling, *Strategy of Conflict*. A lack of transparency is one reason for the security dilemma. See Robert Axelrod, *Evolution of Cooperation* (New York: Basic, 1984); and Charles L. Glaser, "The Security Dilemma Revisited," *World Politics* 50 (October 1997).

23. Kydd, "Sheep in Sheep's Clothing," p. 125.

24. Kydd, "Trust, Reassurance, and Cooperation," *International Organization* 54:2 (Spring 2000), p. 325.

26. See also Kydd, "Sheep in Sheep's Clothing"; and Randall Schweller, "Neorealism's Status-Quo Bias: What Security Dilemma?" *Security Studies* 5 (Spring 1996).

25. Robert Jervis, "Cooperation under the Security Dilemma," *World Politics* 30:2 (January 1978), p. 126.

26. Societies that feel victimized sometimes behave in ways that others find hostile, even though that behavior arises from a sense of vulnerability rather than from aggression. Others may take steps to defend themselves, which then make the victimized society feel even less secure. Recognizing how others interpret behavior can help leaders avoid this trap. For a discussion applying this logic to China and Japan, see Thomas J. Christensen, "China, the US-Japan Alliance, and the Security Dilemma in East Asia," *International Security* (Spring 1992).

27. Nontransparent states can also break out of the security dilemma, but it is more difficult. To do so, they may either send "costly signals" or through a slower means, engage in an iterative process of negotiating concessions on both sides. Costly signals are actions taken by a government to send a credible message about its intentions even in an atmosphere of limited trust. They are intended to convince suspicious states that a government is trustworthy and to demonstrate its commitment to cooperation. Costly signals are most likely to be effective when the recipient understands that the message would be too costly in political or economic terms to send if it was not accurate. An example of a costly signal is Egyptian president Anwar Sadat's trip to Jerusalem in 1977. Because of the strong anti-Israeli sentiment among other Arab states in the region, Sadat's trip sent a very strong message that Egypt desired peace and helped pave the way for the Camp David Accords two years later. Nontransparent states may also break out of the security dilemma through a slow and iterative process of granting concessions to each other, with each concession building a bit more confidence between the parties. As confidence grows, parties can move on to more important issues.

28. Antonia Handler Chayes and Abram Chayes, "Regime Architecture: Elements and Principles," in Janne E. Nolan, ed., *Global Engagement: Cooperative Security in the 21st Century* (Washington, DC: Brookings, 1994), p. 65.

29. On structuring military capabilities to indicate defensive intent, see Catherine M. Kelleher, "Indicators of Defensive Intent in Conventional Force Structures and Operations in Europe," in Lawrence Freeman, ed., *Military Power in Europe* (New York: St. Martin's, 1990); Palme Commission, *Common Security: A Programme for Disarmament*, Report of the Independent Commission on Disarmament and Security Issues under the Chairmanship of Olof Palme (London: Pan Books, 1983); and Jonathan Dean, "Alternative Defense: Answer to NATO's Central Front Problems," *International Security* 54 (1988). See also, Jervis, "Arms Control, Stability and the Causes of War," *Political Science Quarterly* 108:2 (1993).

30. For discussions of the offense defense balance see Jervis, "Cooperation under the Security Dilemma;" George Quester, *Offense and Defense in the International System* (New York: Wiley 1977); Barry R. Posen, "The Security Dilemma and Ethnic Conflict," *Survival* 35:1 (Spring 1993); Sean

M. Lynn-Jones, "Offense-Defense Theory and Its Critics," *Security Studies* 4:4 (Summer 1995); Stephen Van Evera, *Causes of War* (New York: Cornell University Press, 1999); William Rose, "Ethnic Conflict and the Security Dilemma: Some New Hypotheses," *Security Studies* (Winter 2001); Ted Hopf, "Polarity, the Offense-Defense Balance, and War," *American Political Science Review* 85:2 (June 1991), pp. 475-493; and Charles L. Glaser, "Realists as Optimists: Cooperation as Self Help," *International Security* (Winter, 1994–1995), pp. 61–64.

31. In the literature on arms control, the idea of reconfiguring strategic doctrine and force posture to demonstrate defensive intentions has been called nonprovocative defense, nonoffensive defense, and defensive defense. For a discussion of the differences among these concepts, see Geoffrey Wiseman, "Common Security in the Asia-Pacific Region," *Pacific Review* 5:1 (April 1992), pp. 48-50. See also, Andrew Mack, "The Strategy of Non-Provocative Defence: The European Debate," in Desmond Ball and Cathy Downes, eds., *Security and Defence: Pacific and Global Perspectives* (Sydney: Allen and Unwin, 1990); Palme Commission, *Common Security*, and Barry Buzan, "Common Security, Non-Provocative Defence, and the Future of Western Europe," *Review of International Studies* 13:4 (October 1987). For examples of the literature on de-alerting, see Bruce G. Blair, "Lengthening the Fuse," *Brookings Review* (Summer 1995), and Blair, *The Logic of Accidental Nuclear War* (Washington, DC: Brookings, 1993).

32. See Kelleher, "Indicators of Defensive Intent in Conventional Force Structures and Operations in Europe," in *Military Power in Europe*, pp. 164–170.

33. Nolan, *Global Engagement*, p. 4.

34. Ibid.

35. For a discussion see Herbert Wulf, "The Register as an Instrument for Promoting Restraint and Preventing Conflict," in *Developing Arms Transparency*.

36. General Assembly Resolution 46/36L of 9 December 1991, "Transparency in Armaments."

37. Charles Lipson, *Reliable Partners: How Democracies Have Made a Separate Peace* (Princeton: Princeton University Press, 2003), p. 76.

38. Glaser, "The Security Dilemma Revisited," *World Politics* 50 (October 1997), pp. 192–193. See also, Schultz, *Democracy and Coercive Diplomacy*.

39. Shared values and interests also serve as a basis for cooperation between authoritarian states. See Martin Malin, "Is Autocracy an Obstacle to Peace? Iran and Iraq, 1975-1980," in Miriam Fendius Elman, ed., *Paths to Peace: Is Democracy the Answer?* (Cambridge: MIT Press, 1997).

40. For a related argument, see Randall Schweller, "Neorealism's Status-Quo Bias: What Security Dilemma?" *Security Studies* 5 (Spring 1996); and

"Bandwagoning for Profit: Bringing the Revisionist State Back In," *International Security* 19:1 (Summer 1994). Schweller rightly notes that not all states are interested in security alone. Governments are also motivated by desires for influence, power, wealth, territory, and so on. See also Paul Fisher, "Connected: War and Peace in a Wired World," *Daily Telegraph* (May 27, 1999), p. 8.

41. For the classical statement that war is a "continuation of policy by other means," see Carl Von Clausewitz, *On War* (London: Penguin, 1968).

42. Martha Finnemore, *National Interests in International Society* (Ithaca: Cornell University Press, 1996), p. 138.

43. See Ann Florini, "The End of Secrecy," in Bernard I. Finel and Kristin M. Lord, eds., *Power and Conflict in the Age of Transparency* (New York: St. Martin's Palgrave 2000).

44. Iraq, which the U.S. government actively supported for many years, is an example of how a regime can be considered a friend at one time and a foe later, even when the country's leadership stays the same.

45. John Mearsheimer, "The False Promise of International Institutions" *International Security* (Winter 1994–1995). For a discussion of the tragic nature of realist thought, see Michael Spirtas, "A House Divided: Tragedy and Evil in Realist Theory," *Security Studies* 5:3 (Spring 1996).

46. This view is ascribed to "classical" realists such as Hans Morgenthau. See Morgenthau, *Politics among Nations: The Struggle for Power and Peace*, 6th ed. (New York: Knopf, 1985).

47. Domestic politics gives leaders additional incentives to be suspicious and uncooperative in international affairs. To avoid perceptions of weakness or ineffectiveness, leaders may assume the worst when analyzing the behavior of other states, which further reinforces incentives to be suspicious and uncooperative. Under conditions of uncertainty, the political costs of guessing wrong may appear higher than the political rewards of guessing correctly. Politicians do not want to underestimate a threat only to look unprepared later, see their nation victimized by a foreign government due to insufficient capacity to respond, make a cooperative gesture that is not reciprocated, or comply with an international agreement and then find that others have cheated. Such risk aversion is particularly evident in democracies, where citizens can vote politicians out of office. However, authoritarian systems may also discourage political risk-taking.

48. Ernst B. Haas defines nationalism as a "doctrine of social solidarity based on the characteristics and symbols of nationhood." A nation is a "socially mobilized body of individuals who believe themselves united by some set of characteristics that differentiate them (in their own minds) from outsiders and who strive to create or maintain their own state." See Haas, *Nationalism, Liberalism and Progress: The Rise and Decline of Nationalism*, vol. 1. (Ithaca: Cornell University Press, 1997), p. 23.

49. See Immanuel Kant, *Perpetual Peace* (New York: Columbia University Press, 1939). For an excellent analysis of the democratic peace, see James Lee Ray, *Democracy and International Conflict: An Evaluation of the Democratic Peace Proposition* (Columbia: University of South Carolina Press, 1995).

50. John M. Owen, "How Liberalism Produces Democratic Peace," *International Security* (Fall 1994), p. 91.

51. See quote by Harry Harding, in Ezra Vogel, ed., *Living with China: US-China Relations in the Twenty-First Century* (New York: Norton, 1997), p. 176. See also, Edward Mansfield and Jack Snyder, "Democratization and the Danger of War," *International Security* 20 (Summer 1995); and Bruce Russet, *Controlling the Sword: The Democratic Governance of National Security* (Cambridge: Harvard University Press, 1990).

52. See P. Wright, *Conflict on the Nile: The Fashoda Incident of 1898* (London: Heinemann, 1972), pp. 44–45. Quoted in Darrell Bates, *The Fashoda Incident of 1898: Encounter on the Nile* (London: Oxford University Press 1984), p. 153). See T. W. Riker, "Survey of British Policy in the Fashoda Crisis," *Political Science Quarterly* 44:1 (1929), p. 66; R. G. Brown, *Fashoda Reconsidered: The Impact of Domestic Politics on French Policy in Africa 1893-1898* (Baltimore: Johns Hopkins, 1970), p. 112; and William F. Hoeft Jr. "Explaining the Interdemocratic Peace: The Norm of Cooperatively Biased Reciprocity" (Ph.D. diss., Georgetown University, May 18, 1993), pp. 312–322, and p. 396).

53. The effects of transparency also depend on the risk propensities of leaders. If leaders are more likely to accept risk, uncertainty can tempt them to gamble and risk provoking a conflict. If leaders are risk averse, uncertainty may encourage caution. For a discussion, see Paul Huth, D. Scott Bennett, and Christopher Gelpi, "System Uncertainty, Risk Propensity, and International Conflict among the Great Powers," *Journal of Conflict Resolution* 36:3 (September 1992), p. 488.

54. High levels of arms held by Taiwan, Saudi Arabia, and Iran have not led those countries to initiate war and may have deterred war in those regions. Jasjit Singh, "The UN Register: Transparency and the Promotion of Conflict Prevention and Restraint," in *Developing Arms Transparency*, p. 135. See also, F. S. Pearson and M. Brzoska, *Arms and Warfare: Escalation, Deescalation, Negotiation* (Columbia: University of South Carolina Press, 1994).

55. For an excellent discussion of the global implications of the rise and decline of state power, see Robert Gilpin, *War and Change in World Politics* (Cambridge, MA: Cambridge University Press, 1981).

56. Bueno de Mesquita and Lalman, *War and Reason*, p. 250.

57. Peter Duus, *The Rise of Modern Japan* (Boston: Houghton, 1976), p. 227. See also, W. G. Beasley, *The Rise of Modern Japan* (New York: St. Martin's, 1990); and Ronald Spector, *Eagle against the Sun* (New York: Free Press, 1985).

58. Another example of a war due to a closing window of opportunity is the Ogaden War of 1977–1978 in which the government of Somalia attacked Ethiopia when Somali leader Siad Barre perceived that Somalia's arms supply from the Soviet Union might be ending (Pearson and Brzoska, *Arms and Warfare*, p. 234). Given the prospect of losing Soviet support and realizing that giving up the Ogaden War would mean a popular uproar and possibly another coup at home, Barre saw his window of opportunity closing and launched a quick military action to recapture Ogaden and to present the world with a fait accompli. (For an overview of the Ogaden War, see Tom J. Farer, *War Clouds on the Horn of Africa* [New York: Carnegie Endowment for International Peace, 1979]; Bereket Selassie, *Conflict and Intervention in the Horn of Africa* [New York: Monthly Review Press, 1980]; James Dougherty, *The Horn of Africa: A Map of Political-Strategic Conflict* [Cambridge: Institute for Foreign Policy Analysis, 1982]; and Robert Patman, *The Soviet Union in the Horn of Africa* [Cambridge, MA: Cambridge University Press, 1990].

59. For a discussion, see David S. Geller and J. David Singer, *Nations at War: A Scientific Study of International Conflict* (Cambridge, MA: Cambridge University Press, 1998), pp. 68–76. See also, A. F. K. Organski and Jacek Kugler, *The War Ledger* (Chicago: University of Chicago Press, 1980); Robert Gilpin, *War and Change in World Politics* (Cambridge, MA: Cambridge University Press, 1981); and Dale Copeland, *The Origins of Major War* (New York: Cornell University Press, 2000). Organski and Kugler observe that a weaker state may attack at stronger state if the weaker state's power is rising.

60. Singh, "The UN Register," in *Developing Arms Transparency*, p. 136. The dangers of transparency in an atmosphere of mistrust were evident on the subcontinent again in 1986–1987 during the Brasstacks episode. India decided to unilaterally enhance transparency about a major military exercise, code-named Brasstacks, in western India. Such exercises had been held frequently in the past without Pakistan noticing. However, this newfound transparency alarmed Pakistan, which proceeded to mobilize its armor strike forces. The parties managed to resolve the crisis peacefully but the situation between these two rivals that had already fought three wars since independence was extremely dangerous.

61. For empirical evidence to this effect, see James H. Lebovic, "Open to Inspection: Democracies and Transparency in the Conventional Arms Trade" (paper).

62. Singh, "UN Register," in *Developing Arms Transparency*, p. 130.

63. J. David Singer, "System Structure, Decision Processes, and the Incidence of International War," in Manus I. Midlarsky, ed., *Handbook of War Studies* (Boston: Unwin Hyman, 1989), p. 6.

64. See Schelling, *Strategy of Conflict*.

65. For an overview of prospect theory, see Barbara Farnham, ed., *Avoiding Losses/Taking Risks: Prospect Theory and International Conflict* (Ann Arbor: University of Michigan Press, 1995).

66. Quoted from James A. Baker III, in Thomas M. Defrank, *The Politics of Diplomacy* (New York: Putnam, 1995), p. 359. William M. Arkin, "Calculated Ambiguity: Nuclear Weapons and the Gulf War," *Washington Quarterly* 96.4.1 (Fall 1996), p. 3.

67. Arkin, "Calculated Ambiguity," p. 5.

68. Kristin M. Lord and Bernard I. Finel, "Institutional Transparency and Conflict Strategies" (paper presented at the annual meeting of the International Studies Association, Chicago, IL. February 21-25, 1995).

69. David E. Sanger, "U.S. Warns North Korea against Nuclear Test," *New York Times* (May 7, 2005), p. A9.

70. On the trade-off between military capabilities and policy intentions in assessing threats, see Singer, "Threat Perception and the Armament-Tension Dilemma," *Journal of Conflict Resolution* (March 1958).

71. For a discussion of these issues in the context of the Cold War, see Richard Ned Lebow, "Deterrence and the Cold War," *Political Science Quarterly* (Summer 1995).

72. Edward J. Laurance, Siemon T. Wezeman, and Herbert Wulf, "Arms Watch: SIPRI Report on the First Year of the UN Register of Conventional Arms," *SIPRI Research Report, no. 6* (Oxford, England: Oxford University Press, 1993).

73. Kelleher, "Indicators of Defensive Intent in Conventional Force Structures and Operations in Europe," p. 173.

74. Transparency will be most effective when governments agree as much as possible on what types of weapons and behavior are acceptable. According to John Sislin and David Mussington, some military capabilities appear to be particularly dangerous: Destabilizing arms acquisitions are defined as those arms acquisitions that increase perceptions of invulnerability in the state that imports or procures them, or that increase the feelings of vulnerability in others. The offensive or defensive character of particular weapons is not at issue. The central point is the shift in perceptions of weakness and strength held by political elites resulting from weapons acquisitions. Examples of destabilizing capabilities include those that (1) decrease warning time and make successful preemption more possible, (2) provide breakthrough capabilities because of either the quantity or quality of weapons, (3) increase the transparency of a neighbor's military preparations that helps an adversary to pinpoint targets more effectively, (4) provide more or better targets, and (5) generally create hostile feelings. Weapons that have at least one of these effects include ballistic missiles and cruise missiles, advanced strike aircraft, and smart weapons and "low-observable" technologies; tanks and armored combat vehicles, and artillery; and technologies that increase battle management and C3I capabilities.

75. Kelleher, "Indicators of Defensive Intent in Conventional Force Structures and Operations in Europe," in *Military Power in Europe*, p. 166.

76. Singh, "UN Register," p. 132.

77. Pearson and Brzoska *Arms and Warfare*, pp. 250–252. See also, Chaim Herzog, *The Arab-Israeli Wars: War and Peace in the Middle East* (New York: Random, 1982).

78. For a discussion, see Thomas J. Christensen, "China, the US-Japan Alliance, and the Security Dilemma in East Asia," *International Security* (Spring 1992).

79. Charles L. Glaser, "The Security Dilemma Revisited," *World Politics* 50 (October 1997).

80. Kydd, "Trust, Reassurance, Cooperation," p. 341.

81. Quoted in Bruce Russett, *Grasping the Democratic Peace: Principles for a Post-Cold War World* (Princeton: Princeton University Press, 1993), p. 127.

82. The relationship between trust and the security dilemma gives democracies an advantage because its statements are more credible. See Schultz, *Democracy and Coercive Diplomacy*; and Lipson, *Reliable Partners*.

83. Quoted in Murray Hiebert, "The North Korea Mystery," *Far Eastern Economic Review* (October 21, 2004), p. 21.

84. Thanks to Harry Harding for this comparison. See John Ruwitch, "China to Boost Military Spending as it Eyes Taiwan," DefenseNews.com (February 28, 2005), Accessed June 24, 2005. Nathan Hodge, "New Pacific Commander Sees 'Disconcerting' China Buildup," *Defense Daily International* (March 11, 2005), p. 1; Siddharth Srivastava, "India's Military Hungry for More," *Asia Times* (February 16, 2005). Accessed www.atimes.com, June 24, 2005; Pulkit Singh, "Indian Defense Budget Rises 7.8% to $19B," *Journal of Electronic Defense* (April 2005), p. 19.

85. Wiseman, "Common Security in the Asia-Pacific Region," p. 50.

86. For examples of the functionalist literature, see Karl W. Deutsch, *Political Community and the North Atlantic Area: International Organization in the Light of Historical Experience* (Princeton: Princeton University Press, 1957); David Mitrany, *The Functional Theory of Politics* (New York: St. Martin's, 1976); and Joseph S. Nye, *Peace in Parts: Integration and Conflict in Regional Organization* (Boston: Little Brown, 1971).

87. Sumit Ganguly and Ted Greenwood, eds., *Mending Fences, Confidence and Security Building Measures in South Asia* (Boulder, CO: Westview, 1996), pp. 2–3.

88. Pervaiz Iqbal Cheema, "Transparency Measures," in *Mending Fences,* p. 152.

89. Desjardins, pp. 61–62.

90. Spear, "Arms Limitations, Confidence-Building Measures, and Internal Conflict," p. 403. See also, Singh, "UN Register," p. 138.

91. See United Nations, *Comprehensive Study on Confidence-building Measures*, study series 7 (New York: United Nations, Department of Political and Security Council Affairs, 1982), esp. paragraphs 28 and 160, which indicate that misunderstandings were a major cause of conflict. See Johan Jorgen Holst, "Confidence-Building Measures: A Conceptual Framework," *Survival* 25:1 (January/February 1983), pp. 4–5; Richard E. Darilek, in Larrabee and Stobbe; on CSBMs in Russo-Chinese relations, see David Shambaugh, "Pacific Security in the Pacific Century," *Current History* (December 1994); See Peter Jones, "Open Skies: A New Era of Transparency," *Arms Control Today* (May 1992); *A Handbook of Confidence Building Measures for Regional Security*, handbook no. 1 (Washington, DC: Henry L. Stimson Center, 1993). Helsinki Accords introduced CSBMs to Europe (enhanced at the Madrid meeting in 1983, the Stockholm meeting in 1986, and the Vienna meeting in 1990). For a summary of transparency efforts see Hendrik Wagenmakers, "The UN Register of Conventional Arms," *Arms Control Today* (April 1993).

92. For an excellent overview of the literature on arms control and war, see Pearson and Brzoska, *Arms and Warfare*, p. 244. See also, John C. Lambelet, "A Dynamic Model of the Arms Race in the Middle East 1953-1965," *General Systems* 16:1 (1971); John C. Lambelet, "Do Arms Races Lead to War?" *Journal of Peace Research* 12:2 (1975); Partha Chatterji, "The Equilibrium Theory of Arms Races: Some Extensions," *Journal of Peace Research* 11:3 (1974); Paul Diehl, "Arms Races and Escalation: A Closer Look," *Journal of Peace Research* 20:3 (1983); and Diehl, "Arms Races to War: Testing Some Empirical Linkages," *Sociological Quarterly* 26:3 (1985). See also, Erich Weede, "Nation-Environment Relations as Determinants of Hostilities Among Nations," *Peace Science Society International Papers* 24:1 (1973); Weede, "Arms Races and Escalation, Some Persisting Doubts," *Journal of Conflict Resolution* 24:2 (1980); Theresa Smith, "Arms Race Instability and War," *Journal of Conflict Resolution* 24:2 (1980); Rudolph J. Rummel, "Understanding Conflict and War," *War, Power, Peace*, vol. 4 (Beverly Hills; Sage, 1979); and Dina A. Zinnes, "Why War? Evidence on the Outbreak of International Conflict," in Ted Gurr, ed., *Handbook of Political Conflict* (New York: Free Press, 1980). Only one major study has found a strong correlation between armaments to war: Michael D. Wallace, *War and Rank among Nations* (Washington, DC: Heath, Lexington, 1973); and Wallace, "Arms Races and Escalation, Some New Evidence," *Journal of Conflict Resolution* 23:1 (1979), though this work has been criticized for its use of data and statistical methodology.

93. Ronald Mitchell, "Sources of Transparency: Information Systems in International Regimes," *International Studies Quarterly* 42:1 (March 1998).

94. For a review of the UNROCA, see Edward J. Laurance, Hendrik Wagenmakers, and Herbert Wulf, "Managing the Global Problems Created by the Conventional Arms Trade: An Assessment of the United Nations Register of Conventional Arms," *Global Governance* 11:2 (April 2005).

95. Chayes and Chayes, in *Developing Arms Transparency*, p. 207.

96. Ann Florini, *The Coming Democracy* (Washington, DC: Island Press, 2003), p. 188.

97. For a discussion of reputation in international politics, see Jonathan Mercer, *Reputation and International Politics* (Ithaca: Cornell University Press, 1996).

98. Wulf, in *Developing Arms Transparency*, p. 156.

Chapter 3

1. David Kelley and Roger Donway, "Liberalism and Free Speech," in Judith Lichtenberg, ed., *Democracy and the Mass Media* (Cambridge, MA: Cambridge University Press, 1990), p. 90.

2. David A. Lake and Donald Rothchild, "Containing Fear: The Origins and Management of Ethnic Conflict," *International Security* 21:2 (Fall 1996), p. 74.

3. See Michael Dertouzos, *What Will Be: How the New World of Information Will Change Our Lives* (San Francisco: HarperEdge, 1997), p. 218. Similarly, Negroponte argues that "Digital technology can be a natural force drawing people into greater world harmony." See Negroponte, *Being Digital* (New York: Vintage Books, 1995), p. 230.

4. Tom Standage, *The Victorian Internet: The Remarkable Story of the Telegraph and the Nineteenth Century's On-line Pioneers* (New York: Berkley Books, 1998), p. 83.

5. H. D. Forbes, *Ethnic Conflict: Commerce, Culture, and the Contact Hypothesis* (New Haven, CT: Yale University Press, 1997). The original source of the contact hypothesis is Gordon Allport, *The Nature of Prejudice* (Reading, MA: Addison-Wesley, 1954). For a recent overview of contact theory, see Thomas F. Pettigrew, "Intergroup Contact Theory," *Annual Review of Psychology* 49 (1998).

6. Because this chapter looks at the social and social psychological bases of conflict between groups of people, it does not distinguish groups based on what defines them, be it nationality, ethnicity, race, or religion. The chapter accepts group identities as given, regardless of how they are arrived at.

7. Normal Patiz continues, "Will they like us better when they *do* know us in an accurate fashion? Put it this way: We stand a better chance." Quoted in Jane Mayer, "The Sound of America," *New Yorker* (February 18 and 25, 2002), p. 60.

8. To quote J. M. Goldgeier and P. E. Tetlock, "The greater the transparency, the less latitutde there is for slippage between reality and mental representations of reality." See Goldgeier and Tetlock, "Psychology and International Relations Theory," *Annual Review of Political Science* 4:67 (2001), p. 79.

9. Quoted in Barbara Hall, "Seeds of Peace Plants Hopes for the Future: Group Brings Mideast Kids together in US," *Boston Globe* (December 31, 2000), p. L8.

10. The concepts of transparency and the "marketplace of ideas" are not identical but they are conceptually related. Transparency is a condition of openness in which information about the preferences, capabilities, and intentions of governments and other powerful actors or organizations is widely available to a global public. A marketplace of ideas suggests an open exchange of competing beliefs. Both concepts imply wide access to ideas but only the latter implies that those ideas compete. A marketplace of ideas is likely to encourage transparency. Transparency may illuminate a marketplace of ideas. And, the same mechanisms that create transparency—such as an active civil society or an independent media—may also encourage a marketplace of ideas, though that is not necessarily the case. This book uses the "marketplace of ideas" metaphor because this is a widely used concept and the purpose of this book is to assess existing views rather than to introduce whole new concepts for analyzing political phenomena. However, we must also recognize that the marketplace metaphor may not in fact be the most apt. A market metaphor implies a whole set of dynamics, such as the idea that all goods offered are exchanged for some value, which may not in fact be appropriate for this discussion.

11. Some NGOs and international organizations promote communication as a solution to conflict for this reason. For example, UNESCO promoted radio in rural areas and consolidation of the media in Rwanda in order to "advance the cause of peace and democracy." www.unesco.org/webworld/com_media/communication_democracy/ rwanda.htm (accessed 9/30/02). See also, Search for Common Ground's initiatives (www.sfcg.org/act2.cfm?locus=toolbox).

12. Quoted in Benjamin I. Page and Robert Y. Shapiro, *The Rational Public: Fifty Years of Trends in Americans' Policy Preferences* (Chicago: University of Chicago Press, 1992), p. 396. Page and Shapiro also quote the more emphatic statement by John Milton: "Let her and Falsehood grapple; who ever knew Truth put to the worse, in a free and open encounter?" See also, John Stuart Mill, *On Liberty* and Oliver Wendell Holmes, in *Abrams v. US*, 250 US 616, 630.

13. For examples of this argument see Douglas A. Van Belle, *Press Freedom and Global Politics* (Westport, CT: Praeger Publishers, 2000); David Birn, *The Transparent Society: Will Technology Force Us to Choose between Privacy and Freedom?* (Reading, MA: Addison-Wesley 1998), p. 311; and Susan Carruthers, *The Media at War* (London: Macmillan, 2000), p. 24.

14. Interestingly, many textbooks on the causes of war overlook the social psychology of conflict but the popular press as well as some of the scholarly literature on conflict emphasizes the role of group behavior, be those groups national or ethnic. Many of the practical solutions proposed to end international and internal conflicts focus on changing group dynamics within a region or society.

15. Regardless, conflicts of all stripes typically are motivated at least as much by security, political, or economic interests.

16. Francis A. Beer, *Peace against War: The Ecology of International Violence* (San Francisco: W. H. Freeman 1981), p. 275.

17. Carruthers, *Media at War*, p. 44. See also, Ervin Staub, "Individual and Group Identities in Genocide and Mass Killing," in Richard D. Ashmore, Lee Jussim, and David Wilder, eds., *Social Identity, Intergroup Conflict, and Conflict Reduction* (Oxford, England: Oxford University Press, 2001), pp. 177–178.

18. John Mueller, "The Banality of Ethnic War," *International Security* (Summer 2000).

19. For a discussion of the relationship between information and values, see John Zaller, "Information, Values, and Opinion," *American Political Science Review* 85:4 (December 1991), p. 1215.

20. Van Belle, *Press Freedom and Global Politics*, p. 83.

21. See R. J. Rummel, *Death by Government* (New Brunswick, NJ: Transactions Publishers, 1994). See also, Ervin Staub, *The Roots of Evil, the Origins of Genocide and Other Group Violence* (Cambridge, MA: Cambridge University Press, 1989); and Staub, "Genocide and Mass Killing," *Political Psychology* 21 (2000).

22. The argument here is that collective identities are transitory, at least to some extent. That argument is distinct from a primordialist view, which perceives given biological, cultural, and linguistic and religious differences. See Ted Robert Gurr, *Minorities at Risk* (Washington, DC: United States Institute of Peace, (1993) for a similar argument.

23. Social identity theory suggests that getting people to accept superordinate identities is a useful step to reduce intergroup conflict. See Richard D. Ashmore, Lee Jussim, and David Wilder, eds., *Social Identity, Intergroup Conflict, and Conflict Reduction* (Oxford, England: Oxford University Press, 2001), p. 243. See also, Samuel L. Gaertner, John F. Dovidio, Jason A. Nier, C. M. Ward, and B. S. Banker, "Across Cultural Divides: The Value of Superordinate Identity," in Deborah A. Prentice and Dale T. Miller, eds., *Cultural Divides: Understanding and Overcoming Group Conflict* (New York: Russell Sage, 1999). Obviously such redefinitions don't always last forever. The term *Yugoslav* rather than *Croation*, and *Indonesian* versus *Timorese* are only two examples. Identities can also overlap. A person could regard herself as both Malay and Singaporean, for instance.

24. Gurr, *Minorities at Risk*, pp. 3–4.

25. Ibid., p. 4.

26. My thanks for Martha Finnemore for her analysis of this distinction.

27. For a discussion of different theories regarding how people process information in the media, see Carruthers, *Media at War*, p. 8. For a discussion of

how audiences negotiate the meaning of media messages and resist those they don't accept, see J. Fiske, *Television Culture* (London: Methuen, 1987).

28. Philip Converse, one of the leading theorists of mass opinion, argues that people rely on contextual information from elites about how ideas go together and that people respond to cues about what types of political groups favor or oppose an idea. See Converse, "The Nature of Belief Systems in Mass Publics," in David Apter, ed., *Ideology and Discontent* (New York: Free Press, 1964).

29. Primo Levi, "Afterword: The Author's Answers to his Readers' Questions," in *If This Is a Man* and *the Truce* (London: Abacus, 1987), p. 386.

30. Gordon Allport, who first articulated the contact hypothesis in 1954, formalized the idea that acquaintance can increase positive feelings. This academic version of the contact hypothesis has more clearly specified conditions that are lost in the popular translation, namely, that contact between majority and minority groups decreases prejudice only if the groups have equal status, the groups share common goals, the groups need to cooperate to reach a common goal, and that improved contact is reinforced by law or custom. Note that there are levels of analysis problems with contact theory, that is, it is not clear how valid it is to extrapolate from small group behavior to the level of a society. Allport, *The Nature of Prejudice* (Reading, MA: Addison-Wesley, 1954), p. 281. For a discussion of Allport's views, see Forbes, *Ethnic Conflict*. Psychological experiments support the idea that careful and differentiated information about the history, achievements, norms, and lifestyles of the demonized group can help to over come negative stereotypes. Kurt R. Spillmann and Kati Spillmann, "On Enemy Images and Conflict Escalation," *International Social Science Journal* (February 1991), p. 72. Under these conditions, contact changes not only attitudes toward other groups but also may encourage changes in behavior. When humans feel empathy for one another, they may act in ways that make cooperation easier. After looking at the world through others' eyes, they may see how their own behavior seems threatening. This awareness may lead them to change their behavior or rhetoric.

31. Forbes, *Ethnic Conflict*, p. 116.

32. Amy Chua, *World on Fire: How Exporting Free Market Democracy Breeds Ethnic Hatred and Global Instability* (New York: Anchor Books, 2003).

33. Fortunately, transparency can have the opposite effect when more positive changes in norms spread, until a "tipping point" is reached. Malcolm Gladwell, *The Tipping Point: How Little Things Can Make a Big Difference* (Boston: Little, Brown, 2000).

34. For an interesting discussion of how humans evolved to think in terms of in- and out-groups and how these tendencies are overcome, see Michael Shermer, *The Science of Good and Evil: Why People Cheat, Gossip, Care, Share and Follow the Golden Rule* (New York: Henry Holt, 2004).

35. Nancy Wartik, "Hard-Wired for Prejudice? Experts Examine Human Response to Outsiders," *New York Times* (April 20, 2004), p. D5.

36. See the discussion in Jonathan Mercer, "Anarchy and Identity," *International Organization* (Spring 1995), pp. 242–245.

37. Most intergroup conflicts are not violent. Researchers distinguish between competition, the motivation to seek relative gains, from aggression, the motivation to harm the out-group as an end in itself. See Marilynn B. Brewer, "Ingroup Identification and Intergroup Conflict," in Richard D. Asmore, Lee Jussim, and David Wilder, eds., *Social Identity, Intergroup Conflict, and Conflict Reduction* (New York: Oxford University Press, 2001), p. 26.

38. Benjamin I. Page and Robert Y. Shapiro, *Rational Public*, p. 365. See also, James D. Fearon and David D. Laitin, "Violence and the Social Construction of Ethnic Identity," *International Organization* 54:4 (Autumn 2000).

39. Mercer, "Anarchy and Identity," p. 245.

40. Ervin Staub, "Individual and Group Identities in Genocide and Mass Killing," in *Social Identity, Intergroup Conflict, and Conflict Reduction*, p. 161.

41. Ibid., p. 162.

42. For a discussion of how a marketplace of ideas can fail even in a well-developed democracy, see Chaim Kauffmann, "Threat Inflation and the Failure of the Marketplace of Ideas," *International Security* 29:1 Summer 2004).

43. Consider the "Seventeen rules of Tutsi conduct" issued in Bujumbura, Burundi. It reads: Do not trust a Hutu or anyone supposed to be one....Try to locate Hutu residences so that you will know, when the time comes, whom to save and whom to liquidate....Hutu kids are spoiled and insouciant: just get hold of the kid who lost his way, then ask his father, elder brother or mother to come and fetch him, and then kill them all...." René Lemarchand, *Burundi: Ethnic Conflict and Genocide* (Cambridge, MA: University of Cambridge and Woodrow Wilson Center Press, 1996), p. xvii.

44. For a discussion, see Page and Shapiro, *Rational Public*, p. 397.

45. Early democratic thinkers recognized the potential for majorities to abuse minorities even in a democracy. The Federalist Papers, for instance, note that there are times when the public will be "stimulated by some irregular passion, or some illicit advantage, or misled by the artful misrepresentations of interested men" into advocating unfortunate policies. John Stuart Mill also observed this phenomenon and warned that social tyranny—the tyranny of the masses—can be more dangerous to minorities than political oppression by the government. Consequently, Mill recommends that societies adopt laws that protect the rights of minorities and encourages dissent. Free speech and a free press must be balanced by a system of rights that protect minorities against majorities. David Kelley and Roger Donway, "Liberalism and Free Speech," in Judith Lichtenberg, ed., *Democracy and the Mass Media* (Cambridge, MA: Cambridge University Press, 1990), p. 90. Thanks to Jonathan Frankel for his insights regarding the right to free speech and related laws in the United States.

46. These dynamics may have been at work in Nigeria, which, since the election of Olusegun Obasanjo has more freedom of the press, televised public hearings to expose state-sponsored murders and disappearances of the past thirty years, and the opposition has more freedom. But ethnic and religious violence has grown worse since Nigeria became a democracy. More than 6,000 have died in communal clashes in the last three years. "Three Years of Democracy," *Economist* (April 6, 2002), p. 58.

47. See Cynthia Brown and Farhad Karim, eds., *Playing the "Communal Card": Communal Violence and Human Rights* (New York: Human Rights Watch, 1995); and Jack Snyder and Karen Ballentine, "Nationalism and the Marketplace of Ideas," *International Security* (Fall 1996).

48. For a discussion of the marketplace of ideas and democratizing societies, see Mansfield and Snyder, "Democratization and the Danger of War," *International Security* 20:1 (Summer 1995), pp. 29 and 37. For a discussion of how citizens in authoritarian societies are less susceptible to media manipulation, see Ellen Mickiewicz, *Split Signals: Television and Politics in The Soviet Union* (New York: Oxford University Press, 1988); and Ithiel de Sola Pool, "Communication in Totalitarian Societies," in Pool et al., *Handbook of Communication* (Chicago: Rand McNally, 1973).

49. For a discussion of how democratic presses can promote dehumanizing images, see Heikki Luostarinen, "Finnish Russophobia: The Story of an Enemy Image," *Journal of Peace Research* 26 (1989), pp. 123–137.

50. Snyder and Ballentine, "Nationalism and the Marketplace of Ideas," p. 7.

51. Quoted in ibid., p. 9. See also, Larry Diamond, "Rethinking Civil Society: Toward Democratic Consolidation," *Journal of Democracy* 5:3 (September 1994).

52. For a discussion of how such states are susceptible to international conflicts see Mansfield and Snyder, "Incomplete Democratization and the Outbreak of Military Disputes" *International Studies Quarterly* 46:4 (2002). Some of the same dynamics that Mansfield and Snyder observe may also operate in domestic conflicts. See also, Mansfield and Snyder, "Democratization and the Danger of War." Though Mansfield and Snyder focus on international conflicts, the dynamics they discuss appear to apply equally well in the domestic context.

53. Samuel P. Huntington, *Political Order in Changing Societies* (New Haven, CT: Yale University Press, 1968), p. 55.

54. For the sake of simplicity, this chapter assumes that publics are unitary and that there is a general tendency or a general good for citizens as a group. Of course no population is actually this unitary.

55. When antiterrorist ads produced by the U.S. government were shown to focus groups in Jordan, the majority of respondents were simply puzzled, protesting, "But bin Laden is a holy man." Reported in Barbara Amiel, "Is the

Muslim World Still in Denial about September 11?" *Daily Telegraph* (March 4, 2002), p. 20.

56. Forbes, *Ethnic Conflict*, p. 168.

57. The "selective exposure hypothesis," also known as defensive avoidance, was first associated with Leon Festinger. See his *Conflict, Decision and Dissonance* (Stanford, CA: Stanford University Press, 1964). However, note that successive studies showed that specific factors can offset selective tendency, for instance, the message's utility and ease of refutability. For a discussion see Robert Jervis, *Perception and Misperception in International Politics* (Princeton: Princeton University Press, 1976), pp. 143–216; and Ole Holsti, "Cognitive Dynamics and Images of the Enemy: Dulles and Russia," in David Finley, Holsti, and Richard Fagen, eds., *Enemies in Politics* (Chicago: Rand McNally 1976). See also, James M. Goldgeier, "Psychology and Security," *Security Studies* 6:4 (Summer 1997), p. 141; and Spillmann and Spillmann, "On Enemy Images and Conflict Escalation," (1991), pp. 72–73.

58. David Hoffman, "Beyond Public Diplomacy," *Foreign Affairs* (March/April 2002), p. 83.

59. See, for instance, Jervis, *Perception and Misperception in International Politics*.

60. Daniel Drezner and Henry Farrell, "Web of Influence," *Foreign Policy* (November/December 2004). The classic question regarding conflict is not why leaders lead citizens into violent conflict, but why followers follow. In Rwanda and in instances like it, the question is not why some groups tried to persuade others of their superiority over other groups. There are clear material and psychological incentives to do so. The question is why that information was, in the words of communications experts, salient. Why did citizens listen? Why did they actively tune their radios to RTLM before the genocide and why did they not simply disregard the negative information they heard about Tutsi? Most importantly, why did so many Rwandans act on that information and participate in the genocide? Clearly there is more going on in this case then the simple revelation of information and the reaction of individuals. In Rwanda, negative information about the Tutsi fell on receptive ears and, in the din of a rapidly changing environment, seemed relevant and meaningful. Believing that information seems to have satisfied not only the interests of Hutu extremists but also the personal, material, and psychological interests of average citizens. This, the willingness of people to listen to some voices and not others and find some views credible and not others, is something that greater transparency cannot affect. As a result, the availability of information alone is unlikely to affect intergroup relations positively. The content and credibility of that information is crucial and, unless greater transparency is accompanied by the widespread availability of certain types of information, transparency may only make matters worse. Free markets for ideas self-regulate in well-developed democracies where the rule of law, norms of debate, and institutions of political transition are firmly rooted. In

rapidly changing, politically charged societies, however, free markets for ideas may become dangerous to the point of genocide.

61. Forbes, *Ethnic Conflict*, p. 169.

62. Ibid., p. 20.

63. For instance, two major debates in U.S. foreign policy are occurring while this book is being written. On the one hand, there are serious questions about whether the United States can have an alliance with Saudi Arabia despite incredibly different political and cultural values. On the other hand, some Europeans are asking whether Europeans and Americans continue to share enough values or whether increasing differences really threaten the transatlantic alliance or, as one wag put it, whether Americans are from Mars and Europeans are from Venus. Interestingly, both debates are based as much on domestic values as on international policy. In the case of Saudi Arabia, some Americans object to political oppression and discrimination against women in Saudi Arabia. In Europe, many commentators are appalled at American views toward capital punishment, gun control, and welfare—issues that have no impact on American foreign policy. Transparency makes such differences clear and omnipresent.

64. Thomas Friedman, *The Lexus and the Olive Tree* (New York: Farrar, 1999), p. 274.

65. See Gurr, *Minorities at Risk*, p. 124. The pace of change facilitated by greater transparency complicates the project of social reform, particularly in ethnopolitical conflicts. As Gurr, observes, for policies of social reform to be effective, "they must be pursued cautiously but persistently over the long term, slowly enough not to stimulate a crippling reaction from other groups, persistently enough so that minorities do not defect or rebel." The problem is that the speed of change may be out of governments' control, especially when governments are weak. Gurr, *Minorities at Risk*, p. 313.

66. Samantha Power, "Bystanders to Genocide," *Atlantic Monthly* (September 2001), p. 84.

67. Jeffrey Sharlet, "Fierce Debate Divides Scholars of the 1994 Rwandan Genocide," *Chronicle of Higher Education* (August 2001), pp. A16–19.

68. For a discussion of gauging degrees of transparency, see Bernard I. Finel and Kristin M. Lord, "The Surprising Logic of Transparency," in Finel and Lord, eds., *Power and Conflict in the Age of Transparency* (New York: Palgrave Macmillan, 2000), pp. 140–142.

69. The first bloc was comprised of the dominant Hutu party tied to the regime known as the Mouvement républicain national pour la démocratie et le développement or MRNDD, which was allied with the extremist pro-Hutu Coalition pour la Défense de la République (CDR). The second group included the Mouvement démocratique républicain or MDR, the predominantly Tutsi Parti Libéral (PL), and the Parti Social Démocrate (PSD). The FPR, which was

transforming itself from a solely military group into a political party, also participated in the government.

70. Economist Intelligence Unit, *Rwanda Burundi: Country Profile*
(London: 1993–1994).

71. Whereas the FPR received five cabinet seats in the transitional government, the MDR received four, the predominately PL received three, the PSD
received three, the Parti Chrétien Démocratie received one, and the MRNDD
received six; it was the clear loser in the deal. Economist Intelligence Unit,
Uganda, Rwanda, Burundi: Country Report, no. 1 (London, 1993); pp. 19–24.

72. Economist Intelligence Unit, *Rwanda Burundi: Country Profile*
(London: 1993–1994).

73. Gérard Prunier, *The Rwanda Crisis: History of a Genocide* (New
York: Columbia University Press, 1995), pp. 131–132.

74. Edward R. Girardet, "Reporting Humanitarianism: Are the New
Electronic Media Making a Difference?" in Robert Rothberg and Thomas Weiss,
eds., *From Massacres to Genocide* (Washington, DC: Brookings, 1996), p. 55.
Alison Des Forges notes that despite illiteracy in the country, there was a practice
of individuals bringing newspapers back to the country and reading them to
groups. See Des Forges, *Leave None to Tell the Story: Genocide in Rwanda* (New
York: Human Rights Watch, 1999). Thanks to Lee Ann Fujii for pointing this out.

75. Ibid.

76. 1994 CIA World Fact Book. The CIA World Fact Book only men-
tions one FM station because it does not include the FPR's Radio Muhabura, a
weak signal from rebel-held territory in the northern part of the country.

77. See Christine L. Kellow, and H. Leslie Steeves, "The Role of Radio in
the Rwandan Genocide," *Journal of Communication* 48:3 (Summer 1998). The
idea of radio as a development tool was fueled by the development theories of
Daniel Lerner (1958) and Wilbur Schramm (1964).

78. World Development Indicators Database, World Bank.

79. Prunier, *Rwanda Crisis,* p. 164.

80. Economist Intelligence Unit, *Rwanda Burundi.*

81. Ibid., p. 14.

82. Quoted in Alan J. Kuperman, "The Other Lesson of Rwanda:
Mediators Sometimes Do More Damage than Good," *SAIS Review* 16:1 (1996),
p. 230.

83. For more information on the Rwandan genocide, see, for instance,
Philip Gourevitch, *We Wish to Inform You that Tomorrow We Will Be Killed
with Our Families: Stories from Rwanda* (New York: Farrar, 1998).

84. William Ferroggiaro, "U.S. Identified Rwandan Killers on Second
Day of Genocide," *National Security Archive Update* (Washington, DC:

National Security Archives, April 7, 2004), available at www.nsarchive.org. This
information is based on declassified American documents obtained by Freedom
of Information Act requests.

85. It is unclear whether General Habyarimana supported the hard-liners
or reformists immediately before his death. He is accused of sanctioning death
squads and must have known about earlier killings of Tutsi. See Tharcisse
Gatwa, "Ethnic Conflict and the Media: The Case of Rwanda," *Media
Development* 3 (1995).

86. Des Forges, *Leave None to Tell the Story.*

87. Prunier, *Rwanda Crisis*, p. 223.

88. C. Kellow and H. Steeves, "The Role of Radio in the Rwandan
Genocide," *Journal of Communication,* 48:3 (1998).

89. John Mueller, "The Banality of Ethnic War," *International Security*
(Summer 2000), p. 59.

90. Des Forges, *Leave None to Tell the Story.*

91. See Mahmood Mamdani, *When Victims Turn Killers: A Political
Analysis of the Origins and Consequences of the Rwanda Genocide* (Princeton:
Princeton University Press, 2001).

92. Mueller, "Banality of Ethnic War," p. 61.

93. The political and economic context may also help to explain why so
many Rwandans either acquiesced to, or participated in, the killings. Beyond the
culpability of the Rwandan people, several conditions facilitated genocide.
Contrary to its portrayal in the Western press as a "failed state," Rwanda had a
well-organized, highly centralized civil service and a reasonably efficient government. The country had a decent communications system and a small, tightly controlled land area. The government also had the resources to launch the genocide.
It possessed arms from machetes to rocket launchers from suppliers in France,
South Africa, Egypt, and China, making Rwanda Africa's third largest importer
of weapons in 1993. The government paid for the arms with funds from international financial institutions. The World Bank was aware of the arms imports.

94. Rwandese political tradition is one of "systematic, centralized and uncon-
ditional obedience to authority." Prunier, *Rwanda Crisis*, p. 141. For a discussion of
the causes of ethnic conflict, see Michael E. Brown, ed., *The International
Dimensions of Internal Conflict* (Cambridge: MIT Press, 1996), p. 573.

95. For an excellent discussion, see Lee Ann Fujii, "The Diffusion of a
Genocidal Norm in Rwanda." (Paper prepared to the annual convention of the
International Studies Association, New Orleans, March, 2002).

96. Des Forges, *Leave None to Tell the Story.*

97. Linda Melvern, *A People Betrayed: The Role of the West in Rwanda's
Genocide* (London: Zed Books 2000), pp. 70–71; Des Forges, *Leave None to Tell
the Story.*

98. The Journalist Lindsey Hilsum states that the French broadcasts of Radio Rwanda were fairly innocuous but broadcasts in Kinyarwanda were inflammatory. See Hilsum, "The Radio Station Whose Call Sign Is Mass Murder," *Observer* (May 15, 1994), p. 19.

99. The Arusha Accords forbade the government-owned Radio Rwanda from inciting hatred. See Frank Chalk, "Radio Propaganda and Genocide," *MIGS Occasional Paper* (Montreal: Montreal Institute for Genocide and Human Rights Studies, November 1999), p. 2.

100. Prunier, *Rwanda Crisis*, p. 164.

101. Quoted in Melvern, *People Betrayed*, p. 155.

102. Prunier, *Rwanda Crisis*, pp. 210–211.

103. Marlise Simons, "Trial Centers on Role of Press during Rwanda Massacre," *New York Times* (March 3, 2002).

104. African Rights Report, p. 80, quoted in Kellow and Steeves, "Role of Radio in the Rwandan Genocide."

105. Simons, "Trial Centers on Role of Press during Rwanda Massacre."

106. See Kellow and Steeves, "Role of Radio in the Rwandan Genocide."

107. Simons, "Trial Centers on Role of Press during Rwanda Massacre."

108. Quoted in Kellow and Steeves, "Role of Radio in the Rwandan Genocide."

109. René Lemarchand, *Burundi: Ethnic Conflict and Genocide* (Cambridge, MA: University of Cambridge and Woodrow Wilson Center Press, 1996), p. xii.

110. Differentiation between Hutu and Tutsi first escalated during the colonial era when notions of racial superiority led Belgian colonialists to raise Tutsi to positions of higher authority in the administration. Rule by the Tutsi minority continued with Belgian support until the 1950s when the colonial administrators began to allow Hutu into more powerful positions in the government, admit Hutu to secondary schools, and conduct limited elections for advisory government councils. These changes frightened the Tutsi but left the Hutu unsatisfied. When a longtime Rwandan ruler died in 1959, extremist Tutsi rose to power and assaulted a Hutu sub-chief. Hutu groups attacked Tutsi officials in response and the Tutsi retaliated. The attackers killed hundreds before the Belgians restored order. After independence, a 1961 election ended the monarchy and established a Hutu-dominated government, which displaced thousands of Tutsi and sent thousands more into exile. Some of these Tutsi organized attacks against the Hutu government, but the government used the attacks to bolster Hutu solidarity and to emphasize the Tutsi threat. The Hutu government instituted a system of identification cards that identified citizens as Hutu or Tutsi and established an ethnically based quota system for education and government jobs. Hutu leaders realized there was much to gain from attacking the

relatively wealthy Tutsi, and in the late 1960s killed approximately 20,000 and forced another 300,000 to flee the country. Habyarimana seized power in a bloodless coup in July 1973 and ruled the country without much opposition until world coffee prices collapsed and the attacks from the Tutsi FPR, comprised of refugees who had fled Rwanda in earlier crises, increased. To shore up support for his ailing regime, Habyarimana played up anti-Tutsi sentiments and exaggerated the threat from the Tutsi FPR. At one point in 1990, the government even faked a Tutsi attack on Kigali. Des Forges, *Leave None to Tell the Story*.

111. Michele D. Wagner, "All the Bourgmestre's Men: Making Sense of Genocide in Rwanda," *Africa Today* (January/March 1998).

112. For a discussion of this dynamic, see David A. Lake and Donald Rothchild, "Containing Fear: The Origins and Management of Ethnic Conflict," *International Security* 21:2 (Fall 1996), p. 54.

113. Mark Frohardt and Jonathan Temin, "Use and Abuse of Media in Vulnerable Societies," *United States Institute of Peace Special Report* (Washington, DC: United States Institute of Peace, October 2003), p. 3.

114. See Fujii, "Diffusion of a Genocidal Norm in Rwanda," p. 3.

115. See Brown, *International Dimensions of Internal Conflict*.

116. Michael W. Doyle, *UN Peacekeeping in Cambodia: UNTAC's Civil Mandate*, International Peace Academy, Occasional Paper Ser. (Boulder: Lynne Rienner, 1995), pp. 54–55. See also, Dan Lindley, "Collective Security Organizations and Internal Conflict," in Michael Brown, ed., *International Dimensions of Internal Conflict* (Cambridge: MIT Press, 1996); MacAlister Brown and Joseph J. Zasloff, *Cambodia Confounds the Peacemakers 1979–1998* (Ithaca: Cornell University Press, 1998); John Marston, "Cambodian News Media in the UNTAC Period and After," in Steve Heder and Judy Ledgerwood, eds., *Propaganda, Politics, and Violence in Cambodia* (Armonk, NY: M. E. Sharpe, 1996); and Dan Lindley, "Untapped Power: The Status of UN Information Operations," *International Peacekeeping* 11:4 (Winter 2004).

117. "Cambodia—UNTAC [United Nations Transitional Authority in Cambodia]: Facts and Figures" (www.un.org/Depts/dpko/co_mission/untac-facts.html). Accessed May 26, 2004.

118. For a brief discussion, see Frohardt and Temin, "Use and Abuse of Media in Vulnerable Societies," p. 14. See also, Jamie Metzl, "Information Intervention: When Switching Channels Isn't Enough," *Foreign Affairs* (November/December 1997).

119. Even if the contact hypothesis is accurate, it may be a gradual trend and the progression of that trend sometimes may be violent. More knowledge of other people and viewpoints may indeed reduce prejudice and hostility over time, but in doing so it also may encourage people to turn away from old values. This transition may threaten those who cling to old values as well as the power or status of certain groups. Faced with this threat, some groups may defend their values or status violently.

Chapter 4

1. Told to Tutsi FPR major general Kagame, according to a 1997 interview by the journalist Linda Melvern. See Melvern, *A People Betrayed: The Role of the West in Rwanda's Genocide* (London: Zed Books 2000), p. 54.

2. Brian Steidle, "In Darfur, My Camera Was Not Nearly Enough," *Washington Post* (March 20, 2005), p. B02.

3. Identifying the potential for violent conflicts before they break out should be possible if it is true that "dangerous circumstances rarely degenerate without warning into violence." Carnegie Report, p. 44. Michael S. Lund defines preventive action as "sounding alarm bells at the right time and in a salutory and appropriate manner." See Lund, *Preventing Violent Conflict: A Strategy for Preventive Action* (Washington, DC: U.S. Institute of Peace, 1996). For the purposes of this chapter, conflict intervention refers to a spectrum of intervention, including diplomatic, economic, and especially military intervention, including peacekeeping.

4. "Early warning is essential to conflict prevention," writes former congressperson Lee H. Hamilton. Hamilton, "Foreword," in Bruce W. Jentleson, ed., *Opportunities Missed, Opportunities Seized: Preventive Diplomacy in the Post-Cold War World* (New York: Carnegie Commission on the Preventing Deadly Conflict, 2000), p. xi.

5. This phenomenon is popularly known as the "CNN Effect." Key works on the subject include Michael Beschloss, *Presidents, Television, and Foreign Crises* (Washington, DC: Northwestern University, 1993); Lewis A. Friedland, *Covering the World: International Television News Services* (New York: Twentieth Century Fund, 1992); Nik Gowing, "The CNN Factor" (Cambridge: Joan Shorenstein Barone Center, Harvard University, 1994; Steven Livingston and Todd Eachus, "Humanitarian Crises and U.S. Foreign Policy: Somalia and the CNN Effect Reconsidered," *Political Communication* 12 (1995); Susan L. Carruthers, *The Media at War* (London: Macmillan, 2000), pp. 205–243; Edward N. Luttwak, "Is Intervention a Thing of the Past?" *Harper's Magazine* (October 1994), pp. 15–17; Jacqueline Sharkey, "When Pictures Drive Foreign Policy," *American Journalism Review* (December 1993), pp. 14–19; and Warren P. Strobel, *Late Breaking Foreign Policy: The News Media's Influence on Peace Operations* (Washington DC: U.S. Institute of Peace, 1997). For a review of related literature see Eytan Gilboa, "Global Television News and Foreign Policy: Debating the CNN Effect," *International Studies Perspective* (2005).

6. See, for instance, *Preventing Deadly Conflict* (New York: Carnegie Commission on Preventing Deadly Conflict, 1997).

7. Saferworld.co.uk/media/stats/htm. Accessed December 22, 2003.

8. For a discussion of internal conflicts, see Michael E. Brown, ed., *The International Dimensions of Internal Conflict* (Cambridge: MIT Press, 1996).

9. International norms are evolving in ways that justify intervention without the consent of the state in question if lives are in danger. See Martha Finnemore, *The Purpose of Intervention: Changing Beliefs about the Use of Force* (Ithaca: Cornell University Press, 2003); and Bruce Jentleson, "Coercive Prevention: Normative, Political and Policy Dilemmas," *Peaceworks* (Washington, DC: United States Institute of Peace, 2000).

10. Boutros Boutros-Ghali, *An Agenda for Peace,* 2d ed. (New York: United Nations, 1995), p. 45. Note that Boutros-Ghali's initial reference was to preventive diplomacy, a word he later replaced with the phrase "preventive action" to include not just diplomacy but also preventive deployment, disarmament, humanitarian action, and peace-building. See Abiodun Williams, *Preventing War: The United Nations and Macedonia* (Lanham, MD: Rowman & Littlefield, 2000), p. 4.

11. Bruce Jentleson, "Coercive Prevention: Normative, Political, and Policy Dilemmas," *Peaceworks* (Washington, DC: United States Institute of Peace, 2000), p. 6.

12. For a comprehensive discussion of this operation, see Abiodun Williams, *Preventing War: The United Nations and Macedonia* (Lanham, MD: Rowman & Littlefield, 2000).

13. Complicating matters even further, even if individuals find the right information (in this case, data that provides early warning of dangerous conflicts), and interpret it correctly, they must communicate that information to people with the capacity for action. Numerous obstacles litter this process. In the realm of collection and analysis, pertinent information is held within the branches of national governments, international organizations, nongovernmental organizations, and individuals, and there are few systems for sharing this information. Moreover, even those organizations most suited to preventive action, such as the United Nations, do not have the capacity to respond effectively themselves. In the absence of a UN army, the organization must rely on contributions by member states, which make armed forces available to the Security Council under Article xliii of the UN charter. Preventive action, in other words, requires a major international effort to communicate and coordinate. A key question is which types of organizations have the power to either engage in preventive action or encourage others to do so if they are so inclined. At the international level, the UN has both the capacity to monitor disputes and formal mechanisms to convince others to intervene. However, both roles are limited—for some good reasons—by the organization's structure. Ultimately, the UN depends on the capabilities and political will of its member governments in general and the UN Security Council in particular. When the five permanent members of the Security Council do not support intervention, there is little the UN bureaucracy can do except publicly denounce decisions by individual members of the Security Council. On balance, greater transparency aids international organizations like the UN by giving them more information and early warning about brewing conflicts, despite a relatively small bureaucracy. However, access

to information is not generally what prevents the UN from intervening. Good information is a necessary but not sufficient condition for effective preventive action. Though we are now better informed about foreign conflicts, an effective early warning system also depends on effective analysis, communication, institutions, strategies, and tactics.

14. Ignorance of foreign disputes is rarely a legitimate explanation for not preventing violence. Greater transparency makes it hard for leaders to "explain away policy missteps or failures by pointing to the lack of timely or correctly evaluated intelligence." See Alexander L. George and Jane E. Holl, "The Warning-Response Problem and Missed Opportunities in Preventive Diplomacy," in Bruce W. Jentleson, ed. *Opportunities Missed, Opportunities Seized* (New York: Carnegie Corporation, 2000), p. 22.

15. Philip Sherwell and David Wastell, "How Did We Let This Happen? The West Has Known about the Horrors of Kosovo for Months. So Why Was Nothing Done Earlier?" *Sunday Telegraph* (October 4, 1998), p. 22.

16. Walter Lippmann, *Public Opinion* (London: George Allen and Unwin, 1922), p. 226.

17. Peter Viggo Jakobsen, "Focus on the CNN Effect Misses the Point: The Real Media Impact on Conflict Management Is Invisible and Indirect," *Journal of Peace Research* (March 2000).

18. Nik Gowing, "The CNN Factor" (Cambridge: Joan Shorenstein Barone Center, Harvard University, 1994, p. 18.

19. For a discussion of why some international issues are covered and others are not, see William C. Adams, "Whose Lives Count? TV Coverage of Natural Disasters," *Journal of Communications* 36 (1986).

20. Gowing, "CNN Factor."

21. Matthew Vita, "The CNN Effect: TV Playing Extraordinary Role in Setting National Agenda," *Houston Chronicle* (May 7, 1993), p. A19.

22. Today's journalists are technically more able to cover ever more remote conflicts and circumvent countries' communications infrastructures because of innovations such as satellite telephones, yet many obstacles still remain.

23. Jennifer Parmelee, "Sudan's Hidden Disaster: Africa's Longest War Leaves Millions at Risk," *Washington Post* (January 26, 1994), p. A1, quoted in Steven Livingston, "Suffering in Silence: Media Coverage of War and Famine in the Sudan," in Robert I. Roberg and Thomas G. Weiss, eds., *From Massacres to Genocide: The Media, Public Policy, and Humanitarian Crises* (Cambridge, MA: World Peace Foundation, 1996). Livingston and Eachus, "Humanitarian Crises and U.S. Foreign Policy," *Political Communication* 12 (1995), p. 77.

24. Gowing, "CNN Factor," p. 360.

25. See Carruthers, *Media at War*, p. 120.

26. Felicity Barringer and Jim Rutenberg, "For News Media, a Daunting and Expensive Task," *International Herald Tribune* (October 2, 2001).

27. See Carruthers, *Media at War*.

28. Andrew Natsios, "Illusions of Influence: The CNN Effect in Complex Emergencies," in Robert I. Roberg and Thomas G. Weiss, eds., *From Massacres to Genocide: The Media, Public Policy, and Humanitarian Crises* (Cambridge, MA: World Peace Foundation, 1996), p. 150.

29. Quoted in Carruthers, *Media at War*, p. 239.

30. For a discussion, see Steven Livingston, "Suffering in Silence: Media Coverage of War and Famine in the Sudan," in Roberg and Weiss, *From Massacres to Genocide*.

31. Clifford Bob, "Merchants of Morality," *Foreign Policy* 129 (March/April 2002), pp. 36–45.

32. Ibid., pp. 36–37.

33. Experimental research indicates that three key factors are important: the "signal-to-noise" ratio, that is, the strength of the signal relative to the amount of contradictory, confusing, or unrelated information, the expectations of analysts, and the rewards and costs of recognizing the signal correctly. George and Hall, "Warning-Response Problem and Missed Opportunities in Preventive Diplomacy," p. 24.

34. Quoted in Samantha Power, "Bystanders to Genocide: Why the United States Let the Rwandan Tragedy Happen," *Atlantic Monthly* (September 2001).

35. George and Holl argue that fears of crying wolf discourage analysts from voicing concerns. George and Holl, "Warning-Response Problem and Missed Opportunities in Preventive Diplomacy," p. 29.

36. Robert C. DiPrizio's study of humanitarian intervention indicates that the CNN Effect did not have a significant impact in any of the cases he examined. See DiPrizio, *Armed Humanitarians: U.S. Interventions from Northern Iraq to Kosovo* (Baltimore: Johns Hopkins, 2002).

37. See Gowing, "Real-Time Television Coverage of Armed Conflicts and Diplomatic Crises: Does it Pressure or Distort Foreign Policy Decisions?" (Cambridge: Harvard University Press, Joan Shorenstein Barone Center), working paper 94–1 (1996); and Gowing, "Instant TV and Foreign Policy," *World Today* (October 1994), p. 187. See also Warren P. Strobel, "The CNN Effect," *American Journalism Review* 18 (May 1996); Piers Robinson, "The Policy-Media Interaction Model: Measuring Media Power during Humanitarian Crisis," *Journal of Peace Research* (September 2000).

38. See the case studies by Strobel, "The Media and U.S. Policies toward Intervention: A Closer Look at the 'CNN Effect,'" in Chester A. Crocker and Fen Osler Hampson with Pamela Aall, eds., *Managing Global Chaos* (Washington, DC: United States Institute of Peace, 1996).

39. The moral weight of not preventing the genocide in Rwanda may have had some effect and encouraged intervention in Sierra Leone and Congo. However, that effect has been fairly weak. According to the International Rescue Committee, 3.3 million died in Congo in the first four and a half years of civil war, with only limited response from the UN and from powerful governments. This failure is, again, not for lack of information but a lack of political will to commit the necessary resources, especially when the UN and its member governments are already feeling the strain of multiple, ongoing peacekeeping operations.

40. See John E. Mueller, *War, Presidents and Public Opinion* (New York: Wiley, 1973). See also, Mueller, "Domestic Views of Foreign Policy," *National Interest* (Spring 1997).

41. Mueller, *Presidents and Public Opinion*, pp. 65 and 167.

42. Bruce Jentleson, "Coercive Prevention," *Peaceworks*.

43. Warren P. Strobel, "The CNN Effect," *American Journalism Review* 18 (May 1996), p. 32. Moreover, the news media is ultimately a profit-oriented business, which makes it unsuitable as a monitor of looming crises. There are no pictures of possible events and not much of a story. For a discussion, see G. Phil and J. E. T. Eldridge, *Glasgow Media Group Reader: Industry, Economy, War, and Politics*, vol. 2 (London: Routledge, 1995); Lionel Rosenblatt, "The Media and the Refugee," in Robert I. Rotberg and Thomas G. Weiss, eds., *From Massacres to Genocide: The Media, Public Policy and Humanitarian Crises* (Washington, DC: Brookings, 1996).

44. Peter Baker and Dan Balz, "Bush Words Reflect Public Opinion Strategy," *Washington Post* (June 20, 2005), p. A1.

45. Livingston and Eachus, "Humanitarian Crises and U.S. Foreign Policy," *Political Communication* 12 (1995), p. 427.

46. Conversely, when there is less transparency and citizens are not bombarded with information that disconfirms their views, publics may simply look the other way. Disturbingly, Primo Levi claims that most Germans simply acquiesced to Holocaust and "didn't know because they did not want to know." Levi, *The Reawakening: Two Memoirs*, trans. Stuart Woolf (New York: Summit Books, 1986), pp. 377–391, quoted in Smith, p. 224. See also, Daniel Jonah Goldhagen, *Hitler's Willing Executioners: Ordinary Germans and the Holocaust* (New York: Knopf, 1996).

47. Barry M. Blechman and Tamara Cofman Wittes, "Defining Moment: The Threat and Use of Force in American Foreign Policy," *Political Science Quarterly* 114:1 (Spring 1999), electronic version, p. 3.

48. Alison Des Forges, "Rwanda: Genocide and the Continuing Cycle of Violence," Testimony before the Subcommittee on International Operations and Human Rights" (Tuesday, May 5, 1998).

49. Kenneth A. Schultz, "Domestic Political Competition and Transparency in International Crises: The Good, the Bad and the Ugly," *Power and Conflict.* It is important to note that although divided opinion may constrain the threats that democratic governments are able to make, the possibility of divided opinion can also be an asset "when open competition and debate reveal the *strength* of domestic support" and undermine the credibility of a government's policy promise. See Kenneth A. Schultz, *Democracy and Coercive Diplomacy* (Cambridge, MA: Cambridge University Press, 2001), p. xiv.

For an analysis of the impact of transparency on crisis decision making in the Gulf War, see Kristin M. Lord and Bernard I. Finel, "Institutional Transparency and Conflict Strategies" (paper presented at the annual meeting of the International Studies Association, Chicago, IL. February 21-25, 1995).

50. Lawrence Freedman and Efraim Karsh, *The Gulf Conflict 1990-1991* (Princeton: Princeton University Press, 1993), p. 236. For an analysis of the impact of transparency on crisis decision making in the Gulf War, see Lord and Finel, "Institutional Transparency and Conflict Strategies."

51. Alan J. Kuperman, "Rwanda in Retrospect," *Foreign Affairs* (January/February 2000). Note that if the international community had not only announced that it was watching but clearly and credibly committed themselves to punishing the perpetrators, the threat might have been enough to slow or even stop the killings.

52. Hugo Slim, "Dithering over Darfur? A Preliminary Review of the International Response," *International Affairs* 80:5 (2004), p. 816.

53. Ernest J. Wilson III, *Globalization, Information Technology, and Conflict in the Second and Third Worlds* (New York: Rockefeller Brothers Fund, 1998).

54. Clifford Bob, "Beyond Transparency: Visibility and Fit in the Internationalization of Internal Conflicts," in *Power and Conflict in the Age of Transparency*, p. 293.

55. In 1998, President Clinton's apology to the Rwandan people stressed that "there were people like me sitting in offices ... who did not fully appreciate the depth and the speed with which you were being engulfed in unimaginable terror." Samantha Power argues that the choice of the word "appreciate" was carefully considered. See Power, "Bystanders to Genocide," *Atlantic Monthly* (2001).

56. Des Forges, "Rwanda."

57. Holly J. Burkhalter, "The Question of Genocide: The Clinton Administration and Rwanda," *World Policy Journal* (December 1994), p. 90. Des Forges, "Rwanda."

58. Julia Preston and Daniel Williams, "Tepid Response from U.S., World Contributed to Crisis, U.N. Says," *Washington Post* (July 23, 1994), p. A17.

59. Quoted in Michael Barnett, *Eyewitness to a Genocide: The United Nations and Rwanda* (Ithaca: Cornell University Press, 2002), p. 149.

60. General Dallaire has said he could have stopped the genocide with a force of 1,800 troops with enhanced mandate and additional equipment but that option was not considered. Whether UNAMIR or another small force of 5,000 could have intervened to stop the genocide is a matter of much debate, however. Some analysts, like Des Forges, argue that the killings were highly centralized in Kigali, so stopping the killing there would have quelled violence in the rest of the country. The Carnegie Commission argued that there was a window of opportunity from April 7 to 21 when intervention could have stemmed violence in the capital and prevented its spread to the countryside. Alan Kuperman argues that, given the pace of the killings, even a major mission would have failed to save many lives. Still, as Kuperman himself admits, "the hard truth is that even a large force deployed immediately upon reports of attempted genocide would not have been able to save even half of the ultimate victims." Of course, in this case, half the victims is equivalent to hundreds of thousands of people.

61. *New York Times*, May 14, 1994, sec. 1, p. 3.

62. Melvern, *People Betrayed.*

63. Economist Intelligence Unit, *Uganda, Rwanda, Burundi: Country Report*, no. 1 (London, 1993), pp. 19–24.

64. See International Federation of Human Rights, Africa Watch, Interafrican Union of Human Rights, International Center of Rights of the Person and Democratic Development, "Report of the International Commission of Investigation of Human Rights Violations in Rwanda since October 1, 1990, (January 7–21) (Paris and Washington, DC, 1993).

65. Des Forges "Rwanda."

66. The World Bank expressed concern to President Habyarimana before the genocide regarding purchases of arms and the diversion of aid money to support military and not civilian programs.

67. Astri Suhrke and Bruce Jones, "Preventive Action in Rwanda: Failure to Act or Failure of Actions?" in *Opportunities Missed, Opportunities Seized*, p. 238.

68. "Rwanda: Mass Murder by Government Supporters and Troops in April and May 1994" (London: Amnesty International, AFR 47/11/94).

69. Des Forges, "Rwanda."

70. Ibid.

71. For a discussion see Suhrke and Jones, "Preventive Action in Rwanda," p. 242.

72. Barnett, *Eyewitness to a Genocide*, p. 123.

73. Quoted in Melvern, *People Betrayed*, p. 43.

74. Des Forges, "Rwanda."

75. The United States withdrew personnel and nationals on April 9 and 10, and several European governments were close behind.

76. Suhrke and Jones, "Preventive Action in Rwanda," p. 242

77. Jamie Frederic Metzl, "Rwandan Genocide and the International Law of Radio Jamming," *American Journal of International Law* (October 1997).

78. Des Forges, "Rwanda."

79. Melvern, *People Betrayed*, p. 46.

80. Suhrke and Jones, "Preventive Action in Rwanda," p. 253.

81. Memorandum from Deputy Assistant Secretary of Defense for Middle East/Africa, through Assistant Secretary of Defense for International Security Affairs, to Under Secretary of Defense for Policy, "Talking Points on Rwanda/Burundi," April 11 1994, reproduced in William Ferroggiaro, ed., "The U.S. and the Genocide in Rwanda 1994" (Washington, DC: National Security Archive, August 20, 2001). The fact that this document was a briefing paper for a dinner between Under Secretary Frank Wisner and former secretary of state Henry Kissinger suggests that this was unlikely to be the first inkling that genocide was likely. For instance, Kuperman claims that "In Rwanda, Western officials failed to foresee the genocide, despite numerous warning signs, in part because the act was so immoral that it was difficult to picture."

82. "Rwanda: The Rwandan Patriotic Front's Offensive," Defense Intelligence Report, Defense Intelligence Agency, May 9, 1994, reproduced in William Ferroggiaro, ed., "The U.S. and the Genocide in Rwanda 1994" (Washington, DC: National Security Archive, August 20, 2001).

83. Memorandum from Assistant Secretary for Intelligence and Research Toby T. Gati to Assistant Secretary of State for African Affairs George Moose and Department of State Legal Adviser Conrad Harper, "Rwanda—Genocide Convention Violations," reproduced in William Ferroggiaro, ed., "The U.S. and the Genocide in Rwanda 1994" (Washington, DC: National Security Archive, August 20, 2001).

84. William E. Schmidt, "Troops Rampage in Rwanda: Dead Said to Include Premier," *New York Times* (April 8, 1994), p. 1; Jerry Gray, "2 Nations Joined by Common History of Genocide," *New York Times* (April 9, 1994), p. 6; Gérard Prunier, *The Rwanda Crisis: History of a Genocide* (New York: Columbia University Press, 1995), p. 199.

85. Melvern, *People Betrayed*, p. 21.

86. See Samantha Power, "Bystanders to Genocide," *Atlantic Monthly* (2001). Power subsequently won a Pulitzer Prize for her book on genocide.

87. Quoted in Power, "Bystanders to Genocide."

88. This failure to interpret information correctly extended to the RPF. An RPF leader told two scholars that FPR underestimated the impact of the

RTLM radio broadcasts. He remarked, "What they said was so stupid; we did not take it seriously enough." However, the fact that the FPR reached the outskirts of Kigali three days after the genocide started and targeted the RTLM station soon thereafter indicates that FPR was not taken completely by surprise. Quoted in Suhrke and Jones, "Preventive Action in Rwanda," p. 255.

89. Martin Shaw, *Civil Society and Media in Global Crises: Representing Distant Violence* (London: Pinter, 1996).

90. Carruthers *Media at War*, p. 225. See also, L. Hilsumuhj, "Where Is Kigali?" *Granta* 51, (1995).

91. Kuperman, "Rwanda in Retrospect," *Foreign Affairs* (January/February 2000).

92. Barnett, *Eyewitness to a Genocide*, p. 103.

93. Kuperman, "Rwanda in Retrospect."

94. Power, "Bystanders to Genocide," p. 108.

95. Kuperman, *The Limits of Humanitarian Intervention* (Washington, DC: Brookings, 2001).

96. See, for instance, "World Leaders Refused to Hear Cry of Rwanda," *National Catholic Reporter* (July 1, 1994), p. 28.

97. Quoted in Melvern, *People Betrayed*, p. 148.

98. See Power, "Bystanders to Genocide."

99. More transparency might also have exposed stronger government links to extremists and militia groups and either empowered the opposition or compelled supporters of the Habyarimana regime, such as France, to act. Human rights groups or international organizations, armed with such information, might have been able to make a stronger case for intervention. Greater transparency of the government and other powerful organizations in Rwanda before the genocide might also have led the FPR to walk away from the transitional government and to attract more international pressure. This knowledge might have empowered them to counter or at least limit the genocide.

100. See Craig W. Whitney, "At Inquiry, French Officials Say They Tried in Rwanda," *New York Times* (April 22, 1998). See also, Margaret Bald, "France Absolves France," *World Press Review* (February 1999), p. 23.

101. See, for example, George Melloan, "Blame France, If Anyone, for Rwandan Holocaust," *Wall Street Journal* (July 25, 1994), p. A15; and "Rwanda: Guilty Governments," *Economist* (June 3, 1995), p. 37.

102. Barbara Crossette, "Report Says U.S. and Others Allowed Rwanda Genocide," *New York Times* (July 8, 2000), p. A4.

103. The United States has not conducted its own investigation.

104. J. A. C. Lewis, "France Reviews Commitment in Africa," *Jane's Defense Weekly* (January 6, 1999), p. 1.

105. Crossette, "Inquiry Says U.N. Inertia in '94 Worsened Genocide in Rwanda," *New York Times* (December 17, 1999), p. A1.

106. See Secretary of State Colin Powell, Testimony before the Senate Foreign Relations Committee, September 9, 2004.

107. See Slim, "Dithering over Darfur." For additional information on the Darfur Crisis, see the International Crisis Group webpage (www.crisisgroup. org/home/index.cfm?id=3060&1=1#C8). Accessed July 18, 2005. See also the web pages of Amnesty International (www.amnesty.org) and Human Rights Watch (www.hrw.org).

108. See "Do Americans Care about Darfur? An International Crisis Group/Zogby International Survey" (June 1, 2005), available at www.crisis-group.org/home/index/crm?id=349&l=1. Accessed July 18, 2005.

109. Bob Herbert, 'Lifting the Censor's Veil on the Shame in Iraq," *New York Times* (May 5, 2005).

Chapter 5

1. Lester M. Salamon, "The Rise of the Nonprofit Sector," *Foreign Affairs* (July/August 1994). A similar quote by Kookmin University professor Andrei Lankov follows: "[North Koreans] are gradually learning about South Korean prosperity. This is a death sentence to the regime." See James Brooke, " How Electronics Are Penetrating North Korea's Isolation," *New York Times* (March 15, 2005), p. A3.

2. Quoted in Walter Wriston, "Bits, Bytes, and Diplomacy," *Foreign Affairs* (September/October 1997).

3. Wriston argues that transparency empowers citizens "to watch Big Brother" instead of the other way around, unleashing "a virus of freedom for which there is no antidote" that will be "spread by electronic networks to the four corners of the earth." Ibid.

4. As one analyst writes, "The combination of new access to standardized information and new technology, especially the growth of the Internet, has set in motion an irreversible process." Mary Graham, *Democracy by Disclosure* (Washington, DC: Brookings, 2002). Importantly, Graham questions transparency's utility as a tool of public policy—but even she believes that greater transparency is inevitable. Charles Lipson writes that the disclosure of new information in nondemocratic regimes can create a "cascade" that can culminate in "mass resistance to the regime." See Lipson, *Reliable Partners: How Democracies Have Made a Separate Peace* (Princeton: Princeton University Press, 2003), p. 89. Former president Bill Clinton boldly announced that the Internet will make a closed political and economic society "impossible" and ultimately bring down the communist regime. Speech by Clinton (Washington, DC, May 2000). Jamie Frederic Metzl writes simply, "no government can control the global information environment." Metzl, "The International Politics of Openness," *Washington Quarterly* (Summer 1999), p. 12.

5. Thomas L. Friedman, *The Lexus and Olive Tree* (New York: Farrar, 1999).

6. Allen Hammond, "Digitally Empowered Development," *Foreign Affairs* (March/April 2001). National governments in particular will "find their control slipping during the twenty-first century as information technology gradually spreads to the large majority of the world that still lacks phones, computers, and electricity." Joseph S. Nye Jr. *The Paradox of American Power* (New York: Oxford University Press, 2002), p. 47. Or, as Kevin Kelly puts it, "In the network era, openness wins, central control is lost." Kelly, *Out of Control: The Rise of Neo-biological Civilization* (Reading, MA: Addison Wesley, 1994), p. 90, quoted in Darin Barney, *Prometheus Wired: The Hope for Democracy in the Age of Network Technology* (Chicago: University of Chicago Press, 2000), p. 239.

7. The Technologist John Perry Barlow proclaimed to the governments of the world, "You have no sovereignty where we gather....Cyberspace does not lie within your borders." *Declaration of the Independence of Cyberspace* (http://www.eff.org/~barlow/Declaration-Final.html).

8. Quoted in Darin Barney, *Prometheus Wired: The Hope for Democracy in the Age of Network Technology* (Chicago: University of Chicago Press, 2000), p. 238.

9. "[T]here is little that one can do to keep out messages from any other country, or indeed to keep citizens from sending messages wherever they like." Michael A. Froomkin, "The Internet as a Source of Regulatory Arbitrage," in Brian Kahin and Charles Newson, eds., *Borders in Cyberspace: Information Policy and Global Information Infrastructure* (Cambridge: MIT Press, 1997). Quoted in Ronald J. Deibert, "Circuits of Power: Security in the Internet Environment," in James N. Rosenau and J. P. Singh, eds., *Information Technologies and Global Politics* (Albany: SUNY Press, 2002).

10. For a discussion of how NGOs increase public participation in international decision making, see P. J. Simmons, "Learning to Live With NGOs," *Foreign Policy* (Fall 1998).

11. For instance, a hearing before the Committee on Foreign Affairs in the United States House of Representatives, included the observation that there is "nothing the United States government can do to tone down repressive governments better than satellite TV." "Impact of TV on U.S. Foreign Policy" (April 26, 1999).

12. Kenichi Ohmae, *The End of the Nation State* (New York: Free Press, 1995). For a related but more nuanced view see Susan Strange, *Retreat of the State: The Diffusion of Power in the World Economy* (New York: Cambridge University Press, 1996).

13. For a discussion of how market pressures can lead NGOs to compromise their normative agendas, see Alexander Cooley and James Ron, "The NGO Scramble: Organizational Insecurity and the Political Economy of Transnational Action," *International Security* (Summer 2002).

14. Ann M. Florini, *The Coming Democracy: New Rules for a New World* (Washington, DC: Island Press, 2003), p. 32.

15. To give another example, Israeli soldiers have been expressing concerns on web sites and through the news media about the wrongful killing of Palestinians by the Israeli Defense Forces. See Molly Moore, "Israeli Soldiers' Testimony Supports Claims of Abuse," *Washington Post* (December 11, 2004), p. A16.

16. Francis Fukuyama, *The Great Disruption: Human Nature and the Reconstitution of Social Order* (New York: Free Press, 1999), p. 4.

17. Quoted in Randall E. Stross, "A Web of Peace—or War?" *U.S. News and World Report* (November 26, 2001), p. 47.

18. "Clinton Sends to a Wary Congress a Long-Delayed China Trade Bill," *New York Times* (March 9, 2000), p. A1.

19. Quoted in Shanthi Kalathil and Taylor C. Boas, *Open Networks, Close Regimes: The Impact of the Internet on Authoritarian Rule* (Washington, DC: Carnegie Endowment for International Peace, 2003), p. 1.

20· See Anne Wells Branscomb, "Jurisdictional Quandaries for Global Networks," in Linda Harasim, ed., *Global Networks, Computers, and International Communication* (Cambridge: MIT Press, 1993).

21. The communications scholar Hamid Mowlana, for instance, argues that the Shah of Iran fell when television exposed the distance between myth and reality. Before the introduction of television in 1958, the Shah was seen mainly by elites. His infrequent appearances in print and radio gave him an aura of mystery, which he cultivated. When television gave the masses better access to the Shah and to his beliefs, however, the Shah could not live up to the image of the "King of Kings, the Shadow of God, and the Light of the Aryans" he had developed. According to Hamid Mowlana, popular disappointment helped to undermine support for the Shah and to pave the way for his overthrow. Mowlana, *Global Communication in Transition: The End of Diversity?* (London: Sage, 1996), p. 53.

22. Ithiel de Sola Pool, "Communication in Totalitarian Societies," in Pool et al., *Handbook of Communication* (Chicago: Rand McNally, 1973), p. 463.

23. For a discussion of how regime change requires access to alternative ideas to mobilize political opposition, see Geoffry Taubman, "A Not-So World Wide Web: The Internet, China and the Challenges to Nondemocratic Rule," *Political Communication* (April/June 1998). See also, Adam Przeworski, *Democracy and the Market* (Cambridge, UK: Cambridge University Press, 1991).

24. Mary Graham, in her excellent book, *Democracy by Disclosure*, argues that transparency can also help citizens in democratic governments pressure for political change. "Armed with the facts, [citizens] create pressure for change

through what they buy, how they invest, where they work, how they vote, and what groups they join." Graham, *Democracy by Disclosure*, p. 137. "Technopopulism is an optimistic notion: it expresses a belief that transparency can make life better for ordinary citizens...." According to Graham, information can be used by individuals or groups to "influence actions by elected representatives, appointed boards and commissions, regulators, enforcement authorities in agencies, or courts, or to influence, boycotts, demonstrations, or other direct actions by citizens themselves." Ibid., p. 143.

25. Charles Lipson, *Reliable Partners* p. 87.

26. Cathy Hong, "New Political Tool: Text Messaging," *Christian Science Monitor* (June 30, 2005).

27. Quoted in David Birn, *The Transparency Society: Will Technology Force Us to Choose Between Privacy and Freedom?* (Reading, MA: Addison-Wesley, 1998), p. 25.

28. The most commonly cited example of a regime that will be threatened by the Internet is the People's Republic of China, where more than one hundred million Internet users are viewed as increasingly beyond the government's control. Elizabeth Rosenthal, "Web Sites Bloom in China, and Are Weeded," *New York Times* (December 23, 1999), p. A1.

29. Andrew Shapiro, *The Control Revolution* (New York: Century Foundation, 1999), p. 7. See also, Chris Hedges, "Serbs' Answer to Oppression: Their Web Site," *New York Times,* (December 8, 1996), p. A1.

30. Analysts typically focus on the benefits of transparency for democracy. As Florini writes, greater transparency "decentralizes the flow of information, which allows democracy to emerge." Florini, *Coming Democracy*, pp. 15–16.

31. Margaret E. Keck and Katheryn Sikkink, *Activists beyond Borders* (Ithaca: Cornell University Press, 1998); p. 16. According to Keck and Sikkink,

> A transnational advocacy network includes those relevant actors working internationally on an issue who are bound together by shared values, a common discourse, and dense exchanges of information and services. Such networks are most prevalent in issue areas characterized by high value content and informational uncertainty. At the core of the relationship is information exchange. What is novel in these networks is the ability of nontraditional international actors to mobilize information strategically to help create new issues and categories and to persuade, pressure, and gain leverage over much more powerful organizations and governments," in ibid., p. 2.

A flair for drama is helpful in a world bombarded by competing messages. Dorothy Q. Thomas, "Holding Governments Accountable by Public Pressure," in Joanna Kerr, ed., *Ours by Right: Women's Rights as Human Rights* (London: Zed Books, 1993).

32. For a review of the literature on NGOs, see William F. Fisher, "Doing Good? The Politics and Antipolitics of NGO Practices," *Annual Review of Anthropology* 26 (1997). For a case study and an argument that international

NGOs can undercut the power of local NGOs, see Pauline Jones Luong and Erika Weinthal, "The NGO Paradox: Democratic Goals and Non-democratic Outcomes in Kazakhstan," *Europe-Asia Studies* 51:7 (1999).

33. Transparency can also help citizens change the behavior of corporations, without government enforcement. The World Bank points to the success of Indonesia's Environmental Impact Management Agency, which publishes data about industrial pollution. Since companies do not want to be named publicly as polluters that cause serious harm to the environment, they choose to reduce harmful emissions. Florini, "End of Secrecy," in Bernard I. Finel and Kristin M. Lord, eds. *Power and Conflict in the Age of Transparency* (New York: St. Martin's Palgrave 2000), p. 23.

34. For instance, the Swedish organization Space Media Network monitors governments worldwide and publicizes behavior that it finds questionable. The organization made public the first pictures and details regarding the 1986 Chernobyl nuclear disaster as well as preparations for a Soviet space shuttle, a site for Chinese missiles in Saudi Arabia, and a new chemical warfare facility in Libya. James N. Rosenau, *Turbulence in World Politics: A Theory of Change and Continuity* (Princeton: Princeton University Press, 1990), p. 278.

35. Commercial imagery and declassified historical imagery are powerful tools for the NGO policy community, since they allow the public to evaluate government policy and give NGOs data to support proposals for alternative policies. See John Pike, "Public Eye—Lessons Learned" (http://www.globalsecurity.org/eye/lessons.htm). Accessed April 10, 2004.

36. Fredrik Galtung, "A Global Network to Curb Corruption: The Experience of Transparency International," in Florini, ed., *The Third Force: The Rise of Transnational Civil Society* (Washington, DC: Carnegie Endowment for International Peace, 2000), pp. 42–43. See also www.transparency.org.

37. See Keck and Sikkink, *Activists beyond Borders.*

38. Kalathil and Boas, *Open Networks, Close Regimes,* pp. 37–38.

39. The United States, which is not only rich and powerful but also open, is the biggest winner of all. To give just a few examples, the United States funds its intelligence agencies at a cost of billions of dollars per year. Home to many of the world's major providers of high-quality commercial satellite imagery, it is able to shut down surveillance (known as "shutter control") if it deems necessary or simply exercise "checkbook shutter control" and purchase all satellite time over sensitive sites. On shutter control, see John C. Baker, Kevin M. O'Connell, and Ray A. Williamson, *Commercial Observation Satellites: At the Leading Edge of Global Transparency* (Santa Monica, CA: Rand, American Society for Photogrammetery and Remote Sensing (ASPRS), 2001).

40. Despite claims that greater transparency decentralizes control over information, even in civil society that trend benefits the strong most of all. Wealthy NGOs with a global reach, like Amnesty International or World Wildlife Federation, benefit the most. The sheer number of NGOs and the

falling cost of communication empower the strongest NGOs because they can attract attention to their causes amid a cacophony of voices. Attention often leads to success and success leads to financial support, fueling a virtuous cycle that reinforces the "brand" of the mega-NGOs and makes it harder for smaller groups to attract attention and resources.

41. For a good discussion of the International Convention to Ban Landmines, see Florini, *Coming Democracy*, pp. 123–128.

42. Larry Diamond and Marc F. Plattner eds., *The Global Resurgence of Democracy*, 2d ed. (Baltimore: Johns Hopkins, 1996).

43. Jessica Mathews, "Power Shift," *Foreign Affairs* (January/February 1997), p. 8 (electronic version).

44. Ibid.

45. Susan L. Carruthers, *The Media at War* (London: Macmillan, 2000); p. 167. See also Alex Schmid and Janny de Graaf, *Violence as Communication: Insurgent Terrorism and the Western News Media* (London and Beverly Hills: Sage, 1982); and Walter Laqueur, *The Age of Terrorism* (Boston: Little Brown, 1987).

46. See, for instance, Gabriel Weimann, www.terror.net: How Modern Terrorism Uses the Internet," *Special Report* (Washington, DC: United States Institute of Peace, 2004). See also, Ariana Eunjung Cha, "From a Virtual Shadow, Messages of Terror," *Washington Post* (October 2, 2004), p. A 1.

47. Kalathil and Boas, *Open Networks, Closed Regimes.* There is evidence that semi-authoritarian regimes and illiberal democracies are spreading. See Fareed Zakaria, The Future of Freedom: Illiberal Democracy at Home and Abroad (New York: Norton, 2003).

48. As the democracy expert Larry Diamond observers, "the overthrow of authoritarian regimes through popularly based and massively mobilized democratic opposition has not been the norm." Most democratic transitions— "in South Korea, Taiwan, Chile, Poland, China, Czechoslovakia, South Africa, Nigeria, and Benin"—have been protracted and negotiated. The rise of illiberal democracies and semi-authoritarian governments lends credence to this view. Though some of these societies may one day, hopefully, become more democratic, greater transparency can coexist with nondemocratic governments. There are many possible types of governance between complete suppression of information by the government and full openness and democracy. Diamond, "Toward Democratic Consolidation," in Diamond and Marc F. Plattner, eds., *The Global Resurgence of Democracy*, 2d ed. (Baltimore: Johns Hopkins, 1996), p. 227.

49. As a Chinese Communist Party member told a British expert in communication policies, "You do propaganda so much better than we do." Anonymous source (May 24, 2004).

50. Jonathan Krim, "Web Censors in China Find Success," *Washington Post* (April 15, 2005), p. A20.

51. Kalathil and Boas note that "E-government may also increase transparency, which can expose corruption; this could cause a crisis of legitimacy for the regime (especially if corruption is widespread), but it might also bolster the regime's legitimacy if an honest central government is seen to be rooting out endemic corruption. Kalathil and Boas, *Open Networks, Close Regimes*, p. 7.

52. Stuart Ewen, *PR! A Social History of Spin* (New York: Basic, 1996); Douglas A. Van Belle, "Press Freedom and Peace: Theory and Findings," in *Power and Conflict in the Age of Transparency*, confidential interview with Singaporean foreign ministry official, February 2001.

53. See Daniel Lynch, *After the Propaganda State* (Stanford, CA: Stanford University Press, 1999). Lynch argues that the Internet is filled with apolitical content and will not contribute to the formation of an independent civil society.

54. Stephen Haggard, *Pathways from the Periphery: The Politics of Growth in the Newly Industrializing Countries* (Ithaca: Cornell University Press, 1990).

55. "The Internet's New Borders," *Economist* (August 11, 2001), p. 9.

56. Cited in Xiudian Dai, *The Digital Revolution and Governance* (Aldershot, England: Ashgate, 2000), p. 143.

57. See Kalathil and Boas, *Open Networks, Close Regimes*, p. 115.

58. Harvey Nelson, "Caution: Rough Road Ahead," in Edward Friedman and Barrett L. McCormick, eds., *What if China Doesn't Democratize?: Implications for War and Peace* (Armonk, NY: M. E. Sharpe, 2000) p. 266.

59. "The Internet's New Borders," *Economist* (August 11, 2001). Yahoo! is appealing the case.

60. "The Internet in the Mideast and North Africa: Free Expression and Censorship," Human Rights Watch Report (June 1999).

61. For a discussion, see Bernard I. Finel and Kristin M. Lord, "The Surprising Logic of Transparency," *International Studies Quarterly* 43:2 (June 1999), pp. 315-339.

62. Roland Lim, "Singapore mobile phone penetration past 90%: IDA," *IT Asiaone* (December 31, 2004), (http://itasia1.com.sg/newsdaily/news003_20041231.html). Accessed July 19, 2005. See also, *Annual Survey on InfoComm Usage in Households and by Individuals for 2004* (Singapore: InfoComm Development Authority, 2005).

63. "Information Hub," Singapore Fact Sheet Series. Ministry of Information and The Arts, (Singapore, 2001). See www.mita.gov.sg/bksifh.htm.

64. Ibid.

65. "The People," in Ibid.

66. "Measuring Globalization: Who's Up, Who's Down? *Foreign Policy* (January/February 2003), p. 60.

67. Note that there was a short period of political competition from 1963 to 1965.

68. "Singapore: Country Reports on Human Rights Practices 2001" (Washington, DC: Bureau of Democracy, Human Rights and Labor, U.S. Department of State, March 2002).

69. See Garry Rodan, "The Internet and Political Control in Singapore," *Political Science Quarterly* 113:1 (1998), pp. 82–83; Hussin Mutalib, "Illiberal Democracy and the Future of the Opposition in Singapore," *Third World Quarterly* 21:2 (2000), pp. 314–316; and Ran Tarn How, "More Level Playing Field Needed, to be Fair" *Straits Times* (November 11, 2001), p. 42.

70. The editor of the *Straits Times*, Singapore's major daily newspaper, acknowledges the progovernment stance and makes no apologies. *Asiaweek,* September 25, 1992, quoted in Rodan, "Internet and Political Control in Singapore."

71. See Rodan, "The Internet and Political Control in Singapore," p. 68; and "Singapore: Country Reports on Human Rights Practices 2001." See also, "Singapore: J.B. Jeyaretnam—The Use of Defamation Suits for Political Purposes," London: Amnesty International (October 15, 1997).

72. "Singapore: Country Reports on Human Rights Practices 2001."

73. Rodan, "Internet and Political Control in Singapore," p. 65.

74. *Asiaweek* (June 15, 1985), p. 20.

75. Rodan, "Internet and Political Control in Singapore," p. 66.

76. Laurel Teo, "Licence to Speak, or Not?" *Straits Times* (November 18, 2000), p. 14. See also, Chee Soon Juan, "The Government is Terrified of Losing Control, Especially with a Younger Generation Pushing for More Openness—Chee Soon Juan: Speaking Out in Singapore," *Newsweek* (February 15, 1999), p. 54.

77. Rajiv Chandrasekaran, "Restriction-Bound Orators Shun Singapore's Soapbox," *Washington Post* (March 18, 2001), p. A23.

78. For a discussion of regulating the Internet in Singapore, see Sarah B. Hogan, "To Net or Not to Net: Singapore's Regulation of the Internet," *Federal Communications Law Journal* (March 1999); "NetNanny States," *Economist* (September 14, 1996), p. 34; and Peter Lovelock, "Asia Meets the Internet," *China Business Review* (November/December 1996).

79. For discussions regarding the technical means of controlling the Internet as well as circumventing such controls, see Kees Brants, "Policing Democracy: Communication Freedom in the Age of Internet," *Javnost-The Public* 3 (1996).

80. "Industry Guidelines on the Singapore Broadcasting Authority's Internet Policy," Singapore Broadcasting Authority (www.sba.gov.sg/sba/I-guidelines.jsp).

81. Singapore Broadcasting Authority Act, Chapter 297, sec. 1.

82. "Singapore: Country Reports on Human Rights Practices 2000."

83. Quoted in Rodan, "Internet and Political Control in Singapore," p. 80.

84. Ibid., p. 64.

85. "Singapore: Country Reports on Human Rights Practices 2001."

86. Rodan, "Internet and Political Control in Singapore," p. 68. See also, Rodan, "Singapore in 2004," p. 141.

87. "Singapore: Country Reports on Human Rights Practices 2000." For further discussion of self-censorship in Singapore, see *Self-Censorship: Singapore's Shame* (January 2000), by the activist James Gomez. The book was published under the aegis of the Think Centre in Singapore.

88. See Lee Siew Hua, "Citizens' Rights 'Generally Respected,'" *Straits Times* (February 27, 2000), p. 7.

89. For an excellent discussion of Singapore's vulnerability, see Michael Leifer, *Singapore's Foreign Policy: Coping With Vulnerability* (London: Routledge, 2000), chap. 1. See also, Peter Montagnon, "Singapore: Caution Remains the Keyword," *Financial Times* (March 28, 2000), p. 6.

90. Leifer, *Singapore's Foreign Policy*, p. 5.

91. Ibid., p. 20. See also, *Environment and Security in Pacific Asia*, Adelphi Papers, no. 319 (London: Institute for International and Strategic Studies [IISS] 1998).

92. "Background Note: Singapore" (Washington, DC: Bureau of East Asian and Pacific Affairs, U.S. Department of State, April 2005. See www.state.gov/t/pa/ei/bgn/2798.htm. Accessed July 19, 2005.

93. See Leifer, *Singapore's Foreign Policy*.

94. Lee Lai To, "Singapore in 1999: Molding the City-State to Meet Challenges of the 21st Century," *Asian Survey* 40:1, 207.

95. Alan Sipress and Ellen Nakashima, "Militant Alliance in Asia Is Said to Seek Regional Islamic State," *Washington Post* (September 20, 2002), p. A16.

96. Agence France Press (February 18, 2005).

97. See Leifer, *Singapore's Foreign Policy*; Mutalib and Heng Chee Chan, *Singapore: The Politics of Survival* (London: Oxford University Press, 1971).

98. "Defence," Singapore Fact Sheet Series. Ministry of Information and The Arts (Singapore, 2001). See www.mita.gov.sg/bksdfc.htm. This principle has existed since the country's beginnings. In 1966, Lee Kuan Yew made this point, arguing that "The reflexes of group thinking must be built to ensure the survival of the community, not the survival of the individual; this means a reorientation of emphasis and a reshuffling of values." Quoted in Leifer, *Singapore's Foreign Policy*, p. 44.

99. "CIA World Factbook 2004." See www.cia.gov/cia/publications/fact-book/rankorder/2004rank.hrml. Accessed July 19, 2005.

100. "Global Competitiveness Report" (Geneva: World Economic Forum 2004-2005); "IMD World Competitiveness Yearbook 2005" (Lausanne, Switzerland: Institute for International Management, 2005).

101. Amirt Prakash, "Singapore Unemployment Rate Rises," *International Herald Tribune* (February 1, 2005). For a discussion of Singapore's economic success, see Garry Rodan, *The Political Economy of Singapore's Industrialization: National State and International Capital* (London: Macmillan 1989).

102. Leifer, *Singapore's Foreign Policy*, p. 2.

103. See Wayne Arnold, "Growth Pace Slackens in Singapore," *New York Times* (October 12, 2004), p. W1. See also, "Banking," Singapore Fact Sheet Series. Ministry of Information and the Arts (Singapore, 2001).

104. Quoted in Leifer, *Singapore's Foreign Policy*, p. 3.

105. For an opposing view, see Adrain Leftwich, "Governance, the State and the Politics of Development," *Development and Change* 25 (1994); and Jose Maria Maravall "The Myth of the Authoritarian Advantage," *Journal of Democracy* 5: 4 (1994).

106. See *Straits Times* (July 26, 1965).

107. Zuraidah Ibrahim, "75.3%—Resounding Win for PAP," *Straits Times* (November 4, 2001), p. 1.

108. See, for instance, *World Competitiveness Yearbook 2005* (Lausanne, Switzerland: International Institute for Management Development, 2002). A summary press release can be found at www.miti.gov.sg/public/EDA/frm_EDA_Default.asp?sid=9&sid=195.

109. See Fareed Zakaria, "The Rise of Illiberal Democracy," *Foreign Affairs* (November/December 1997); Daniel Bell et al. (eds.), *Towards Illiberal Democracy in Pacific Asia* (New York: St. Martin's, 1995); D. Brown, *The State and Ethnic Politics in Southeast Asia* (London: Routledge, 1994); and K. Hewison, R. Robinson and G. Rodan, eds., *Southeast Asia in the 1990s: Authoritarianism, Democracy and Capitalism* (St. Leonards: Allen and Unwin 1993). See also, "Singapore, China and the 'Soft Authoritarian' Challenge," *Asian Survey* (March 1994). For an opposing view, see Adrian Karatnycky, "The Decline of Illiberal Democracy," *Journal of Democracy* (January 1999). For an argument that Singapore is authoritarian, see J. B. Tamney, *The Struggle over Singapore's Soul: Western Modernism and Asian Culture* (New York: Walter de Gruyter, 1996).

110. For a discussion of elections in Singapore, see Garry Rodan, "Elections Without Representation: The Singapore Experience under the PAP," in R. H. Taylor, ed., *The Politics of Elections in Southeast Asia* (New York: Woodrow Wilson Center Press and Cambridge University Press, 1996). See also,

Chan Heng Chee, *The Dynamics of One Party Dominance: The PAP at the Grassroots* (Singapore: Singapore University Press, 1976). On the purpose of elections when there is no viable opposition, see Murray Edelman, *Constructing the Political Spectacle* (Chicago: University of Chicago Press, 1988). For a critique of the rise of "red carpet" MPs, see Lam Pang et al., "Lack of Competition Will Hurt PAP and nation," *Straits Times* (November 10, 2001), p. 26.

111. Christopher Tremewan, *The Political Economy of Social Control in Singapore* (Basingstoke, Macmillan and New York: St. Martin's, 1994), p. 181.

112. See Leifer, *Singapore's Foreign Policy*, pp. 18–19; and Beng-Huat Chua, *Communitarian Ideology and Democracy in Singapore* (London, and New York: Routledge, 1995).

113. Fareed Zakaria, "Culture Is Destiny: A Conversation with Lee Kuan Yew," *Foreign Affairs* 73:2 (March/April 1994), pp. 109–126. For a discussion of "Asian Values," see Neil A. Englehart, "Rights and Culture in the Asian Values Argument: The Rise and Fall of Confucian Ethics in Singapore," *Human Rights Quarterly* (May 2000); Bilahari Kausikan, "Governance that Works," *Journal of Democracy* (April 1997); and Kishore Mahbubani, "Can Asians Think?" *Times Books International* (1998).

114. Nathan Gardels, "City of the Future: What America Can Learn from Post-Liberal Singapore," *Washington Post* 11 (February 1996), quoted in Rodan, "Internet and Political Control in Singapore," p. 76.

115. "Censorship in Singapore," Channel NewsAsia/Gallup Poll, results released July 11, 1999 (http://can.mediacorpnews.com/polls/bottom-past.htm). See also, Chua Lee Hoong, "A New Paradigm Needed for Singapore Press," *Straits Times* (November 13, 1999), p. 66. The 2003 Report of the Censorship Review Committee suggests a different picture, noting that a survey of 1,000 Singaporeans indicated that 53 percent felt that the government should relax its censorship of material for adults. However, the focus of that report was on entertainment content and issues such as sex and violence rather than politics.

116. Thomas Friedman, *The Lexus and the Olive Tree* (New York: Farrar, 1999), p. 144.

117. Hussin Mutalib, "Illiberal Democracy and the Future of the Opposition in Singapore," *Third World Quarterly* 21:2 (2000), p. 338. See also Peter Self, *Government by the Market?: The Politics of Public Choice* (London: Macmillan 1993); and Samuel P. Huntington, *The Third Wave* (Norman: University of Oklahoma Press, 1991).

118. "Censorship in Singapore," Channel News Asia/Gallup Poll, results released July 11, 1999 (http://can.mediacorpnews.com/polls/bottom-past.htm).

119. See George Yeo, "Young PAP—Recasting the Net," *Petir* (May/June 1993), p. 19.

120. "PM Goh's Vision of a New Era for Singapore," *Straits Times* (June 7, 1997), pp. 40–41.

121. Ibid.

122. Garry Rodan, "Singapore in 2004: Long Awaited Leadership Transition," *Asian Survey* 45, 1 (2005), p. 140.

123. Ibid. For the government's description of the plan, see www.singapore21.org.sg.

124. Sheila McNulty and Peter Montagnon, "Getting Ready to Take a More Relaxed Approach: Singapore Is Poised for Further Economic Liberalization," *Financial Times* (March 13, 2000), p. 21.

125. John Aglionby, "One Small Step for Singapore," *Guardian* (April 28, 2001), p. 18.

126. "Singapore: Country Reports on Human Rights Practices 2000."

127. Mutalib, "Illiberal Democracy and the Future of the Opposition in Singapore," p. 337.

128. "The Political Transition," *Straits Times* (August 24, 2004).

129. See Rodan, "Internet and Political Control in Singapore," p. 65; T. J. S. George, *Lee Kuan Yew's Singapore* (London: Andre Deutsch, 1983); and Dennis Bloodworth, *The Tiger and the Trojan Horse* (Singapore: Times Books International, 1986).

130. See Rodan, "Singapore in 2004."

131. Joshua Kurlantzick, "End of the Nanny State? Singapore Cautiously Embraces Change," *The World & I* (July 2001).

132. For a discussion on the relationship between competitive politics and press freedom see Douglas Van Belle, "Press Freedom and Peace," in Bernard I. Finel and Kristin M. Lord, eds., *Power and Conflict in the Age of Transparency* (New York: Palgrave, 2000), pp. 118–122.

133. The idea that control over information is necessary to prop up dictatorships can be observed widely. See, for example, Blaine Harden, "How to Commit the Perfect Dictatorship," *New York Times* (November 26, 2000).

134. Data from Reporters Sans Frontières, quoted in Florini, *Third Force*, p. 223.

135. See Shanthi Kalathil and Taylor C. Boas, "The Internet and States Control in Authoritarian Regimes: China, Cuba and the Couterrevolution," Global Policy Program working paper, no. 21 (Washington, DC: Carnegie Endowment for International Peace, July 2001).

136. David Banisar, "Freedom of Information and Access to Government Records around the World" (London Privacy International, May 2004).

137. See Yuen Foong Khong "Singapore: A Time for Economic and Political Engagement," in Alastair I. Johnson and Robert S. Ross, eds., *Engaging China: The Management of an Emerging Power* (New York: Routledge, 1999).

For a discussion of how the Internet could aid the Communist Party in the short term (and how the Internet could potentially undermine the party in the long term), see Nina Hachigian, "China's Cyber-Strategy," *Foreign Affairs* (March/April 2001).

138. Jim Yardley, "A Hundred Cellphones Bloom, and Chinese Take to the Streets," *New York Times* (April 25, 2005), p. A1. See also, Jonathan Krim, "Web Censors in China Find Success."

139. Douglas Jehl, "A Saudi Prince with an Unconventional Idea: Elections," *New York Times* (November 28, 2001). On the Internet in Saudi Arabia, see Michael Dobbs, "Online Agitators Breaching Barriers in Mideast," *Washington Post* (October 24, 2001), p. A10.

140. For a discussion, see Neal Lane, "The Openness Imperative," *Foreign Policy* (March/April 2001); and David Albright, "Secrets that Matter," *Bulletin of the Atomic Scientists* (November/December 2000).

Chapter 6

1. Pervaiz Iqbal Cheema, "Transparency Measures," in Sumit Ganguly and Ted Greenwood, eds. *Mending Fences: Confidence and Security Building Measures in South Asia* (Boulder, CO: Westview Press, 1996), p. 154.

2. Quoted in Ben Brantley, "A Torn Land of Torn Hearts Lost in a Mist of Deception," *New York Times* (November 18, 2004).

3. This view paraphrases Martha Finnemore's definition of persuasion: "Persuasion involves changing what people value and what they think is right or good." See Finnemore, *The Purpose of Intervention* (Ithaca, NY: Cornell University Press, 2003), p. 152.

4. See Joseph S. Nye Jr., *Soft Power: The Means to Success in World Politics* (New York: Public Affairs, 2004).

5. Anthony in Malcolm Chalmers, Mitsuro Donowaki, and Owen Greene, eds., *Developing Arms Transparency: The Future of the United Nations Register*, Bradford Arms Register Studies, no.7 (University of Bradford and Center for the Promotion of Disarmament and Non-Proliferation, Japan Institute for International Affairs, 1997), p. 93. Anthony notes that, because of the marginal costs of increasing transparency of military capabilities, it is necessary to "isolate categories of items that could serve as reasonable indicators of military capability within the much larger pool of items bought by the military."

6. Transparency regimes can reveal arms buildups as well as adherence to arms control regimes. Greece and Turkey engaged in an open arms race in the mid-1990s, for example, despite participation in the United Nations Register of Conventional Arms (UNROCA). Both countries did keep acquisitions below the threshold required by the CFE treaty, however, to avoid CFE penalties.

Herbert Wulf, "The Register as an Instrument for Promoting Restraint and Preventing Conflict," in *Developing Arms Transparency*, p. 156.

7. David Kelley and Roger Donway, "Liberalism and Free Speech," in Judith Lichtenberg, ed., *Democracy and the Mass Media* (Cambridge, MA: Cambridge University Press, 1990), p. 90. For a discussion of how democratic presses can promote dehumanizing images, see Heikki Luostarinen, "Finnish Russophobia: The Story of an Enemy Image," *Journal of Peace Research* 26 (1989), pp. 123–137.

8. Jack Snyder and Karen Ballentine, "Nationalism and the Marketplace of Ideas," *International Security* (Fall 1996), p. 7.

9. Benjamin I. Page and Robert Y. Shapiro, *The Rational Public: Fifty Years of Trends in Americans' Policy Preferences* (Chicago: University of Chicago Press, 1992), p. 365.

10. As the McCarthy period and the internment of Japanese Americans during World War II shows us, however, under conditions of threat, even highly developed democracies like the United States can produce cultures in which voices in favor of protecting minority rights—in this case those of communists and Japanese Americans—are either too intimidated to speak or simply drowned out. For a discussion of John Stuart Mill's views on the tyranny of the majority, see Jill Gordon, "John Stuart Mill and the 'Marketplace of Ideas," *Social Theory and Practice* (Summer 1997). See also David Kelley and Roger Donway, "Liberalism and Free Speech," in *Democracy and the Mass Media*, p. 90.

11. Federalist Papers, no. 63.

12. Snyder and Ballentine, "Nationalism and the Marketplace of Ideas," p. 6.

13. People—and governments—also make mistakes, regardless of their resources. To give an example, despite intelligence budgets of billions of dollars per year, the U.S. government wrongly believed that its stocks of ballistic missiles had fallen significantly below those of the former Soviet Union, that the Soviet economy was 59% the size of the American economy when the figure was closer to 33%, and that the former Soviet Union continued to be a viable state until the very eve of its collapse. In 1992, for instance, a CIA official testified that Russia had 30,000 warheads "plus or minus 5,000" and even that wide-ranging estimate was later questioned. "Testimony of Larence Gershwin before the House Defense Appropriations Subcommittee," May 6, 1992, quoted in Steve Fetter, "A Comprehensive Transparency Regime for Warheads and Fissile Materials," *Arms Control Today* (January/February 1999). On the accuracy of this projection, see William J. Broad, "Russian Says Soviet Atom Arsenal Was Larger than West Estimated," *New York Times* (September 26, 1993), p. A1.

14. See Robert Jervis, *Perception and Misperception in International Politics* (Princeton: Princeton University Press, 1976), p. 143.

15. Social practices reduce uncertainty. For a discussion, see Nicholas Greenwood Onuf, *World of our Making: Rules and Rule in Social Theory and*

International Relations (Studies in International Relations) (Columbia: University of South Carolina Press, 1989).

16. For example, after the unfortunate fatal shooting of an Italian intelligence agent by American troops in Iraq in March 2005, an investigation failed to arrive at a shared conclusion by the American and Italian governments. The reason was that even after examining the evidence jointly and agreeing on many facts, they disagreed about what conclusions to draw. See Daniel Williams and Bradley Graham, "U.S., Italy Fail to Agree on Agent's Death in Iraq," *Washington Post* (April 30, 2005), p. A9.

17. Andrew Kydd, "Trust, Reassurance, Cooperation," *International Organization* 54:2 (Spring 2000), p. 341.

18. Quoted in Bruce Russett, *Grasping the Democratic Peace: Principles for a Post-Cold War World* (Princeton: Princeton University Press, 1993), p. 127.

19. Identities can also lead people to misinterpret actions. For instance, as Michael Barnett notes in his work on the Middle East, Iraq failed to recognize that Saudi Arabia would side against it in the Gulf War of 1990 because the Iraqi government viewed Saudi Arabia as an Arab state instead of as a sovereign state. This interpretation caused Saddam Hussein to interpret information in a certain way. In such cases, transparency may have little effect in changing predisposed views about identity, especially over short periods of time. Barnett, "Institutions, Roles and Disorder: The Case of the Arab State System," *International Studies Quarterly* (September 1993); also, Barnett, "Sovereignty, Nationalism and Regional Order in the Arab System," *International Organization* 49:3 (Summer 1995).

20. Using transparency to promote accountability requires careful planning to produce positive results, however. To give an example, Mary Graham observes, "Reporting systems could create conflicting incentives. In principle, public disclosure...was essential for accountability, but in practice it might drive reporting of errors underground....More requirements for transparency might produce less knowledge." Graham, *Democracy by Disclosure* (Washington, DC: Brookings, 2002), pp. 118–119.

21. We should recognize that groups are complex and may support both positive and negative goals. To give an example, several NGOs in the Middle East have come under attack for supporting radical Islamic terrorist groups, but also feed the hungry.

22. For a critical view of how the U.S. government deployed its advantages in the marketplace of ideas, see Chaim Kaufmann, "Threat Inflation and the Failure of the Marketplace of Ideas," *International Security* (Summer 2004).

23. On shutter control, see John C. Baker, Kevin M. O'Connell, and Ray A. Williamson, *Commercial Observation Satellites: At the Leading Edge of Global Transparency* (Santa Monica, CA: Rand: American Society for Photogrammetry and Remote Sensing (ASPRS), 2001).

24. Because deliberate acts of openness are political signals of intentions and identity, it is easy to see why analysts equate this type of transparency with positive outcomes such as less corruption, less pollution, less cheating on arms control agreements, more accountability for governments, and more voice for the governed. See, for example, Ann Florini, *The Coming Democracy* (Washington, DC: Island Press, 2003). Florini's excellent work on this subject focuses almost entirely on deliberate acts of transparency.

25. Consider the Cold War export control regime known as CoCom, which sought to limit access of nonmember countries to certain technologies with military applications. Sharing sensitive technology with non-CoCom countries was discouraged because members feared it would be used to threaten their interests. For a discussion, see Michael Mastanduno, *Economic Containment: CoCom and the Politics of East-West Trade* (Ithaca: Cornell University Press, 1992).

26. For a good analysis and overview, see Bruce Berkowitz, "We Collected a Little, and Assumed a Lot," *Washington Post* (February 1, 2004), p. B1.

27. For a discussion of this initiative, see Ian Gary, "Do Oil and Democracy Mix?" Democracy at Large 1:3 (Washington, DC: IFES, 2005).

28. Nocholas Wood, "Video of Serbs in Srebrenica Massacre Leads to Arrests," *New York Times* June 3, 2005), p. A3.

29. For a recent discussion of framing in the domestic context, see Matt Bai, "The Framing Wars," *New York Times Magazine* (July 17, 2005).

30. As a RAND report on politics in the information age notes, success "may ultimately be about whose story wins." John Arquilla and David Ronfeldt, *The Emergence of Noopolitik: Toward an American Information Strategy* (Santa Monica, CA: RAND Corporation, 1999), quoted in Nye, *Soft Power*, p. 106.

31. Often, people take their cues from opinion leaders, so persuading those opinion leaders to change their minds can have an important ripple effect and, for this reason, Track II and Track III diplomacy—meetings of unofficial, but powerful individuals who communicate with officials—can help highly regarded leaders explain government policy and persuade others. They are also excellent for listening and understanding why others might object to a particular policy. Because participants in such dialogues are not officials, they may be more credible messengers and hence, have more influence. They have more freedom to speak their minds and more freedom to explore new approaches to problems.

32. For a discussion, see Daniel Patrick Moynihan, *Secrecy* (New Haven: Yale University Press, 1998).

Index

SUNY Series in Global Politics

James N. Rosenau, Editor

List of Titles

American Patriotism in a Global Society—Betty Jean Craige

The Political Discourse of Anarchy: A Disciplinary History of International Relations—Brian C. Schmidt

Power and Ideas: North-South Politics of Intellectual Property and Antitrust—Susan K. Sell

From Pirates to Drug Lords: The Post—Cold War Caribbean Security Environment—Michael C. Desch, Jorge I. Dominguez, and Andres Serbin (eds.)

Collective Conflict Management and Changing World Politics—Joseph Lepgold and Thomas G. Weiss (eds.)

Zones of Peace in the Third World: South America and West Africa in Comparative Perspective—Arie M. Kacowicz

Private Authority and International Affairs—A. Claire Cutler, Virginia Haufler, and Tony Porter (eds.)

Harmonizing Europe: Nation-States within the Common Market—Francesco G. Duina

Economic Interdependence in Ukrainian-Russian Relations—Paul J. D'Anieri

Leapfrogging Development? The Political Economy of Telecommunications Restructuring—J. P. Singh

States, Firms, and Power: Successful Sanctions in United States Foreign Policy—George E. Shambaugh

Approaches to Global Governance Theory—Martin Hewson and Timothy J. Sinclair (eds.)

After Authority: War, Peace, and Global Politics in the Twenty-First Century—Ronnie D. Lipschutz

Pondering Postinternationalism: A Paradigm for the Twenty-First Century?—Heidi H. Hobbs (ed.)

Beyond Boundaries? Disciplines, Paradigms, and Theoretical Integration in International Studies—Rudra Sil and Eileen M. Doherty (eds.)

International Relations—Still an American Social Science? Toward Diversity in International Thought—Robert M. A. Crawford and Darryl S. L. Jarvis (eds.)

Which Lessons Matter? American Foreign Policy Decision Making in the Middle East, 1979—1987—Christopher Hemmer (ed.)

Hierarchy Amidst Anarchy: Transaction Costs and Institutional Choice—Katja Weber

Counter-Hegemony and Foreign Policy: The Dialectics of Marginalized and Global Forces in Jamaica—Randolph B. Persaud

Global Limits: Immanuel Kant, International Relations, and Critique of World Politics—Mark F. N. Franke

Money and Power in Europe: The Political Economy of European Monetary Cooperation—Matthias Kaelberer

Why Movements Matter: The West German Peace Movement and U. S. Arms Control Policy—Steve Breyman

Agency and Ethics: The Politics of Military Intervention—Anthony F. Lang, Jr.

Life After the Soviet Union: The Newly Independent Republics of the Transcaucasus and Central Asia—Nozar Alaolmolki

Information Technologies and Global Politics: The Changing Scope of Power and Governance—James N. Rosenau and J. P. Singh (eds.)

Theories of International Cooperation and the Primacy of Anarchy: Explaining U. S. International Monetary Policy-Making After Bretton Woods—Jennifer Sterling-Folker

Technology, Democracy, and Development: International Conflict and Cooperation in the Information Age—Juliann Emmons Allison (ed.)

Systems of Violence: The Political Economy of War and Peace in Colombia—Nazih Richani

The Arab-Israeli Conflict Transformed: Fifty Years of Interstate and Ethnic Crises—Hemda Ben-Yehuda and Shmuel Sandler

Debating the Global Financial Architecture—Leslie Elliot Armijo

Political Space: Frontiers of Change and Governance in a Globalizing World—Yale Ferguson and R. J. Barry Jones (eds.)

Crisis Theory and World Order: Heideggerian Reflections—Norman K. Swazo

Political Identity and Social Change: The Remaking of the South African Social Order—Jamie Frueh

Social Construction and the Logic of Money: Financial Predominance and International Economic Leadership—J. Samuel Barkin

What Moves Man: The Realist Theory of International Relations and Its Judgment of Human Nature—Annette Freyberg-Inan

Democratizing Global Politics: Discourse Norms, International Regimes, and Political Community—Rodger A. Payne and Nayef H. Samhat

Landmines and Human Security: International Politics and War's Hidden Legacy—Richard A. Matthew, Bryan McDonald, and Kenneth R. Rutherford (eds.)

Collective Preventative Diplomacy: A Study of International Management—Barry H. Steiner

International Relations Under Risk: Framing State Choice—Jeffrey D. Berejikian

Globalization and the Environment: Greening Global Political Economy—Gabriela Kütting

Sovereignty, Democracy, and Global Civil Society—Elisabeth Jay Friedman, Kathryn Hochstetler, and Ann Marie Clark

United We Stand? Divide and Conquer Politics and the Logic of International Hostility—Aaron Belkin

Imperialism and Nationalism in the Discipline of International Relations—David Long and Brian C. Schmidt (eds.)

Globalization, Security, and the Nation State: Paradigms in Transition—Ersel Aydinli and James N. Rosenau (eds.)

Identity and Institutions: Conflict Reduction in Divided Societies—Neal G. Jesse and Kristen P. Williams

Globalizing Interests: Pressure Groups and Denationalization—Michael Zürn (ed., with assistance from Gregor Walter)

International Regimes for the Final Frontier—M. J. Peterson

Ozone Depletion and Climate Change: Constructing A Global Response—Matthew J. Hoffmann

States of Liberalization: Redefining the Public Sector in Integrated Europe—Mitchell P. Smith

Mediating Globalization: Domestic Institutions and Industrial Policies in the United States and Britain—Andrew P. Cortell

The Multi-Governance of Water: Four Case Studies—Matthias Finger, Ludivine Tamiotti, and Jeremy Allouche, eds.

Building Trust: Overcoming Suspicion in International Conflict—Aaron M. Hoffman

Global Capitalism, Democracy, and Civil-Military Relations in Colombia—Williams Avilés

Complexity in World Politics: Concepts and Methods of a New Paradigm—Neil E. Harrison

Technology and International Transformation: The Railroad, the Atom Bomb, and the Politics of Technological Transformation—Geoffrey L. Herrera